HELLENISTIC QUEENS

A STUDY OF WOMAN-POWER IN MACEDONIA, SELEUCID
SYRIA, AND PTOLEMAIC EGYPT

FIGURE 1.

A FOURTH CENTURY HELLENISTIC QUEEN, PROBABLY AMASTRIS.

THE JOHNS HOPKINS UNIVERSITY
STUDIES IN ARCHAEOLOGY

No. 14

EDITED BY DAVID M. ROBINSON

HELLENISTIC QUEENS

A STUDY OF WOMAN-POWER IN MACEDONIA, SELEUCID
SYRIA, AND PTOLEMAIC EGYPT

BY

GRACE HARRIET MACURDY

PROFESSOR OF GREEK IN VASSAR COLLEGE

BALTIMORE: THE JOHNS HOPKINS PRESS
LONDON: HUMPHREY MILFORD
OXFORD UNIVERSITY PRESS

1932

Printed in the
United States of America
by the J. H. Furst Company
Baltimore, Maryland

To HENRY NOBLE MacCRACKEN

ἀνδρὶ φιλοκάλῳ καὶ φιλοσόφῳ καὶ φιλανθρώπῳ

THE PUBLICATION
OF THIS BOOK WAS MADE POSSIBLE
BY A GRANT FROM THE
LUCY MAYNARD SALMON
FUND FOR RESEARCH
ESTABLISHED AT VASSAR COLLEGE
JUNE, 1926

PREFACE

In the following investigation of woman-power in the Hellenistic centuries I have confined my study to the three chief dynasties, Macedonia, Seleucid Syria, and Ptolemaic Egypt. Since the statement is so generally made with regard to the queens of these royal houses that in them a woman is the equal of a man, it has seemed to me desirable to attempt to arrive at a clear idea of what is meant by this equality and to discover whether it prevailed alike in all three dynasties. As a matter of fact Strack pointed out the truth when he observed that it was in Egypt that " the emancipation of the queens " took place. In a paper published in 1927 I showed that there was no trace of equality in power between king and queen in early Macedonia and that the Macedonians were in principle opposed to any " regiment of women." Tarn has strikingly said: " If Macedonia produced perhaps the most competent body of men the world had yet seen, the women were in all respects the men's counterparts." Yet in spite of the notable achievements of women, which Tarn summarizes in his following sentence, the truth is that very few of the queens in Macedonia and in Seleucid Syria possessed any political power at all and that only gradually in Egypt did a woman become the equal of a man as ruler.

In this book I have considered the question of woman-power from the time of the early royal women in Macedonia, whose names occur only on the occasion of their marriage, when they are given by father or brother to some prince with whom a treaty of alliance is made, down to the last queen of Macedonia, Laodice wife of Perseus. I have then discussed the position of the queens of Seleucid Syria and of Ptolemaic Egypt, from the founding of those dynasties to the last Seleucid and Ptolemaic queens, whose position and power were reflected in the vassal queens of Pontus and Mauretania under the Roman Empire.

I have also discussed the question of the character of these queens, who are generally reputed to have been wicked. This reputation rests, as does the statement that they possessed power equal to that of the men, on the acts of a few of the many who were queens in the Hellenistic centuries. Of these few it may be said that if they were in nature and character the counterparts of the men, they should be judged by the same standard. If the women are to be compared to tigresses (a favorite simile for them) we must admit that the Macedonian blood produced tigerish men.

I have not attempted to give a romantic reconstruction of the lives of any of the queens, but have stated the chief facts that have been preserved about each of them. Since a picture of the civilization of the Hellenistic Age and of its social and economic background is presented in important and well-known works by the great authorities on this period, Beloch, Bevan, Bouché-Leclercq, Ferguson, Rostovtzeff, Tarn, and others, I have felt it unnecessary to include in a book of this compass and design what can so much better be found in the works of these authors. I have confined myself to the matters which involve the lives and characters of the queens and their political position. In the Introduction I have stated at some length the points on which I differ from prevailing views.

Professor David M. Robinson of Johns Hopkins University, the editor of the series in which this book appears, has been indefatigable in the reading of manuscript and proof and in the discovery of errors. I thank him for his tireless labor and for many suggestions, for which I am deeply indebted to him. I owe a great debt of thanks also to my former pupil, Miss Sarah Morris, for the invaluable aid which she has given me in the preparation of the Index and in reading proof. I am under obligations to the Trustees of the British Museum for photographs made for me in that Museum of sculpture, vases, and a coin. For similar kindness I thank Dr. L. D. Caskey, who sent me photographs of sculptures and medallions in the Boston Museum of Fine Arts.

Mr. Edward T. Newell has generously permitted me to use photographs of coins in his collection and Mrs. Agnes Baldwin Brett has most kindly aided me with material from the Numismatic Museum in New York. I thank them both for their kindness and I thank also the Director of the Fogg Art Museum in Cambridge, Massachusetts, who has allowed me to use a photograph of the head of Amastris (or Olympias) which is in that museum.

The reading for this book has been done chiefly in the Reading Room of the British Museum and in the Vassar College Library. To the staff of both these libraries, from whom I have received much courteous assistance, I offer my thanks. Miss Fanny Borden, Librarian of the Vassar College Library, has done me great service by procuring books for my use from the libraries of Harvard, Yale, Columbia, and Princeton Universities. I am grateful to my colleagues of the Vassar Classical Journal Club for the interest which they have taken in my work.

Finally I express my gratitude to the members of the Committee on Research of Vassar College, who awarded me from the Lucy Maynard Salmon Fund for Research the sum necessary for the publication of this book.

G. H. M.

Poughkeepsie, New York,
    January, 1932

CONTENTS

LIST OF ILLUSTRATIONS

HELLENISTIC QUEENS

A STUDY OF WOMAN-POWER IN MACEDONIA, SELEUCID SYRIA, AND PTOLEMAIC EGYPT

INTRODUCTION

From the latter part of the fourth century B. C. for about three hundred years before the Christian era women of Macedonian blood in the Hellenistic kingdoms established by the Successors of Alexander the Great showed a remarkable capacity for ruling in the manner of the kings of whom they were wives and daughters. They possessed to an extraordinary degree, "greater than the measure of women", as is said of them in ancient historians,[1] the qualities of energy, political foresight, daring, and courage which distinguished the men who took the world in their hands after Alexander's death. These women had great prestige and influence and in some cases great political power, though this last did not come to them as it came to the men by direct inheritance or by conquest, but through the doorway of marriage, which often afforded them opportunity to act as regent for an absent husband, or for a minor child, or as co-regent with a husband whose weakness of character allowed a queen of strong nature to come forward as co-ruler. If, as happened in the last period of the Lagid rule in Egypt, the throne came to a daughter in default of male heirs, a husband as closely connected as possible with the reigning house was sought with all haste as consort for the queen.

The influence of these queens upon the events of their times and the history of their countries was very great. The earliest Macedonian woman to take a part in political affairs of whom history tells is Eurydice, mother of Philip the Second, the last is the famous Cleopatra VII of Egypt. Cleo-

---

[1] Diod. XIX, 67; Arrian, *Succ.* I, 40.

1

patra has never lacked historians, poets, and dramatists to
tell the story of her life, but many of her predecessors are
all but completely ignored by historians ancient and modern
and are, when mentioned, often condemned *en masse* as
unscrupulous, cruel, and wanting in all the gentler virtues.
Justin, who loves to denounce the crimes of queens, has done
his worst by some of them, and some modern historians refer
to the whole line of queens or to individuals among them as
Megaeras, hyaenas, tigers, and criminals. The crimes of
which they are accused are dynastic murder and infidelity
to their marriage vows. Tarn however has noted the fact
that they were *not* licentious;—" no lover is anywhere recorded " for the third century queens.[2] Those whose actions
appear most culpable followed in their feminine way the
rules of political procedure established and observed by kings
whose cruelties are often condoned by the words " political
necessity ". Among these queens are some women notable for
loyalty and kindness and others whose lives were lived in
quietness, of whom we know little or nothing except that they
were the wives of kings. It has often been noted that especially among the Lagids in Egypt the queens remained
vigorous and capable at a time when the kings were degenerate and worthless. It is to their strong character and their
political understanding—σύνεσις πραγματικὴ καὶ τόλμα [3]—qualities which Diodorus ascribes to a Hellenistic princess, that
they owed their influence. About their power exaggerated
statements are sometimes made and in a sweeping assertion
what is true of some of them in this regard is attributed to all.
It is the design of this book to set down the important facts
which are known about the lives of the queens in Macedonia,
Syria, and Egypt, from the time of Eurydice, mother of Philip
the Second of Macedon, to the end of the Seleucid and Lagid
lines, and to define, so far as possible, the kind and extent
of power possessed by the women in the various dynasties.

---

[2] *Hellenistic Civilisation*, p. 51.

[3] Diod. *loc. cit.*

The case against the character of these queens is put by Mahaffy, with the passionate rhetoric of the Celt, in writing of two of them, Tryphaena, wife of Antiochus VIII of Syria, and her sister Cleopatra, wife of Antiochus IX. He says of them:—" These ladies show the usual features ascribed to Ptolemaic princesses—great power and wealth, which makes an alliance with them imply the command of large resources in men and money; mutual hatred; disregard of all ties of family and affection; the dearest object fratricide—such pictures of depravity as make any reasonable man pause and ask himself whether human nature had deserted these women and the Hyrcanian tiger of the poet taken its place." [4] In the fine flow of his invective Mahaffy forgets the circumstances of the two women of whom he is at the moment writing, and ascribes to the murdered queen Cleopatra, of whom no evil is known, who was first the victim of her mother's tyranny and then of her sister's jealousy, the odium of her own murder. It should be noted that Tryphaena's " dearest object " was to prevent her husband from marrying her sister and not abstract " fratricide ".

With equal inaccuracy Mahaffy writes with regard to the last Cleopatra of Egypt:—" and yet she was of a race in which almost every reigning princess for the last two hundred years had been swayed by like storms of passion, or had been guilty of like violations of common humanity. What Arsinoe, what Cleopatra, from first to last, had hesitated to murder a brother or husband, to assume the throne, to raise and command armies, to discard or adopt a partner of her throne from caprice in policy or policy in caprice." [5]

These highly colored and frequently quoted words give a distorted picture of the whole female dynasty and an entirely false one of several Arsinoes and Cleopatras, who were guilty of no crimes against humanity, but, so far as we are informed, lived lives without reproach, in some cases the victims of the

---

[4] Mahaffy, *Ptolemaic Egypt*, pp. 213-214.
[5] Mahaffy, *Empire of the Ptolemies*, pp. 445 f.

crimes of others. Polybius [6] writes of the tragic orphan girl, Arsinoe III, that she endured insult all her life long; and the other Arsinoes, with the exception of the great queen Arsinoe II, have no evil recorded against them, while of the Cleopatras of Egypt only the third and the seventh made use of the means that are so often condoned in the case of kings as crimes of political necessity. Mahaffy's remark about their taking and discarding partners of their thrones is singularly beside the mark in the light of the fact that the discarding of partners in the House of Ptolemy was done by kings; for examples, Ptolemies I, II, and VII.

The Berenices whom he admits by implication into the company of wicked queens have an excellent reputation for virtues of courage and kindness; only the last one is accused of dynastic murder. She is said to have ordered the execution of the vulgar Seleucid pretender who was brought from Syria to marry her.[7] The only Laodice of Syria to commit this crime was the first queen of that name, wife of Antiochus II and mother of Seleucus II and Antiochus Hierax. In a significant expression of the doctrine of equal rights in political murder for queens, Beloch maintains that her actions were justified by the rules then prevailing, and declares that in taking such measures to insure the rights of her sons she followed the precedents always followed by kings in such a case. He suggests that Alexander the Great on coming to the throne went to a far greater length in political murder. Cassander has often been defended on the ground that his cruelties had always some political aim in view. Laodice's are defended on the same grounds by Beloch.[8]

The other Laodices of Syria appear to have lived uneventful lives and to have done no violence to husband, son or rival. The Seleucid queen of whom most evil is told is Cleopatra Thea of Syria, who is said to have poisoned her eldest

---

[6] Polyb. XV, 25a.

[7] Strabo, XVII, 796; Cassius Dio, XXXIX, 57.

[8] Beloch, IV¹, pp. 675 f., n. 1.

son Seleucus and to have attempted to poison her second son
and co-regent Antiochus. If we grant to the historians who
condemn the whole line of Hellenistic queens of Macedonian
descent as a succession of monstrously inhumane women
Laodice I and Cleopatra Thea of Syria and, with some strong
reservations in their favor, Arsinoe II, Cleopatra III, and Cleopatra VII of Egypt as examples of unscrupulous queens who
were "no unequal rivals of the men" in political crime as
well as political genius, there still remain many of these
royal women who were blameless in their lives so far as history
tells of them, and there is probably hardly a Macedonian or
Hellenistic king whose political misdeeds do not outnumber
those of any queen who was guilty of such action. Plutarch's
remarks on these prevailing dynastic murders are well known,
but I will quote them in this connection. He says of the
Antigonids: "This house alone was free from such crimes
for several generations. In all the other lines there were
murders of children and murders of mothers and of wives;
and as for destroying the lives of brothers this was accepted
as generally binding as an axiom of geometry and the uni-
versal first principle of safety for kings." [9] It is evident that
if the old Macedonian blood continued to produce tigress
princesses,[10] it was because it was tigerish in the male line as
well.

The chief value of a daughter of a Hellenistic monarch was
her importance at the making of a treaty or alliance [11] when
her father bestowed her hand together with an imposing
dowry upon some king or prince with whom he was entering
into close relations. It may account for the rarity of brother-
and-sister marriage among the Seleucids that the princesses
were found so useful by their fathers when they were binding

---

[9] Plut. *Dem.* III.

[10] Bevan, *House of Seleucus* II, p. 60.

[11] Cf. Hdt. I, 74 (about a treaty of peace between the Lydians and
the Medes)—οὗτοί σφι καὶ τὸ ὅρκιον οἱ σπεύσαντες γενέσθαι ἦσαν καὶ γάμων
ἐπαλλαγὴν ἐποίησαν· Ἀλυάττην γὰρ ἔγνωσαν δοῦναι τὴν θυγατέρα Ἀρύηνιν
Ἀστυάγεϊ τῷ Κυαξάρεω παιδί.

other kings to them politically that none were left to marry
their brothers. This employment of the daughters of the
royal house has a very long history. The names of the early
Macedonian princesses occur only in this connection.

It appears that no actual political power belonged to a
princess of any of the houses by right of birth. In Macedonia the marriage with a princess or widow of a king might
bring the kingship nearer for an ambitious successor—witness the eagerness of all the Successors to marry Cleopatra,
daughter of Philip and Olympias and widow of Alexander
of Epirus,—and Cassander found his marriage with Thessalonice profitable in his progress toward the throne.[12]
Among the Ptolemies women reached a great height of power,
but up to the late period they arrived at it through marriage,
as the daughters of the Lagids had no claim to inherit so long
as legitimate male descendants were living.[13] Beloch holds
that bastard sons had precedence of the female heirs. Only
in the decline of the royal house in Egypt was the kingdom
left to a daughter, Berenice III, or to a daughter and son,
Cleopatra VII and her brother Ptolemy. And for Berenice,
a middle-aged woman, a youth, her nephew, was brought at
once as a husband. He killed her in less than three weeks.

A Seleucid queen is mentioned occasionally as having been
proclaimed queen. Stratonice, wife of Antiochus I, is said by
Appian and Plutarch to have been appointed by Seleucus as
monarch with her husband when the old king gave his son
his own wife and the charge of the eastern kingdom.[14] And
Polybius says that when Laodice daughter of Mithradates was
married to Antiochus III at Seleuceia-at-Zeugma with great
pomp, he brought her to Antioch and proclaimed her queen

---

[12] Cf. Köhler, *Makedonien unter König Archelaos, Sitzungsberichte
d. Preuss. Akad.*, 1893, p. 491. "The ἐπίτροπος (guardian) belonging
to the royal houses after winning the confidence of the people to a
high degree was often proclaimed king." Cf. also Strack, *Dynastie
der Ptolemäer*, p. 77.

[13] Strack, *Dynastie der Ptolemäer*, p. 75; Beloch IV¹, p. 377, n. 1.

[14] Appian, *Syr.* 61; Plut. *Dem.* XXXVIII.

(βασίλισσαν ἀποδείξας). Such proclamation would confer prestige and potential power as regent in her husband's absence or in the minority of a son.[15] Only in these exceptional circumstances did a queen have the power of a king, and that power was secure against a palace cabal or against the claims of the nearest male relative, whether son or brother or husband, only when the queen herself had an extremely strong character and will and the ability to defend herself.

Contests of this sort occurred chiefly in Egypt in the case of such queens as Cleopatra II, Cleopatra III, and Cleopatra VII. In Macedonia after the tempestuous struggles of Olympias and Eurydice to gain royal power there was a succession of quiet queens, of so little importance for the government of the state that the very names of some of the last are uncertain. The fact that the queens in Macedonia lacked eponymous priestesses and all the pomp and paraphernalia that went with deification and a state-worship,[16] made their position more obscure than that of the Lagid and Seleucid queens. No Macedonian queen ever issued coins in her own right nor had her likeness and name stamped on the coins issued by her husband. The last Macedonian queen, Laodice, wife of Perseus, did not have this honor in Macedonia, but if it is true that as widow of Perseus she married her brother Demetrius I of Syria, her head appears with that of her brother-husband on coins struck by him which bear his name and title.

The legally subordinate position of the Ptolemaic queens even at the highest point of their influence and power has been shown by Kahrstedt[17] from the evidence of the coins. The head of the living queen is placed only on copper of her husband's coinage and without her name, whereas the head and the title of the deified queen are placed on both gold and

---

[15] Cf. also Beloch, IV[1], pp. 375 ff.

[16] Beloch, IV, 1, pp. 372 f.

[17] Kahrstedt, *Frauen auf antiken Münzen, Klio*, X, 1910, pp. 261 ff.

silver coins. This is the rule for the time of Ptolemy Philadelphus. "In other words the dead queen is on an equality with the living king, for the king imprints both gold and silver coins with his image and name and is by the law of the state God." [18] Cleopatra VII was the only princess of the house of Ptolemy to exercise a right of coinage of her own and not as representative of a king.[19] Among the Seleucids Cleopatra Thea issued, apparently for one year only (125 B. C.), silver coins with her head, name, and titles. But one example is in existence,[20] and it is probable that after her first year as regent the issue was recalled as being too great an innovation.[21] The title βασίλισσα when found on the coins of various queens who were acting as regents for an absent husband, or for minor sons, and on those of Cleopatra in her own right, does not mean "the wife of the king", but "a female king".[22] It is a title deriving from Macedonia and in vogue there in the time of Olympias and Alexander and doubtless long before.[23]

In Macedonia the strongest and most domineering of the royal women were defeated in their attempts to secure for themselves permanent power. Olympias was frustrated by Antipater, the regent, and at last, after all her struggles, was killed by Antipater's son Cassander. Cynane, Philip's daughter and wife of the rightful king, who never reigned, Amyntas, was killed by Alcetas as she demanded for her daughter the right to marry the king and be queen of Macedonia. That daughter, Eurydice, with all her mother's spirit, was checked in her youthful arrogance by Antipater and was killed in the struggle with Olympias. After this generation of queens of an Amazonian spirit had passed away in Mace-

[18] *Ibid.* 267.
[19] *Ibid.* 274 ff.
[20] This coin is in the British Museum.
[21] Kahrstedt, 279 f.
[22] Kahrstedt, p. 269; Macurdy, *A.J.P.* XLIX, 1928, pp. 276 ff.
[23] Theopompus ap. Athen. XIII, 595; Macurdy, *loc. cit.* p. 281.

donia, a country which Alexander said would never endure a
woman for its king, the queens were quiet or quiescent.
Stratonice, wife of Demetrius II, when repudiated by her
husband showed the temper of the fourth century queens in
her attempt to rouse the Seleucid king against Demetrius and
in her domination of Antioch for six months, during the
absence of Seleucus. But she too fell in the contest with the
king whom she had hoped to marry. Antipater, the old
regent, on his dying-bed exhorted his country never to let a
woman rule them, and the Macedonians obeyed his words.[24]

It was the Arsinoes, Berenices, and Cleopatras of Egypt
who shared the royal power and themselves often ruled when
the chance offered. In Syria besides Laodice I and Cleopatra Thea, whose careers do not equal in length and splendor
those of the Ptolemaic female monarchs, the Seleucid queens
of the greatest prominence were daughters of the Ptolemaic
house. The last of them, the indomitable old queen Cleopatra Selene, had been the wife of Ptolemy VIII of Egypt
before she married three of the Seleucid kings. We hear of
her from Cicero in her old age as claiming the throne of Egypt
for herself and her two sons.

The two Hellenistic queens whose goodness is most greatly
praised by ancient historians are Phila, wife of Demetrius I,
whose life is described in the account that follows of the
queens of Macedonia; and the other a woman who was not
of royal blood, but the wife of a king and mother of two
kings of Pergamum. This was Apollonis, wife of Attalus I.
Polybius [25] writes of her that for many reasons she was worthy
of distinguished mention. She was of a bourgeois family
and became queen. She kept this high position to the end
of her life because of the nobility of her character, her dignity,
and her understanding of what became a ruler. She had four
sons, to all of whom she showed an incomparable affection and
loyalty. When on a visit with her to her native city of

---

[24] Diod. XIX, 11, 9.
[25] Polyb. XXI, 20.

Cyzicus her sons took her about with them to the temples and the sights of the city, walking with her and supporting her on either side. The sight of this filial and democratic conduct won great applause from the people of Cyzicus, who compared the young men to Cleobis and Biton of old.

When the day of the Macedonian-Hellenistic queens was over, after the death of the last and most splendid of them, Cleopatra VII of Egypt, there remained in the Roman world which had swallowed up Hellenism vassal-queens who ruled their lands and issued coins in their own right. The most important and interesting of these are Cleopatra of Maure-tania, wife of the scholar-king, Juba; Dynamis of Bosporus; and Pythodoris of Pontus-Bosporus. Cleopatra was half Ptolemaic-Macedonian and half Roman, the child of Mark Antony and Cleopatra. Dynamis ruled the kingdom of Bosporus for many years, sometimes sharing power with one of her four successive husbands [26] and sometimes alone. She was a grand-daughter of the great Mithradates, with Maeotian or Sarmatian blood from her mother.[27] Rostovtzeff in his history of her and her dynasty says of her that she was doubt-less one of the most eminent women of that complex epoch. " Her history reminds us to a great extent of the clever, energetic, and ambitious women, wicked wives of many hus-bands, who appeared at the Hellenistic courts after Alex-ander." [28] Pythodoris was perhaps of mingled Asiatic and Roman blood.[29] Her mother was, according to Mommsen, Antonia, daughter of Mark Antony and his cousin Antonia, so that Pythodoris herself had a strong Antonian strain in

---

[26] Rostovtzeff, " Queen Dynamis of Bosporus," *J.H.S.* XXXIX, 1919, pp. 99, 102, 104; *Iranians and Greeks*, pp. 151 ff.

[27] *Iranians and Greeks*, p. 152.

[28] *J.H.S.* XXXIX, 1919, p. 98.

[29] Dessau (*Eph. Ep.* IX, pp. 691 ff.) argues against Mommsen's identification of Antonia Euergetis of the inscription *O.G.I.* 277 with Antonia, daughter of Mark Antony, and denies that Pythodoris was his grand-daughter. Cf. also, *Römische Kaiserzeit*, II, 2, pp. 618, 621, n. 1. Cf. Mommsen, *Eph. Ep.* I, 1873, pp. 270-276.

her. Her father was Pythodorus, a wealthy citizen of Tralles to whom Mark Antony gave his daughter, as Mommsen argues, about the year 34 B. C. Pythodoris married Polemon of Pontus, who had been the third husband of Dynamis, and ruled with him until his death, when she succeeded to the kingdom. Strabo,[30] who writes of her as a contemporary, says that she is a good woman ($\sigma\acute{\omega}\phi\rho\omega\nu$) and able to control a state ($\delta\upsilon\nu\alpha\tau\grave{\eta}$ $\pi\rho\upsilon\acute{\iota}\sigma\tau\alpha\sigma\theta\alpha\iota$ $\pi\rho\alpha\gamma\mu\acute{\alpha}\tau\omega\nu$). She was a great queen, ruling an extensive kingdom with the aid of a son who did not aspire to the kingship. On her coins she put her own legend, but, since she was a vassal of Rome, not her own head, but that of Livia or of some other member of the imperial family.[31]

She had the title of Philometor,[32] and this, Mommsen says, testifies to the glory of her descent from the Roman *gens* Antonia, as does that of her mother Antonia, who was called Euergetis [33] since it was she who brought honor and the imperial favor to her daughter Pythodoris and her children. The daughter of Pythodoris, Antonia Tryphaena, married Cotys, king of Thrace, and she too ruled in Pontus as guardian and regent for her son Polemon II; her head and her name appear on the obverse of the early coins. The Hellenistic custom of having the mother of the minor king act as his guardian and as regent thus survived to the middle of the first century A. D.[34]

Pythodoris, if Mommsen is right, owes her eminence and doubtless her high spirit and capacity for ruling to the blood of Mark Antony and his cousin Antonia. Cleopatra Selene owes hers to both of her parents, Mark Antony and Cleopatra of Egypt. And Mark Antony, who desired to found by his

---

[30] Strabo, XII, 3, 29, p. 555.
[31] Kahrstedt, *op. cit.*; Head, *Hist. Num.* p. 503, Rostovtzeff, *J.H.S.* XXXIX, 1919, p. 94, n. 10.
[32] *O.G.I.* 376, 377.
[33] *O.G.I.* 377.
[34] Kahrstedt, *op. cit.* p. 302.

marriages and *amours* many noble and royal families,[35] had queens and kings and emperors among his descendants in Africa, in Pontus, in Thrace, Armenia, and in Rome. The strong character and will of Dynamis perhaps owed something to Maeotian blood and the old tradition of matriarchy which prevailed among the Maeotians.[36]

In these vassal-queens the tradition of the Hellenistic queens comes to an end. The queens of the great dynasties had in the art of governing often kept pace with the men; in war they naturally were inferior. Many of them were like the men in an inordinate love of power; the best of them show a spirit of loyalty and self-sacrifice unknown to the kings; the worst do not equal the worst of the kings in depravity and cruelty. Some of them are blamed for marrying several times, but these marriages were political and often forced upon them. Lovers are conspicuously absent from their lives. Their desires and gifts lay in the field of government and political power; and looking at their achievements in this domain we may use Plutarch's famous words as their epitaph—" They were no unequal rivals of the men."

---

[35] Plut. *Ant.* XXXVI.
[36] Rostovtzeff, *Iranians and Greeks*, pp. 33, 156.

CHAPTER I

QUEENSHIP IN MACEDONIA

EARLY MACEDONIAN ROYAL WOMEN

Gygaea, Stratonice, and Cleopatra

The queens of the Ptolemaic dynasty beginning with Arsinoe II were often so powerful and so distinguished that historians have been misled by their splendor into attributing a similar prestige and position to the royal women of old Macedonia. The importance of the queenship in Egypt, and to a less conspicuous degree in Seleucid Syria, has often been regarded as a Macedonian tradition, perhaps going back to some northern form of inheritance in the female line, such as that which Droysen [1] believed existed in Epirus. Oldfather [2] argues for some ancient form of " Mother-right " in Locris also. Whatever may have been the case with other northern tribes, Macedonia appears to have been always strictly patriarchal. Alexander the Great remarked with reference to his mother Olympias, when she took charge of affairs in Epirus, " The Macedonians will never endure to have a woman for their king." [3] Alexander here uses the technical word for kingship, whereas Aristotle, in the second book of the *Politics*,[4] when speaking of the power of women in warlike and military tribes uses the word γυναικοκρατούμενοι and makes it clear that he is speaking of the influence of women over men who hold authority rather than the power of women ruling directly.

To disprove the notion that women [5] in the old Macedonian

---

[1] Droysen, *Geschichte des Hellenismus*, I, p. 95, n. 2.

[2] Oldfather, *P.W.* XIII, 1225 ff.

[3] Plut. *Alex.* LXVIII.

[4] Aristotle, *Politics*, II, 9, 6. Cf. also V, 11, 11.

[5] Bevan, *House of Seleucus*, II, pp. 279 f.

kingdom mingled in political affairs as openly as the men it is enough to note that all the royal women who are mentioned in the accounts of early Macedonian history are completely at the disposal of the reigning kings, their fathers or brothers, who give them in marriage together with a large sum of money in order to buy some political advantage from the prince to whom the lady is given. The first Macedonian princess named is Gygaea; [6] she was given with a great dowry by her brother Alexander the philhellene to a Persian nobleman Bubares, who had come to Macedonia at the head of a commission to investigate the death of Persian envoys, assassinated by order of Alexander. The king is said by Herodotus to have quashed the proceedings by his diplomacy in giving Bubares the princess and the dowry. Gygaea is mentioned again by Herodotus as mother of a son Amyntas, named for his maternal grandfather, and given by the Great King an important town of Phrygia, Alabanda, to govern.

Stratonice [7] is the next woman of royal rank whose name occurs. Her brother Perdiccas, son of Alexander, made use of her in the same manner in which his father had employed Gygaea, to get himself out of a military difficulty. In 429 B. C. he bought the retreat of Seuthes the Thracian from the borders of Macedonia for the price of Stratonice as a wife and a sum of money. In the reign of Archelaus, son of Perdiccas (413-399 B. C.), that monarch when pressed by a war against Sirrhas and Arrhabaeus [8] gave his two daughters in marriage, the older to a king of Elimeia, whose name is not given (it was formerly believed to be Sirrhas), and the younger either to his own son by a previous marriage or, according to an emendation accepted by several scholars, to Amyntas, son of Arrhidaeus. The names of the two daughters of Archelaus are not given, but the younger one given, according to the emended reading,[9] to Amyntas, son of Arrhidaeus, may have been named Gygaea. That name oc-

---

[6] Hdt. V, 21 and VIII, 136.

[7] Thuc. II, 101, 6.

[8] Aristotle, *Politics*, V, 1311 b.

[9] Hoffmann, *Makedonen*, p. 160.

curs (in a corrupted form) in Justin VII, 4. Justin says that Amyntas had by Gygaea three sons, Archelaus, Arrhidaeus, and Menelaus. Beloch [10] thinks that Gygaea was descended from Menelaus, brother of Perdiccas, because of the name of her youngest son. The names of the two eldest suggest that the boys were perhaps given the names of two grandfathers, king Archelaus, father of Gygaea, and Arrhidaeus, father of Amyntas.

After Gygaea, daughter of Amyntas I, Stratonice, sister of Perdiccas II, and Gygaea, wife of Amyntas III, only one other royal Macedonian woman of the fifth century is known, the first of the Macedonian princesses and queens to bear the name Cleopatra, later so famous in the Ptolemaic line. She was the wife of Perdiccas the Second, to whom she bore a son, and as queen-widow married Archelaus, the illegitimate son of her husband, who succeeded him as king and was, Thucydides says, the most efficient and energetic of all the Macedonian kings,[11] doing more to strengthen Macedonia by roadmaking, fortifications, and the reconstruction of the army than the eight preceding kings together had done. He was a patron of the arts and introduced the worship of the Muses, or greatly furthered that worship in Macedonia.[12] It was at his court that Euripides, in exile from Athens, wrote the *Bacchae* and the *Archelaus*. Nevertheless he is accounted by Plato a most abominable tyrant. It is in the well-known passage about him in the *Gorgias* [13] that Cleopatra's name occurs. This passage and one in Aristotle give us what scanty information we have of her life. It appears from Plato that her son by Perdiccas was seven years old at the time when Archelaus murdered him. Plato tells the manner of his death: the child was pushed into a well by his half-brother, who told his mother Cleopatra that the little boy while chasing his pet goose had fallen into the well by

[10] Beloch, III², pp. 66 ff.
[11] Thuc. II, 100 ff.
[12] Diod. XVII, 16; Arrian, *An.* I, 11, 1.
[13] Plato, *Gorgias,* 471 c.

accident. It follows from the phrases used by Plato that his brother was at the time his guardian, and "should have reared him to manhood and given him his rightful kingdom ". Since the boy was so young, we may infer that Cleopatra was married by Perdiccas in his late life. Archelaus was the son of a slave-mother, according to *Gorgias* 471a. His father certainly acknowledged him, for his name appears as "Archelaus (son) of Perdiccas" among the ambassadors who negotiated the treaty with Athens in 422 B. C.[14] Perdiccas died in 413 B. C., and Archelaus probably became guardian of the child and married Cleopatra immediately. The passage in Aristotle [15] which mentions Cleopatra's name is the evidence for her marriage to Archelaus. It reads (in the unamended form, which is probably right) : " When hard pressed in war against Sirrhas and Arrhabaeus, he gave his elder daughter to the king of Elimeia and the younger to his son Amyntas, thinking that by this arrangement that son and his son by Cleopatra would be less likely to quarrel."

It is inferred from this passage that Cleopatra had three children by Archelaus, the two daughters and the son mentioned here,[16] but as Perdiccas survived until 413, daughters of Cleopatra by Archelaus would not have been of marriageable age at the time of this arrangement. Archelaus was killed in 399 B. C. Beloch suggests that the elder daughter was the child of a former marriage of Archelaus, and the younger one the child of Cleopatra.[17]

These early queens were entirely passive in political affairs, and their names are known to us only through the use made of them by the kings. The very earliest queen in Macedonia who appears in story is a good house-wife, who baked the bread for the royal household in the king's house at Lebaea in Upper Macedonia, where the little Perdiccas and his brothers tended the horses, cows, and lambs on the king's farm, before they became, according to the story in Herodo-

---

[14] *I.G.* I[2], 71.

[15] Aristotle, *Politics* V, 1311 b.

[16] P. W. XI[1], sp. 734.

[17] Beloch, III[2], p. 64.

tus [18] themselves rulers in Macedonia. From the time of that folk-tale queen down to Eurydice, daughter of Sirrhas, wife of Amyntas, and mother of the great Philip, there is no trace of woman-power in what is recorded of Macedonian history.

EURYDICE I OF MACEDONIA

Eurydice I was the daughter of the mysterious Sirrhas, who is variously regarded as king of Elimiotis (Droysen), son of Arrhabaeus of Lyncestis (Newman), an Illyrian (Hoffmann), and king of Orestis (Beloch). The opinion of Newman was based on the old false translation of Strabo VII, 326,—"and Sirrha (or Irrha) was his daughter". The meaning of course is, "and daughter of Sirrhas" or Irrhas, referring to Eurydice. The passage in Strabo shows that the mother of Eurydice was daughter of Arrhabaeus. Eurydice is called an Illyrian by Plutarch,[19] by Libanius, and by Suidas. Beloch [20] says that she could not have been an Illyrian, since the Macedonian kings did not take their chief wives from the Illyrians. But this point is not established for the early Macedonian kings, and there is little or no evidence about whom they married.

Her husband had been married before he married her to a lady named Gygaea, according to Justin,[21] who may have been a daughter of Archelaus. Eurydice bore him three sons, Alexander, Perdiccas, and Philip, and one daughter Eurynoe. If we are to believe Justin, Eurydice was the prototype of all the most wicked queens of Macedonian blood in later Macedonia, in Seleucid Syria, and in Ptolemaic Egypt. Justin relates that from love of her son-in-law Ptolemaeus of Alorus she plotted against the life of her husband and was detected by her daughter, who revealed her mother's guilt. Justin says

---

[18] Hdt. VIII, 136 ff.

[19] Plut. *De. Educ. Puer.* XX, 14; Libanius, Westermann, *Biogr.* 296; Suidas, *s. v.* Κάρανος.

[20] Beloch, III², p. 79.

[21] Justin, VII, 4.

3

that her husband pardoned her for the sake of his children,
not knowing that she was to be deadly to them. It is said
in the scholium on Aeschines II, 32 that she helped Ptolemaeus kill her son Alexander, who became king at his father's
death in 370 B. C.[22] Justin says that Eurydice was responsible for his death. The young king was murdered at a war-
dance of the Macedonians called " telesias "[23] and Ptolemaeus
Alorites then governed as regent for three years. As he
issued no coins, it appears that he did not assume the title
of king, but kept the promise made to Pelopidas[24] to keep
the kingship for the young princes Perdiccas and Philip.
Aeschines[25] is authority for his title of *epitropos*. He was
perhaps an illegitimate half-brother of the heirs, as stated
by Diodorus.[26] No doubt he and Eurydice were about the
same age, as she was the second wife of Amyntas. When the
young Perdiccas was old enough to take a hand in affairs, he
had Ptolemaeus killed and reigned for five years.[27] Justin
heaps up the sum of Eurydice's crimes by saying that she
killed Perdiccas and was not deterred from her murderous
deed by the sight of his pitiful little son. This story is
admitted to be false, as we have the testimony of Diodorus[28]
and of Marsyas that Perdiccas was killed in battle with the
Illyrians. Hogarth,[29] who takes Justin's accounts at their
face value, thinks that the " Lyncestian Athaliah ", bent on
avenging her lover Ptolemaeus, found an opportunity five
years after his death and kindled the Lyncestians to war upon
Perdiccas, in order that the latter might fall in battle. There
is no proof of this, and the theory ascribes to Eurydice a
political power that she can hardly have possessed. It seems

[22] Cf. Beloch, III², p. 57.

[23] Marsyas ap. Athen. 629 d.

[24] Plut. *Pelop.* XXVI.

[25] Aeschines, II, 28 f.

[26] Diod. XV, 71, 1; 77, 5 (Vogel in the Teubner text deletes the
words for " son of Amyntas " and " brother " in these passages.)

[27] Diod. XV, 77, 5; schol. on Aeschines II, 32.

[28] Diod. XVI, 2; Marsyas, *loc. cit.*

[29] Hogarth, *Philip and Alexander*, p. 41.

likely that Justin used and embroidered upon some scandal-mongering source which blackened the memory of Eurydice, and, finding the crimes of a woman more piquant than those of a man, devolved the murder of Alexander from Ptolemaeus on Eurydice, adding the murder of Perdiccas and the touch about the " *parvulus filius* ". The better authorities [30] state that Ptolemaeus killed Alexander. Justin does not mention the name of Ptolemaeus (though he refers to Eurydice's love for her son-in-law), and he ascribes the murder of Alexander entirely to the queen.

In the speech of Aeschines known as " The False Legation ", we have a picture of Eurydice given by a man who was a contemporary of her son Philip, and one whose testimony deserves consideration as being by far the closest in time to the events of Eurydice's life. In that speech delivered in 343 B. C. either Aeschines finds it politic to refer to Eurydice as a woman who acted for the good of her children and was betrayed by false friends, or else that was the fact. In either case it looks as though Eurydice could not have been such a desperate villain as Justin has painted her, or her name would not have been used by Aeschines to move the heart of her son.

In his speech Aeschines tells a very vivid and dramatic story about Eurydice's summoning Iphicrates, the Athenian general, to her help after the death of her husband and her son Alexander. There is no suggestion of the participation of Eurydice in the plot to kill her son, but Aeschines does say that she had been betrayed by those whom she thought her friends. The story is told in the account of a speech which Aeschines made before Philip on the occasion of the famous embassy in 346 B. C. He says that he said to Philip: " Your mother Eurydice summoned Iphicrates and, as all those who were there present testify, she put your brother Perdiccas in his arms and set you, a little boy, upon his knee and said to him, ' Amyntas, the father of these children, when he was alive, made you his son and counted Athens his friend, so you

---

[30] Diod. XV, 71; Plut. *Pelop.* XXVII.

personally are a brother of these boys and politically a friend
to us.' She then made a strong plea for the children, and herself, and the kingdom." Aeschines mentions the fact that he
criticized in his speech Ptolemaeus of Alorus, who was regent
at the time of Eurydice's interview. Iphicrates gave Eurydice the assistance for which she asked and drove the pretender Pausanias out of Macedonia. If she was an acknowledged murderess and adulteress, it does not seem likely that
Iphicrates would have been moved by her plea or that
Aeschines would have dared recall her to Philip.

A dedication by her to the Muses which is quoted by
Plutarch in his essay on " The Education of a Child "[31]
gives a pleasant piece of information about her; Plutarch
speaks of this as an apt expression of maternal love on the
part of a woman who though " an Illyrian and thrice barbarian," still took to study late in life for the sake of her
children. The true reading in the first line was restored by
W. R. Paton.[32] The dedication translated reads as follows:

> Eurydice, daughter of Irrhas, offers this shrine to the Muses,
> Glad for the wish of her heart granted by them to her prayer,
> Since by their aid she has learned, when mother of sons
>   grown to manhood,
> Letters, recorders of words; learned how to read and to write.

The Eurydice of this charming dedication and of the interview with Iphicrates does not resemble the Eurydice of Justin.
The stories which he repeats against her character may have
originated in the marriage with Ptolemaeus of Alorus after he
had killed her son, king Alexander. This marriage may have
been forced upon her. A similar case was that of Cleopatra,
wife of Perdiccas, who married her step-son when he was
regent for her minor son. It is reasonable to think that
Ptolemaeus was a close connection of the royal family, perhaps son of Amyntas, as Diodorus says; it is difficult to
believe that his marriage with the daughter of Amyntas and
the alleged adulterous relation with the queen-mother would

---

[31] Plut. *De. Educ. Puer.* XX, 14.
[32] Cf. Wilamowitz, *Hermes*, LIV, 1919, p. 71.

have been enough to induce the Macedonians to choose him as ruler and regent for Perdiccas and Philip after he had murdered their brother Alexander. Plutarch [33] speaks of the hostilities between Ptolemaeus and the young king Alexander, and says that Pelopidas had been summoned by both Ptolemaeus and Alexander to be arbiter of their quarrel and to help the injured party. This indicates that Ptolemaeus had some sort of case or claim and strengthens the statement of Diodorus, expunged from the text by Vogel, that he was a son of Amyntas. The question deserves attention in considering the law of inheritance and also in connection with woman-power in Macedonia. If Ptolemaeus was raised to power and practically became king [34] through his relation to the queen-mother, it is important evidence of the influence and power of the queen in the Macedonian state. The queens before Eurydice evidently had no independent power, and there is no other evidence of such power in her case. But if Ptolemaeus was, like Archelaus, a bastard son, but one possessed of ambition and strong qualities, he may very well have wished to emulate the great monarch, and it appears that in the case of the strong man, the Macedonians were not always meticulous about legitimacy in their royal family, occasionally preferring a competent monarch with the bar sinister to a weak legitimate heir.[35]

It seems not improbable that Eurydice was forced by dynastic reasons, or by the threats of Ptolemaeus himself, to marry this prince, who was the husband of her daughter, a fact for which we have Justin's statement. Plutarch says nothing of the marriage with Eurynoe, though he mentions a son of Ptolemaeus, who was given by him to Pelopidas as pledge of his fair-dealing with Perdiccas and Philip. Eurydice may have been, not a " mala bestia," [36] but an unfortunate and gifted woman, whose marriage with the guardian of

---

[33] Plut. *Pelop.* XXVI.

[34] Diod. XV, 76, 77.

[35] Beloch, IV¹, pp. 376 (with notes).

[36] Taylor, quoted in Dobson, *Oratores Attici*, XII, 25.

the royal children appears to have been the natural Macedonian custom. The power which she possessed from her natural gifts, whether resulting from an indomitable will or from the charm of beauty, or from both, should not be confused with the question of political power, for which there is not a shred of evidence in her case. As queen-widow she must have possessed large estates and great prestige. The qualities inherited from her very likely contributed more to the greatness of her son Philip than those inherited from Amyntas.

What her end was we do not know. The last mention of her is the false story in Justin of her murder of Perdiccas.[37] Justin loves to write on crimes of queens and would always choose the slanderous tale among his sources. But for his account of her and for that of his slavish copier Orosius, Eurydice would not have come down in history as the " Lyncestian Athaliah ",[38] but as the first queen of Macedonia who learned to read and write and as a mother devoted to the interests of her children. But to know the truth about her we need to know the sources of Justin's account.

OLYMPIAS AND HER DAUGHTER CLEOPATRA

Olympias, the wife of Philip the Second of Macedon and mother of Alexander the Great, was the great-granddaughter of Tharyps, king of the Molossians in Epirus and the first of his rude tribe to become familiar with the Greek language and customs. He was given citizenship at Athens[39] and introduced the Greek alphabet and some of the Greek humane laws into his land.[40] Neoptolemus, father of Olympias, and his father Alcetas had remained in the philhellene tradition and traced their descent to Achilles and his son Neoptolemus. From the time of Alcetas the members of the royal family received Greek names. It was said that Olympias was de-

---

[37] Justin, VII, 5, 4.

[38] Hogarth, *Philip and Alexander,* p. 41.

[39] *I.G.* II, 1, 115.

[40] Plut. *Pyrrhus,* I.

scended both from Pyrrhus, son of Achilles, and from
Helenus, son of Priam,[41] who was the ancestor of the Chaonian
kings, and it is possible that her mother was a Chaonian.[42]

She could hardly have been born before 375 B. C., since her
marriage took place in 357 B. C. and she was, according to
Plutarch, still a child at the first meeting with Philip, who was
himself a youth, but old enough to fall in love with Olympias
and to ask her uncle [43] Arybbas for her hand. The meeting
was at Samothrace, to which sacred island both of the young
people had been brought for the purpose of being initiated
into the Mysteries. Hogarth, who habitually refers to Olympias as "the Jezebel of a Queen" or "the wild harridan",
declares that "A votary of the Cabiric mysteries before marriage was open to more than suspicion." [44] He appears to over-
look her tender years at the time of her initiation and the
fact that her uncle, the king, had brought his royal niece to
Samothrace for the ceremony. If it was an initiation into
unchastity, as Hogarth suggests, the fact that the young princesses and princes were sent to Samothrace for initiation
throws a lurid light on the moral standards of the royal
families of Epirus and Macedon. Hogarth does not take into
account the wide-spread influence of the worship of the Cabiri
and the significance of that worship for the Macedonian royal
house.[45]

It is stated that the name given to Olympias in childhood
was Myrtale,[46] and the names Polyxene and Stratonice [47] are
also mentioned as hers. There are other cases among the
Macedonian princesses of an additional name or names, some-

[41] Tzetzes on Lyc. 1439. Theopompus, *F.H.G.* I, p. 317.

[42] Klotzsch, *Epirotische Geschichte*, pp. 54-5.

[43] Plutarch wrongly calls Arybbas a brother of Olympias.

[44] *Philip and Alexander*, p. 137.

[45] Cf. Kern, *Griechische Religion*, p. 240; P. W. 10², sp. 1415, *s. v.*
Kabeiroi.

[46] Justin, II, 7. 13.

[47] *Plut. De Pyth. Or.* 401. Plutarch remarks that these changes of
name have a significance behind them and gives examples of such.

times assumed like that of Eurydice or Cleopatra on a significant occasion, such as becoming queen. I suggest that the
name Olympias was taken at the request of her husband after
the birth of her son Alexander in 356 B. C. At that time
Philip had just captured Potidaea. While he was still there
three runners came to him with three different messages of
good fortune: his general, Parmenio, had won a great battle
in Illyria, his racehorses had won the victory at Olympia,[48]
and his wife had borne him a son, Alexander, of whom the
soothsayers prophesied that a child born among so many
victories would never know defeat. The name Olympias
appears for the first time as a proper name as a name of this
queen, and it is probable that the former Myrtale or Stratonice
or Polyxene was now called by this name of good omen for
herself and her son. Liddell and Scott confuse the common
noun and the proper name in translating Diod. XVIII, 65,
where it is said that the Athenians held Olympias in high
respect—τὴν Ὀλυμπιάδα πολυωρηκότες. They render the phrase
" having carefully observed it ", i. e., the festival.[49]

The child born of Hellenized barbarians in the Molossian
land,

Where the Sun turns his steeds to the twilight.[50]

was destined by birth and nature to a stormy life. But if
she had not met her fate, as the saying is, on the island of
Samothrace when she was but a girl in years, the drama of
her life would have been played to the end among her own
tribesmen with no lasting effect on the history of the world.
The meeting of the two young barbarians on the sacred isle,
a meeting of eagle natures, was pregnant with the fate of
nations and civilizations. Plutarch says that Philip fell in
love with Olympias. However that may be, there can be no
doubt that the marriage was a political arrangement between

---

[48] Philip had coins struck with his victorious chariot on them.
Cf. Plut. *Alex.* IV.

[49] Liddell and Scott, *s. v.* πολυωρέω.

[50] Euripides, *Alcestis*, 594, Gilbert Murray's translation.

Arybbas and Philip. It was the rule with these northern
tribes to cement a peace treaty or an alliance by the giving of
a princess in marriage, and Philip notably kept up the practice of political marriages even after his marriage to Olympias.
Young as he was at the time he had probably already married
more than once.[51] His Illyrian wife Audata, who took the
name Eurydice at her marriage, was probably given to him
by Bardylis in 358 B. C., when Philip after sweeping victories
made " a glorious peace " [52] with the Illyrians and returned
to his own country to find his name on every tongue and
himself unboundedly popular because of his Illyrian campaign.
The fruit of this marriage was his daughter, Cynna, or
Cynane, whose only child was later queen of Macedon and
a victim of the jealousy of Olympias in the latter's old age.
His first wife was perhaps Phila, an Elimiot princess, who
appears to have died childless. Beloch [53] supposes that Phila
as a Macedonian was a legitimate wife and Philip's queen,
while Audata came from a country from which Beloch says
the kings of Macedon took only " Nebenfrauen ", or subordinate wives, who would not have the title of queen, even
though they were of royal birth and lived at Philip's court.
His children by his various wives appear to have been brought
up in his palace, and Olympias may have found at least
Audata-Eurydice and her little daughter there when she
came from Epirus to be chief queen. The fact that the
Illyrian princess took the name Eurydice, which had a tendency to become dynastic like the name Cleopatra in Egypt,
indicates that she may from the time of her marriage have been
regarded as queen of Macedon until Philip found an alliance
with the Molossians of greater advantage than one with
Bardylis. The situation from any point of view must have
been difficult and full of occasions for jealousies and wrang-
lings.

---

[51] Beloch, III², pp. 68 f.
[52] Diod. XVI, 8.
[53] Beloch, III², p. 68.

The especial object of Olympias' hatred in the royal household was the child Arrhidaeus, son of a Thessalian lady (some
say a dancing-woman) called Philinna.[54] Whether this son
of Philip was older or younger than Olympias' son Alexander is disputed. He is said by Plutarch to have been
a charming and princely little boy of fine promise, whose
intellect Olympias undermined by the steady administration
of drugs.[55] Although he became king after the death of
Alexander the Great, he always was reckoned deficient in
mind. Besides the two children just mentioned there were in
the palace, if we may believe Satyrus,[56] other offspring of
Philip with their mothers as well, chiefly princesses whom
he married as part of the ceremony of treaty-making and
had brought home to be under one roof with his queen.

Olympias and Philip had two children in quick succession,
Alexander, born in 356 B. C., and Cleopatra two years later.
The marriage of such a man and woman, violent and strong
of will as they both were, could not avoid disaster; neither
one of them could bring happiness to anyone else. It may be
that the love of which Plutarch writes persisted for the first
few years of marriage, especially as Philip was in these years
chiefly away from home, engaged in conquering Chalcidice
and Thrace. He left great power in his wife's hands while
he was off campaigning, and love of power and an obstinate
determination to have her own way lay at the foundation of
the young queen's character. In 351 B. C. she induced Philip
to summon her young brother of twelve or thirteen years to
come and live at their court.[57] She planned to have her little
Cleopatra marry this heir to the Molossian throne, a plan
which was realized when Cleopatra was old enough to marry.

In all the dissensions and rivalries among her husband's

---

[54] Satyrus, *F.H.G.* III 161; Ptolemaeus, son of Agesarchus, *F.H.G.*
III, p. 67; Justin XIII, 2, 11.

[55] Plut. *Alex.* LXXVII.

[56] *F.H.G.* III, 161; Athen. XIII, 557 b.

[57] Justin, VIII, 6, 5.

wives and paramours and their children Olympias appears to have shown at times a sense of humor. When Philip fell madly in love with one of his Thessalian [58] mistresses, he made the well-known witchlore of the Thessalian women his excuse to Olympias, telling her that the girl had made him a victim of magic arts. Olympias had the girl brought to her presence and examined her, finding her a young person of beauty, good sense, and good breeding. Whereupon she said to her, " This is all nonsense about your magic herbs and potions. You have magic in yourself." She had a reputation for making *bons mots,* an instance of which is quoted in the story that she said of a young man who married a lady who was fair but frail, that he had married " with his eyes only " and not his common sense. And she made light of [59] the story that went about that her son Alexander was the son of Zeus, quite wittily saying " Will Alexander never stop getting me into trouble with Hera! "

Plutarch tells of the wild rites which she introduced among the Macedonian women who worshipped Dionysus. She had the power of snake-charming, which Plutarch [59a] speaks of as a barbaric *trait* brought in by the young queen. She taught the Macedonian maenads to carry great tamed snakes which wound themselves about their Bacchic wands and peered from the ivy crowns on their heads. Their husbands did not like the innovation, and Plutarch says that Philip conceived a dislike for the marriage-bed of Olympias because of her pet snakes which frequented it. He is inclined to ascribe the whole tissue of tales about the god who appeared to Olympias in the form of a snake to these uncanny pets of the Epirote princess.

---

[58] Plut. *Conjug. Praecept.* 141 B-C. Beloch (III², pp. 169 ff.) thinks that the Thessalian girl must have been either Philinna, mother of Arrhidaeus, or Nicesipolis, mother of Thessalonice.

[59] Plut. *Alex.* III. The word ἀφοσιοῦσθαι (cf. also Plato, *Legg.* 752 D) is equivalent to " crossed herself " in modern formulas of averting evil.

[59a] Plut. *Alex.* II. Cf. Maenad with snake and thyrsus on r. f. amphora E 253 in the British Museum.

The impulses that drove Olympias to the hills for the wild
Bacchic rites found another outlet in her violent outbursts of
frenzied rage when her will was crossed. She was a woman
of genius, and probably always close to the borderline of
insanity. " A passionate and jealous woman " is the description given by Plutarch [60] of her nature, and Arrian [61] speaks
of her as " obstinate, violent, and interfering ". Her husband
had a vent for his passionate nature and his genius in his constant and successful labours for the unification and aggrandizement of Macedon, and he had the vices, accounted in Macedon soldier-like and manly, of drunkenness and lust. No
lover of Olympias is named except the serpent-god and Zeus.
It is clear that she, like the Macedonian queens in general,
was virtuous in the restricted sense of that word. Hogarth
feels sure that there was some contemporary scandal about
her, which he says Attalus tipsily blurted out when he prayed
at the marriage of his niece to Philip for a legitimate heir to
the throne. The sting of the word γνήσιος for Alexander, in
fact, was that Attalus asked the Macedonians to pray for a
true Macedonian [62] to be born from the two *Macedonians,*
Philip and Cleopatra. Philip's other children had been the
children of Illyrians, Thessalians and Thracians, and the
Molossian Olympias, and might all be regarded as *nothoi,*
bastards, from the old Macedonian point of view. The connection in Plutarch's narrative shows that the question is that
of Philip's many wives and paramours, who had brought
the royal harem into a desperate state of rival claims and
bitter quarrels for precedence. Most of these ladies were
daughters of kings or great chiefs, and it might well be said
by them that a Molossian was no better as a " legitimate "
queen of Macedon than the rest of them. Compare what
Beloch says about Phila as a Macedonian princess and so a
legitimate queen.[63]

Olympias had charge of the early education of her son and

---

[60] Plut. *Alex.* IX.   [62] Cf. Beloch, III², p. 68.
[61] Arrian, VII, 12.   [63] Beloch, III², p. 68. Cf. also III², p. 79.

her daughter, for whom she had a large number of instructors. At the head of the teachers of Alexander she placed a noble kinsman of her own, Leonidas, a man of great austerity of life, who brought up his young charge to endure hardship and not to fear danger, and to avoid luxury. In the later Macedonian houses in Egypt and Syria oriental luxury and self-indulgence were rampant, but in these early days Philip could boast to an effeminate officer from Tarentum who desired a hot bath that Macedonian ladies bathed in cold water even in child-birth. Olympias chose her tutors for her children from Epirus and Acarnania, places even less touched by the softness of civilization than Macedonia. Cleopatra shared as much as a girl might in this strenuous education, for the royal women of these hardy northern stocks had to be familiar with the dangers of the hunt and the forest and even, it is said, of the battlefield. In her later life she showed the boldness and courage that were hers both by inheritance and by the education which her mother gave her.

Considering the care which she bestowed upon her children, her devotion to their interests, and her attachment to the Macedonian cult of Bacchus, one perhaps might say that according to Macedonian standards Olympias in her early married life was a good and religious woman. That her temper was rendered the fiercer because she had to live with the wives and mistresses of her husband is undoubtedly true, and if the story of her undermining the intellect of the little prince Arrhidaeus is not an invention of an enemy, she is like some wicked heroine of the Greek tragedy, Clytemnaestra or Medea for choice, whom evil passions drive to monstrous deeds.

She was bitterly opposed to the proposed marriage of Arrhidaeus to the daughter of Pixodarus, the rich satrap of Caria, as she thought that this was too high a match for him. She declared that Philip was bringing Arrhidaeus forward as an heir to his throne by this alliance, and she succeeded in stirring up Alexander to the point that he sent a message to Pixodarus, asking him to choose him for his son-in-law rather than his " bastard and fool " of a brother. Pixodarus was glad enough to make the exchange, but the affair so angered Philip that he reproached Alexander bitterly and told him that he ought to feel shame at the thought of marrying a barbarous Carian woman, whose father was no better than a slave to the king of Persia. He proceeded to exile the friends of Alexander who had advised him to this step, among them young Ptolemy, who was later the first Macedonian king of Egypt. This episode took place in the year 337-336 B. C., after Philip had married Cleopatra, niece of Attalus, and after Olympias had retired to Epirus.[64]

After Olympias and Philip had lived together for nearly twenty years Philip fell in love with a young Macedonian lady, who bore the name Cleopatra. She was the niece of Attalus, and it was at their wedding, at which Alexander was present, that the celebrated remark was made by Attalus, which has already been discussed, about the hope of a legitimate heir now being born. Alexander hurled his wine cup at Attalus, crying out "Knave! do you account me a bastard?" Philip, drunk like his guests, started at his son with drawn sword, but fell between the banqueting couches, at which his son said those famous words, "Sirs, here is your hero who plans to cross from Europe to Asia, who has been floored in crossing from couch to couch."

After this episode he took his mother Olympias back to her native Molossia (337 B. C.) and he went to Illyria for a time, but soon returned at his father's request.[65] In Epirus Olympias' young brother Alexander was reigning. He had succeeded to the throne of the Molossians in 342 B. C. at the age of twenty, at which time his uncle Arybbas went into exile in Athens. It is highly probable that Olympias endeavored to rouse her brother to war against Philip for his insult to her and her family in taking a new queen; she was not successful in this, and very likely she was ready to urge her brother to accept the offer of her daughter's hand, which Philip now made to him in order to strengthen the connection

---

[64] Plut. *Alex.* X. [65] Plut. *Alex.* IX.

between Macedon and Epirus against the Illyrians. The marriage took place in the late autumn of 336 B. C. between the twenty-eight-year-old uncle and the eighteen-year-old niece. Philip celebrated the marriage of his daughter with the Epirote king at Aegae with great splendor.[66] Guests were present from all parts and gold crowns were brought to him from every city, even from lately conquered Athens. At dawn of the day following the wedding, statues of the Twelve Gods were carried into the temple, where crowds had been waiting all the night for the spectacle, and a statue of Philip was borne in with the others. Attended by his friends, the king of Macedon in all the strength and fineness of his prime—he was forty-six years old—stood for a moment in his white robe at the entrance, between the two Alexanders, his son and his son-in-law. A man darted out from the throng and stabbed the king with a short Celtic sword. The assassin was at once seized and killed. He had a grievance against Philip, but it was believed that Olympias had planned the murder and had horses placed in readiness for those in the plot to escape to Epirus.[67]

She was placed in an extraordinarily good strategic position by Philip's death. All that she could have gained if she had succeeded in inducing her brother to make war on Philip was hers, and more. Her daughter was queen of the Molossi and her son was king of Macedonia. She now had a home and a high position in both kingdoms, and she chose Macedonia, in the hope that her son would make her regent during his absence in Asia. Alexander knew his mother and his Macedonians too well to set her as ruler over them and left Antipater in control, but Olympias was restored to her old position of queen in the palace where there were no more

---

[66] Diod. XVI, 94; Justin, IX, 6.

[67] Plut. *Alex.* X; Justin, IX, 7, 3 f. Justin says that Olympias placed a gold wreath on the head of the murderer as his body hung on a cross, that she burned his body above the ashes of her husband, and had a tomb built for him in which she had rites of expiation performed every year.

wives of Philip to rouse her wrath. She had his young Cleopatra with the child whom she had borne a short time before
Philip's death cruelly murdered.[68]   Alexander reproached
his mother for this abominable act, but himself took the
precaution of killing all the remaining members of Cleopatra's
family before he left for Asia.[69]   Philip had placed them in
important positions, and they constituted a menace to
Alexander, who found it advisable to put to death all possible
claimants to the throne.   Among these was his uncle Amyntas, who had been the rightful heir in 359 B. C. when Philip
assumed authority as guardian of his five-year-old nephew.
Amyntas is called king in a Lebadean inscription [70] of 350
B. C., of course a courtesy title.   He was the husband of
Alexander's half-sister Cynane. Philip must often have wished
that this daughter of his with her bold and high spirit
and fighting power had been a son. She had once killed an
Illyrian queen in battle when fighting under Philip.[71]   She
now retired to bring up her little girl Adea-Eurydice in a
castle of her own.   The palace at Pella had no room for two
such women as Olympias and her step-daughter Cynane.

From the time of her husband's murder until 331 B. C.,
a period of five years, Olympias remained mistress of the
Macedonian court. She had a very strong influence over her
absent son, with whom she kept up a vigorous correspondence,
but she failed to get that political power on which her heart
was set. She hated the regent Antipater and they were constantly at odds with one another. A stream of letters from
Olympias and from her enemies went to Alexander, who
loved his mother and knew that she was unswervingly loyal
to him, but also knew that the judgment of a woman of such
desperate passions could not be trusted. Antipater and his
friends wrote of the stubborn self-will, the violence and

---

[68] Justin, IX, 7, 12.

[69] Justin, XI, 5, 1.

[70] *I.G.* VII, 3055, 9.

[71] Polyaenus VIII, 60.   Berve suggests the campaign of 344-3
B. C. for the time of this exploit (*Alexanderreich*, II, p. 229).

meddlesomeness of the queen.[72] The king did not allow his
mother to meddle with his friendships or to interfere with
his military arrangements, but their natures were so much
alike that he understood her and sent soft answers to her
violent letters. Once indeed, on receiving a letter from Antipater which contained a long list of his mother's misdoings,
he said to Hephaestion that Antipater was unware that one
of his mother's tears would wash out the complaints of a
thousand letters.[73] Although Antipater finally prevailed
against her, the struggle took so much of his strength that
on his dying bed the old man solemnly warned the Macedonians never to let a woman rule them.[74] From his contests
with two women, Olympias and the girl-queen Eurydice, step-
grand-daughter of Olympias, the old regent became a confirmed anti-feminist.

The vengeful and rancorous nature of Olympias gave itself
full rein in these letters to her son. Once she sends a pleasant
letter.[75] She discovered a fine cook, Pelignas, and sent him
with an accompanying letter to her son in Asia: " Receive
from your mother the cook Pelignas. He understands how all
the sacrifices of your family are offered and also the orgiastic
and Bacchic sacrifices which Olympias offers."

In 331 B. C. she had made herself so detested at the Macedonian court that she was ordered by Alexander to refrain
from any further attacks on his friends and to stop meddling
in politics. This strong tone on his part followed her slander
against Amyntas, son of Andromenes, who was triumphantly
acquitted by the Assembly of the Macedonian army and
restored to his honor and office.[76] It was impossible for the
queen to remain at court after such a humiliation, and she
retired to Epirus, where her daughter Cleopatra was regent
during the absence of her husband Alexander I of Epirus on

[72] Arrian, VII, 12, 6.
[73] Plut. *Alex.* XXXIX.
[74] Diod. XIX, 11.
[75] Athen. XIV, 659 ff.
[76] Arrian, III, 27, 3; Curtius, VII, 1, 1.; 2, 10.

4

his Italian campaign. After his death at Pandosia in the
winter of 331-330 B. C., his wife continued to act as regent
and guardian of their four-year-old son, Neoptolemus. In
Epirus Olympias could again play a grand part, and when
her son sent to her and to his sister, queen Cleopatra, splendid
spoil after his great victories,[77] she dedicated magnificent
crowns at Delphi.[78]   Although Alexander deprived her
of political power in Macedon, it was said that he declared
that all his fighting and toiling would be crowned when his
mother Olympias should be consecrated as one of the Immortal Gods.[79] She of course could do less mischief in the
rôle of a goddess with a cult than as a queen with political
power, and to look forward to such deification on the return
of her son doubtless pacified her fierce temper and recompensed her in part for her defeat in the contest with Antipater.[80]   Plutarch says (Alex. 27) that Alexander wrote to
his mother that the oracle of Ammon had imparted to him
certain secrets, which he would divulge on his return to her
alone.

The most authentic account of Olympias which we possess
appears in a speech by the Athenian orator Hyperides [81] which
is dated by Schaefer in the year 330 B. C. It was delivered
after her retirement to Epirus; and the picture in Hyperides
corresponds to that which is found in the later historians.
She is overbearing and dramatic; Hyperides has himself
twice protested in the Athenian Assembly against the in-
justice and impropriety of the letters brought by her envoys,
in which she attacks the Athenians because they have sent a
new face and hands, made by their best artists, for the gold
and ivory statue of Dione at Dodona and also beautiful and

---

[77] Plut. *Alex.* XXV.

[78] Ditt. *Syll.*³ I, 252, N. 5 ff.; Keil, *Hermes*, XXXVII, 1902, pp.
511 ff.

[79] Curtius, IX, 6, says: "quandocumque excesserit vita."

[80] For the Macedonian opposition to worship of royalty cf. Beloch,
IV¹, pp. 372 f.

[81] Hyperides, *Euxen.* 24 ff.

expensive adornments for the goddess, and a deputation to conduct a costly sacrifice in the temple, all of which was done in obedience to an oracle in which Zeus of Dodona had ordered them to renew the statue. Olympias, in words quoted by Hyperides, writes, " This Molossian land in which the temple is, is mine, and it is not for you Athenians to lay a finger on a stone in that temple." She had sent to the temple of Hygieia in Athens a votive cup (phiale), probably of gold, for the hand of the statue of the goddess to hold, and Hyperides pertinently asks " And is Olympias, forsooth, to be allowed to adorn our temples, while we are not permitted to adorn those in Dodona even when the god himself has told us to do it? " [82]

After the death of her brother, King Alexander of Epirus, in Italy, Olympias sent her widowed daughter to Macedon to make what trouble she could for the regent Antipater. The old queen remained in Epirus as regent and guardian for Cadmeia and Neoptolemus, the royal children. It may be that mother and daughter were too much alike in their imperious natures to get along together in the government of the Molossians,[83] but it is probable enough that since Olympias herself could not return to Macedon because of her feud with Antipater, Cleopatra went willingly to oppose the regent and to strengthen her own influence with the Macedonians and with her brother. When he was told that his mother had stayed in Epirus and his sister had come to Macedon, he laughed and said that his mother had chosen the better part, for the Macedonians would never suffer a woman to be king over them.[84] It was in 325 B. C. that Cleopatra went to Macedon to watch the progress of events in that country. There was no one in Epirus who could sufficiently oppose the tyrannous rule of Olympias, and her despotic ways made her

---

[82] *Op. cit.* 26. Hyperides speaks of her melodramatic accusations— τὰς τραγῳδίας καὶ κατηγορίας.

[83] This is the opinion of Berve (*Alexanderreich*, II p. 212).

[84] Plut. *Alex.* LXVIII.

an object of hatred [85] in her native land. It is not known whether she continued to keep the children of her daughter with her or if they went later to their mother in Macedon.

The death of Alexander increased her passionate hatred for Antipater, for she had been biding her time in Epirus, waiting for that day when Alexander should return in glory to give her not only divine honors, but to make her again what she longed to be, queen of the Macedonian court, triumphant over the hated regent. His son Iollas was cupbearer to Alexander and had given him his wine on the day of his death. Olympias spread the story that the king had been poisoned by Iollas at the instigation of Antipater and that the poison had been procured by Aristotle and conveyed by Cassander. Six years after the death of Alexander she had his son Nicanor murdered and desecrated the grave of Iollas.[86] She would have liked to wipe out the entire family, but Cassander was destined to make the last move in the terrible game of assassination at which both Olympias and he were so proficient, and in the end he killed the old queen. But much was to happen before that.

At the moment she planned to secure control of Macedonia by a marriage of her daughter, whose most distinguished lineage and high position as queen in Epirus made all the Successors turn their thoughts to her. Olympias thought that Leonnatus, the popular and handsome satrap of Phrygia,[87] who was related to the royal house through some kinship with Eurydice, mother of Philip the Second, would prove the strongest opponent of Antipater and her own best support. She accordingly had Cleopatra write to him to come to Pella to marry her and to be king of Macedonia. He had been brought up with Alexander and Cleopatra as a boy, and was not unlike Alexander in beauty and height, a resemblance which he endeavored to increase after the king's death by imitating his personal traits, such as his way of wearing long

---

[85] Pausan. I, 11, 4.
[86] Diod. XIX, 11.
[87] Plut. *Eumenes*, III.

hair.[88] Leonnatus was impetuous and easily carried away by enthusiasm, and old associations and the ambition which each of the Successors cherished led him to accept Cleopatra's proposal. He came with his troops to Europe, nominally to assist Antipater, and indeed it fell out so, for he was forced to fight to free Antipater from Lamia, where the Greek troops had him enclosed. He was killed at Crannon in the first battle with the Greeks in Thessaly.[89] His death was a fearful blow to Olympias, while Antipater, who had been informed of the intrigues between Leonnatus and Olympias, was glad to have him dead and his troops at his own disposal.

Now that the plan of Olympias had ended in disaster for herself and triumph for the regent, she turned her thought to the commander-in-chief of the troops in Asia, Perdiccas, as the most brilliant match for her daughter, since he possessed prestige and power that with her aid could make him ruler of Macedonia and give his mother-in-law a proud place there and vengeance on the regent and his family. So she sent Cleopatra to Asia to offer herself to Perdiccas, who would have been very glad to marry her but for the *embarras de richesse* in the way of splendid offers of marriage that presented themselves to him. Antipater also at once sent his daughter, Nicaea, escorted by her brother Iollas and by Archias,[90] to be the bride of Perdiccas, who, forced to choose between the enmity of Olympias and that of Antipater, was indeed between the devil and the deep sea. It was a sad dilemma, and whatever he did was certain to be the mistaken course. He was eager to be king of Macedonia and was already the guardian of the two kings, Arrhidaeus, the dullard, and Alexander the infant. He feared the power of the regent most and decided to marry his daughter for the present,[91] secretly sending word to Cleopatra that he was intending to put Nicaea away and marry her later. The political value of a marriage with Cleopatra was realized by Antipater, Anti-

---

[88] Suidas *s. v.* Λεοννάτος.
[89] Plut. *Phocion*, XXV.
[90] Arrian, *Succ.* I, 21.
[91] Diod. XVIII, 23.

gonus, Ptolemy, and Lysimachus, and when the plan of Perdiccas to marry her and seize the throne was told by Antigonus on his flight from Asia to Antipater and Craterus, it
proved the ruin of Perdiccas. Cleopatra was thereafter kept
in Sardis under close watch, each general being intent on pre-
venting a marriage with her that should disturb the balance
of power, except if it might be in his own interest. So
Olympias was again checkmated by the old regent.

Her rule in Epirus, where she was greatly hated, was at
this time threatened by the return of the younger branch of
the royal family, which had been driven into exile by Philip in
342 B. C., at the time when the young brother of Olympias,
Alexander, was made king in place of her uncle Arybbas. The
exiles found refuge in Athens and there were given the same
honors and privileges that had been in the past conferred
upon Alcetas and Tharyps, the phil-Athenian father and
grandfather of Arybbas.[92] The decree which confers these
privileges also enjoins upon the Athenian generals to assist
Arybbas and his children to recover their ancestral sovereignty. This was not achieved for them by the help of Athens,
but in the case of Arybbas, if he is the Aryptaeus of Diodorus XVIII, 11, by treachery to Athens in the Lamian war, in
which, as we are told in the passage just referred to, the Molossians under Aryptaeus were false allies to the Greeks and
treacherously aided the Macedonian cause. Justin says, however, that Arybbas grew old in exile.[93] In any case his son
Aeacides returned to Epirus, doubtless through the influence of Antipater, and perhaps also the old king, who had
once taken his niece to Samothrace and had negotiated for
her the marriage that made her queen of Macedon and mother
of Alexander the Great, returned with him. Nothing is known
about Arybbas after this time,[94] but his son Aeacides [95] now

---

[92] *I.G.* II, 115.
[93] Justin, VII, 6, 12.
[94] Klotzsch, *Epirotische Geschichte*, pp. 75, 97 ff.
[95] Pausan. I, 11, 3.

appears as ruler in Epirus, in close conjunction with Olympias, who controlled him completely. Deprived as she was of both son and daughter, as Cleopatra was practically imprisoned in Sardis, she had her sole hope for power in her cousin. The young Neoptolemus, the crown-prince, was only eleven years old, and Olympias, who was now over fifty, welcomed the presence of Aeacides as commander of troops at her side.

Antipater, her enemy, died in 319 B. C., with a warning on his lips to his fellow-countrymen never to let a woman rule them. The grim relentless queen, biding her time in Epirus, waiting for Fate to bring her back to Macedonia, haunted his last hours. And now Olympias had her day, a brief one, as the drama of her life moves on to its close with the inevitability of a Sophoclean drama. Antipater,[96] to the disgust of his son Cassander, had recommended Polyperchon as his successor, as regent and guardian of the Two Kings. Polyperchon was the oldest living of the Macedonian officers who had served under Alexander, and the Macedonians had a great regard for him. One of the two Kings was mentally incompetent and the other but four years old. A danger threatened the new regent from the jealousy of Cassander,[97] who thought that his father should have chosen him to succeed him instead of Polyperchon.

Polyperchon now took a bold step. He had a conference [98] of leading Macedonian nobles, in which it was decided that the regent should invite Olympias to return to Macedonia and assume charge of the little Alexander, acting as his guardian and with royal rank. Cassander was as bitterly hated by her as ever Antipater had been, for he had, she believed, taken poison to his brother Iollas to drop in the wine which her son drank; but she did not trust Polyperchon and

---

[96] Diod. XVIII, 48.

[97] Diod. XVIII, 49. Schwahn, *Klio*, 1931, p. 316. Schwahn points out that a prime-minister could not appoint his successor. He shows that the choice must have been made by the Assembly of the Army.

[98] Diod. *loc. cit.*

wrote to her friend Eumenes [99] in Asia, asking his advice and
suggesting that the proposal perhaps came from one who
was seeking royal power for himself. Eumenes counselled
delay—things were still in a precarious way and the fighting
had not yet decided which of the Successors would prevail.
He was steadfastly her friend and always insisted that oaths
be taken in the name of " Olympias and the Two Kings ".[100]
Although the invitation to return to Macedonia was repeated
by Polyperchon in very urgent words when Cassander began
to oppose him openly, Olympias still delayed. It is commonly
said by historians that Roxane and the little Alexander
were sent by Polyperchon after the death of Antipater to be
under the protection of Olympias in Epirus. I have elsewhere [101] shown that this theory is erroneous and comes
from a misunderstanding of Diodorus. Polyperchon was too
cunning a politician to let the Kings out of his grasp. It was
a cardinal rule with the old regent Antipater, impressed upon
him when he took charge of the Two Kings in Asia, by his
son Cassander,[102] always to have the Kings with him. Polyperchon, when he became guardian of the royalties, also kept
them near him.

Olympias still waited in Epirus; she had waited long for
her return and, almost sixty as she was, she was still possessed
of an indestructible strength and demoniac power that inspired with fear and awe of her all who came into her presence.
But when she saw that a young girl, her husband's grand-
daughter, Adea-Eurydice, the queen of Philip Arrhidaeus, en-
dowed with as indomitable a nature as her own, was getting
the control of Macedonia which she had been seeking for herself for so many years, but which had always eluded her grasp,
then in a storm of jealous rage and hatred for the young
queen, she roused her cousin Aeacides to join Polyperchon
with his troops at the border to invade Macedon. It was

[99] Diod. XVIII, 58.

[100] Plut. *Eumenes*, XII.

[101] Article to be published in *J.H.S.*

[102] Arrian. *Succ.* I, 42, μήτε πόρρω τῶν βασιλέων ἀποχωρεῖν.

Polyperchon's last throw of the dice, for he had been defeated in Peloponnesus, and Eurydice had appointed Cassander in his place as regent and had moulded the will of her imbecile husband to utter obedience to her own wishes. Polyperchon had still " a shot in the locker ", for he had little Alexander with whose person he could bargain with friend or foe, and he now told Olympias that he would put her and the child on the throne of Macedonia.[103] At Euia [104] on the border two armies met, that of Olympias and Aeacides and that of Eurydice and Philip Arrhidaeus. The name of the place perhaps seemed to Olympias to promise good fortune to her, a life-long votary of the Euian god, and she entered battle like a bacchanal [105] with the beat of the Dionysiac drums, while Eurydice wore the armor of the Macedonian infantry who had put her husband on the throne against the will of the nobles. Olympias with her bacchanal array may well have been thinking of the help once given an old Macedonian king in battle by the maenads from the hills, who turned the tide of battle against his enemies with their magic thyrsi without striking a blow.[106] And a miracle *was* wrought for her, for when the Macedonian soldiers saw their old queen advancing, they were so struck by her majesty and her noble air, so like that of her glorious son, that they remembered that she was the wife of their great Philip and mother of their great Alexander and came over to her side,—a proud moment for the old queen. Philip the king was captured with his followers and then Eurydice, as she was making off for Amphipolis with Polycles, one of her councillors. Then came one of those episodes that reveal life and what we call history as tragic action such as appears on the stage of Aeschylus and Sophocles and Shakespeare. It is sufficient to translate the narrative of Diodorus.

" In this way Olympias captured the king and queen without risk to herself and secured the royal power. In her good fortune she did not display common humanity, but imprisoned

---

[103] Diod. XVIII, 49. 4; 65. 10.   [105] Duris ap. Athen. 560 f.
[104] Diod. XIX, 11.   [106] Polyaenus, IV, 1.

Eurydice and her husband and proceeded to torture them. She had them shut into a little room, into which barely enough food to sustain life was pushed through a small aperture; day after day her unhappy victims suffered this lawless treatment from her until her conduct scandalized the Macedonians and moved their pity for the king and the queen. She then hired some Thracians to stab Philip. He had been king six years and four months. For Eurydice she destined a more subtle vengeance, for the young queen displayed no fear and sent word by her messengers that she, not Olympias, was queen of Macedonia. Olympias did not regard the young queen's rank or pity her for the stroke of fortune. She now sent Eurydice a dagger, a rope, and a bowl of hemlock-poison, bidding her choose the death she should die. She herself afterward was brought low and met the end which her cruelty merited. Eurydice cursed her before the messenger who brought the gifts, and prayed that Olympias might receive the like. She then wiped the blood from her husband's wound and wrapped him in a robe. She took off her own girdle and hanged herself without shedding a tear for her own fate, her pride unbroken by the blows of fate ".[107]

A heroic girl, just twenty years old.

Olympias, perhaps feeling that her time was shortening, proceeded to kill her enemies, so far as she could lay hands on them. The Macedonians were revolted by her atrocious conduct and remembered the dying words of Antipater. It was clear enough, says Diodorus, that this sort of régime could not last in Macedonia. The *peripeteia* of the drama of Olympias came when Cassander returned from the Peloponnesus, mad with rage at the murder of his brother and friends and the king and queen. Olympias could expect no mercy from him. He evaded the Aetolian allies of Olympias and Polyperchon and arrived on the scene with his army.[108] Olympias put in command of her troops a man who had been the devoted body-guard of her son in Asia, Aristonous. She fled

---

[107] Diod. XIX, 11.   [108] Diod. XIX, 35.

to Pydna, taking with her the little Alexander and his mother Roxane, the little Deidameia, daughter of Aeacides, betrothed to Alexander, Thessalonice, daughter of Philip by a Thessalian lady, the daughters of Attalus, and many other ladies of rank. Some cavalry from Ambracia and some soldiers who had been attached to the court of Pella joined her, and some of Polyperchon's elephants were driven into the town, though Cassander had captured most of them. She had hopes of help from enemies of Cassander in Greece and in Macedonia, from her cousin Aeacides, whose little daughter was with her, and from Polyperchon. All these hopes failed her; Aeacides was defeated and deposed, Polyperchon's soldiers deserted to Cassander for bribes, and Cassander proceeded to blockade Pydna from sea to sea.

Pydna was now filled with such horrors from siege and starvation that the most hardened soldiers were sickened. Some of the Ambraciots resorted to cannibalism, when the horses and mules had been eaten. The elephants were fed on sawdust. Cassander received all deserters kindly, and small wonder that many slipped away to join him. He sent such deserters to their homes to tell the tale of the horrors in Pydna and so to crush all danger of any rising in favor of Olympias, who would not surrender, although her men were dying of hunger. Outside her walls only Monimus and Aristonous remained faithful to her, Monimus at Pella and Aristonous at Amphipolis. Finally Olympias despaired of help from them or from Polyperchon, and attempted to escape by sea from the place in which the stench and pestilent filth were so awful as to threaten the lives of the besieged, among whom were delicately-reared court-ladies and little children. Cassander learned of her attempt through a deserter and seized the boat in which she was planning to sail. All possibility of escape was gone, and Olympias sent to ask her bitter enemy for terms. She received a promise of her personal safety. Monimus in Pella surrendered when he heard that the queen was in Cassander's hands; Aristonous held out in Amphipolis until Olympias wrote to him to surrender. He was killed by Cassander because he had been dear to Alexander, whom Cassander had feared and hated, and was loyal to his house. Cassander then got relatives of those whom Olympias had killed to accuse her [109] before the National Assembly of the Macedonians. She was not allowed to be present and was condemned to death. Cassander still feared her so much that he offered to provide a safe-conduct by sea for her to Athens, an offer which the queen saw to be a treacherous one, knowing that she would be killed or drowned on the voyage if she accepted it. She demanded that she be allowed to plead her cause before the Assembly. Cassander knew what the result would be if the easily-moved Macedonians should see and hear their old *basilissa* pleading before them, and sent two hundred men to murder her in the palace. When she stood before the assassins in her majesty, they were abashed and went away. She was their queen, and they could not kill her who had been so greatly beloved by their great Alexander. Then Cassander sent some relatives of those whom she had slain, and these men stabbed her. She looked at the assassins without uttering any cry for mercy and died, a trapped lioness.

Cassander at once married Thessalonice and, regarding himself as a member of the royal family because of this marriage, he had the bodies of Eurydice, Arrhidaeus, and Cynane brought to Aegae for splendid burial. It is not recorded whether or not Olympias was buried in this ancient place of burial for Macedonian kings and queens.

The genius and remarkable temperament of Olympias are more apparent in the life of her son, who inherited so much from her, than in her own, so harassed and uneasy. She was the first of the Macedonian queens to show that thirst for political power combined with unscrupulous and unbounded ambition which marks many of the later women of this extraordinary northern breed. Her great contribution to

---

[109] Diod. XIX, 51.

the world was Alexander, who inherited from his mother his fiery nature and his romantic beauty. There was a strong bond of love between them, and there is no evidence that he ever loved any woman except his wild and passionate mother, on whom he wished to confer divinity, and whom he cherished to his life's end. Both of them were the cause of the deaths of many men for political reasons and for personal revenge. Alexander sometimes bitterly repented his murderous deed, but it is not recorded that Olympias felt remorse for any of her cruelty. It would be of interest to compare the murders committed by Philip and Alexander or at their instigation, with those of Olympias. Even in Macedonia at that time murder seemed less pardonable and more hateful when committed by a woman, and the ferocity with which Olympias pursued her victims shocked both Epirotes and Macedonians, peoples used to deeds of violence.[110] Those of her qualities which appear in her son were less detrimental in a soldier and conqueror than in a woman, whose weapons had chiefly to be intrigue, slander, and bursts of passion. She was worsted in all her struggles with men—with Philip, though it is possible that she instigated his assassination, with Antipater, who outgeneralled her and died with a warning against her on his lips, and with Cassander, who killed her.

Of her husband Hogarth [111] says that perhaps no man or woman ever loved him. Olympias possessed the hearts of her children, Alexander and Cleopatra, and the friendship of Eumenes and of her relative, king Aeacides. It may be that if we knew more of her life with her children and those of Philip who were brought up with hers, such as Thessalonice, who was with her at Pydna, we might catch a glimpse of gentler feeling and possibly a greater humanity than we are warranted in attributing to her by any record of her that has reached us.

---

[110] Diod. XIX, 11. 9.
[111] *Philip and Alexander of Macedon*, p. 44.

She died in the year 316 B. C., as did her friend Eumenes. Her daughter Cleopatra was left surrounded by treachery and plots, with nothing but an indomitable will inherited from both parents to sustain her. It was the faithful Eumenes who had urged Perdiccas to marry Cleopatra, and it was he who brought to the queen in Sardis the message of Perdiccas, after he had married Nicaea, that he would put away Antipater's daughter when an opportunity came and marry Cleopatra. The news of this message leaked out and so alarmed Antigonus that he rushed to Europe with the tale, taking with him his young son Demetrius. Antipater and Craterus were so shaken on hearing that Perdiccas was planning a marriage which not only was an insult to his father-in-law Antipater, but would as well make him (virtual) king of Macedon (ὡς βασιλεύς)[112] and end their own power, that they gave up the Aetolian campaign and marched to Asia, sending word to Ptolemy in Egypt, who had his own score to settle with Perdiccas, of the projected marriage, which threatened the ambitions of all the Successors. Cleopatra's hope to become queen of Macedonia was ended when Perdiccas fell by the hands of assassins, his own generals, at the Nile, and Seleucus and the rest of his followers went over to Ptolemy. She mourned, not for Perdiccas, but for the throne which had again escaped her. When Antipater was close to Sardis, Arrian[113] says, Eumenes was on the point of attacking him with his cavalry, but Cleopatra sent messages to him which convinced him that it would be better for her ambitions if he should desist, as she feared that such an attack on the regent by her friend would make her unpopular in Macedon if she should have a hand in bringing on war. In spite of this intervention on her part, in consequence of which Eumenes marched away from Sardis to Phrygia, Cleopatra did not escape an angry scene with Antipater. He reproached her with her friendship with Perdiccas and with Eumenes, and she stood up to him with all a man's spirit (κρεῖσσον ἢ κατὰ

---

[112] Diod. XVIII, 25, 3; Arrian. *Succ.* I, 24.
[113] Arrian, *Succ.* I, 40; Plut. *Eumenes*, VIII.

γυναῖκα) and gave him insult for insult. Antipater realized that he had a true Macedonian princess to deal with, whom he could not quell, and they came to terms and made peace with one another.[114]

Antipater was an inveterate matchmaker and gave his daughters to the most promising Successors, Perdiccas, Craterus, Ptolemy, and he doubtless had his eye on Cleopatra for one of his sons if not for himself. This was true of all the Successors, who, Diodorus [115] says, all saw the enormous value of a marriage with her for one who had for his heart's desire the kingship of Macedonia. Cassander did not succeed in this ambition by a marriage with Cleopatra, but he did achieve his end later by marrying her illegitimate half-sister Thessalonice.[116]

In 308 B. C., Cleopatra, tiring of her semi-captivity in Sardis, decided to go to Egypt to marry Ptolemy, but the prefect of Sardis, who was under orders from Antigonus to watch her, prevented her leaving the city, and following further orders from his chief, sent some women to kill her. Antigonus was eager to avoid the odium of having killed a royal princess of Macedon and queen of Epirus, and therefore put to death the women who had carried out his orders and gave Cleopatra a very splendid funeral.[117]

· Like Philip's other daughters, Cynane and Thessalonice, Cleopatra was murdered by men who feared her power and prestige. She had occupied a very high place in her world, as daughter of Philip and Olympias, beloved sister of Alexander the Great, and wife of king Alexander of Epirus. The fate of her eldest child, her daughter Cadmeia, is not known, though she evidently grew to womanhood and perhaps married, since Plutarch [118] tells, evidently from some source inimical to Neoptolemus, that her brother, king Neoptolemus, at a banquet at her house (κωμάσας παρὰ τὴν ἀδελφὴν Κάδμειαν)

---

[114] Arrian, *loc. cit.*
[115] Diod. XX, 37.
[116] Cf. Beloch, IV¹, p. 377, n. 1.
[117] Diod. XX, 37.
[118] Plut. *Pyrrhus*, V.

told her of a plot to kill Pyrrhus, at the time joint-king of
Epirus, with poison. Neoptolemus, who was the younger
child of Cleopatra, was king of Epirus from 317 B. C. to
his death in 296 or 295 B. C.[119] Pyrrhus, informed of the
plot, invited him to a sacrifice and killed him at the feast. So
the tradition of death by assassination in the royal house of
Macedonia was maintained in the case of Cleopatra's son,
who was at the time of his assassination the last of the
legitimate descendants, of whose fate we know, of Philip and
Olympias.

CYNANE AND ADEA-EURYDICE

Audata, the mother of Cynane, may have been the first
wife of Philip the Second. She was very likely the daughter
of Bardylis and was probably, as has been already suggested,
given by the Illyrian prince to Philip to bind the treaty made
between them in 358 B. C. We know of Audata nothing but
her Illyrian blood and name, together with the fact that she
took the name Eurydice at her marriage with Philip. This
change of name points, perhaps, to her having been regarded
for a time as a " legitimate " wife, that is, one whose children
could inherit the kingship. The daughter born to her and
Philip, but for her sex, might have been a great soldier like
her father. She was of the wild, fierce, fighting type of
women who flourished among the Illyrian nobility. When
Cynane was only a girl—she was about a year older than
Alexander—she is said to have fought under her father in an
Illyrian campaign and to have killed an Illyrian queen.[120]
Philip had kept in the background of his reign the rightful
heir to the throne by the law of direct succession, his nephew
Amyntas, who was only five years old at the death of his
father, king Perdiccas; Philip had reigned at first only as
his guardian. When Cynane was seventeen or eighteen years

---

[119] Plut. *Pyrrh.* V; Klotzsch, pp. 157 f.
[120] Polyaen. VIII, 60; Duris ap. Athen. XIII, 560 f. Abel, *Makedonien vor König Philipp*, p. 121.

old [121] she was given as a wife to this Amyntas by her father.[122] This marriage, which must have taken place about 340 B. C., was of short duration, as Alexander killed her husband on a charge of treason before he set out for Asia. Whether the charge was true or not, it was for Alexander's interest to have his cousin, who had a clear claim to the throne, out of the way before he left the country. It is not unlikely, if Cynane's later action is taken into consideration, that she urged her husband to push his claims for the succession after Philip's death. In the northern campaign of 335 B. C., Alexander was aided by a young king of the Agriani, Langarus, whom he invited to come to Pella, promising him the hand of the young widow.[123] He evidently thought that Macedon would be safer in his absence if his bold sister was in the barbarous north. But Langarus fell ill and died, and it is unlikely that her pride and her ambition for her daughter would have allowed her to marry the young barbarian in any case. It is recorded that she refused all offers of marriage, preferring to be the widow of Amyntas.[124] Her daughter was reared by her in a manly way, taught hunting and fighting, and was as bold and adventurous as Cynane. Cynane was a wealthy princess and able to support an army of mercenary troops, with which she marched to Asia after the death of Alexander, taking Eurydice to marry her to the new king, Philip Arrhidaeus, who was her own half-brother. At the crossing of the river Strymon the regent Antipater met her with his troops and tried to turn her back, but she forced her way across. She was opposed by Alcetas, brother of Perdiccas, who threatened her life if she did not desist from her demand that her daughter be married to the king. Before the fierce array of armed Macedonians she declared

---

[121] Berve, *op. cit.* II, 229.

[122] Probably 344-3 B. C. See Berve, II, 229.

[123] Arrian, I, 5, 4. The Agrianian javelin-men were among Alexander's best fighting-men. Cf. Tarn, *Hellenistic Military and Naval Developments*, pp. 21 f.

[124] Polyaen. *loc. cit.*

that Philip's grand-daughter should be queen of Macedon, even though she herself paid for it with her life; she defied Alcetas and denounced him for his treachery toward the blood of Philip. He had her struck down, as she stood defying him; the soldiers, frenzied at the sight of their murdered princess, howled with rage against him and threatened revolt if the marriage for which she gave her life was not at once arranged.[125] Perdiccas saw the fatal stupidity of his brother's act and had the marriage ceremony performed in all haste, though he must have cursed the fate that forced this on him, for he was planning to marry Cleopatra and to become king himself in place of the dullard, Arrhidaeus. The death of Cynane and the ambitious schemes of Perdiccas were reported to Antipater and Craterus in Macedonia by Antigonus, "dwelling on the tragedy of her fate", says Arrian, and the report sealed the doom of Perdiccas.

The girl Eurydice, who saw her mother die and heard the roar of the Macedonian army demanding that she should be the queen of Arrhidaeus, not unnaturally thought that she had henceforth at her command the soldiers who had turned to her in flaming rage against the murderer of her mother. We cannot wonder that she now demanded to have a voice in all that was discussed and that the temporary commanders of the army, Peithon and Arrhidaeus, should do nothing without her consent. From the moment of her marriage she determined to rule Macedonia. She knew herself to be of the royalty of the land through both father and mother, and scorned the upstart generals who were fighting among themselves for a share of the spoils left by Alexander. In the first glow of the army's enthusiasm for her she prevailed over the Guardians, but they soon found her dictatorial temper unendurable and told her that she must keep out of political affairs until the arrival of Antipater and Antigonus.[126] Antipater found things in a desperate state when he arrived at Tri-

---

[125] Polyaen. VIII, 60; Arrian, *Succ.* I, 22-24.
[126] Arrian, *Succ.* I, 30-31.

paradeisus; the army was on the point of revolt, as they had not received the money promised them by Alexander, and Eurydice inflamed them against him. She was supported by her secretary Asclepiodorus and by Attalus (which Attalus is uncertain), and her fiery speeches so roused the soldiers that the old regent barely escaped with his life, and the other leaders, Antigonus and Seleucus, were threatened. Antipater finally succeeded in pacifying the soldiers and came to terms with Eurydice, putting an end to her intrigue with the army by taking her and her husband together with Roxane and the infant king Alexander back to Macedonia.[127]

Antipater's death in 319 B. C. was a cause of joy to an old woman in Epirus and a young woman in Pella. His last words were a warning to the Macedonians never to let a woman rule them.[128] These two women, his constant enemies, were as strong-willed and able as any of the Successors, but they had to deal with men who did not like a woman's authority. Eurydice found that the new regent Polyperchon was a new foe. He was Guardian of the two Kings and at first took them everywhere with him. He was afraid of Eurydice and, for the protection of the child-king, who he feared might be killed by her, he summoned the grandmother to come from Epirus to be guardian of her grandchild, with the right to wear the diadem of royalty. The thought of the old queen's coming to such a position of power was deadly for Eurydice, and she lost no time in making connections with Cassander, Polyperchon's enemy and rival, who was determined to be regent in the old man's place. The late tale [129] that she bought Cassander with the price of her person is an invention; her passion was for power, not love-intrigue. While Polyperchon was touring Greece against Cassander, she ruled at Pella and finally got her husband back out of Polyperchon's grasp. She then appointed Cassander regent (Justin,

---

[127] *Ibid.* 42, 44.
[128] Diod. XIX, 11.
[129] Orosius, III, 23.

XIV, 5; Diod. XVIII, 75). Polyperchon, deprived of his office and defeated in Peloponnesus, still had in his power the little king and his mother Roxane. He now persuaded Olympias to come back to Macedon, to put down the girl-queen and rule there as guardian of the royal child. Nothing but the thought of the girl in the place for which she had striven all her long life and the knowledge that the hated Cassander was now regent brought Olympias again to the land she had left in humiliation and anger, bested by Antipater. With her came her cousin and co-ruler Aeacides at the head of an Epirot army. Eurydice foolishly did not await Cassander's arrival and risked battle in command of the Macedonian troops at the border town Euia. How the two queens came into battle, the old one in Bacchic array and the young one in the armor of a Macedonian soldier, and how the army at the sight of the old queen changed sides, and how Olympias captured and killed Arrhidaeus and Eurydice has already been told. Eurydice died like an Antigone of the Attic stage.[130]

THESSALONICE

Philip's daughter Thessalonice was the child of Nicesipolis,[131] a Thessalian lady, perhaps a relative of Jason of Pherae. She appears to have had a softer nature than his daughters by Illyrian and Epirote mothers, and we do not hear of her in public life and warfare. As her mother died when she was only three weeks old, she was probably reared by her step-mother Olympias, who was still living at Pella as Philip's queen at the time of her birth, some time between 346 B. C. and 340 B. C. She may have gone to Epirus with Olympias in 338 B. C. or in 331 B. C., but nothing is known

---

[130] Soph. *Ant.* 1222, βρόχῳ μιτώδει σινδόνος καθημμένην.

[131] Beloch (III², p. 69) says that the story told in Plut. *Conjug. Praecept.* 23, p. 141, about the Thessalian girl who was said to have exercised magic upon Philip, must refer to either Philinna, or Nicesipolis. Since Olympias was kind to the girl in question and apparently had charge of Thessalonice, the girl was very likely Nicesipolis, mother of Thessalonice.

of her life until the flight to Pydna in which she accompanied
the old queen. Cassander spared the lives of the innocent
refugees Deidameia, Thessalonice, and the others, and at once
married Thessalonice. Her spirit, perhaps never strong, must
have been broken by the horrors of that siege, and no Macedonian princess would have rejected the opportunity to marry the
ruler of Macedonia. She may have been nearing thirty years
at this time. Why she had not married earlier we can only
guess; it may be that Olympias kept her from marriage in
order that no more " pretenders " to the throne might be born.
Her three sons became kings of Macedon, but for all their
great names, Philip, Antipater, and Alexander, and their
splendid descents from Philip and from Antipater they were
shadows or worthless, and soon passed. The fate of Thessalonice was no happier in the end than that of Philip's other
daughters.

Cassander was proud of his wife's birth, which made him
a member of the royal family and in line for the succession to
the throne.[132] In 311 B. C. in a Council of the Successors
he was appointed Commander of Europe until such time as
the young king Alexander should come of age. Accordingly
he had the boy and his mother, who were under guard at
Amphipolis, killed and their bodies hidden. Two years later
he persuaded Polyperchon to have the young Heracles, son
of Alexander and Barsine, killed instead of bringing him to
Macedon to inherit the crown, as Polyperchon had been planning to do. So Cassander removed all male claimants for the
kingship and at the same time gratified an ancient and deep-
seated hatred of Alexander, whose very statue when he came
upon it suddenly at Delphi made him turn sick and faint as
he remembered the blows he had once received from the king

---

[132] Cf. Beloch. IV¹, p. 377, n. 1. Beloch says that even illegitimate
sons had precedence of the female line in inheritance of the kingship
and that only after the royal house was extinct (in the male line)
was Cleopatra, sister of Alexander, heir (Diod. XX, 37, 4). Thessalonice was perhaps counted as a legitimate daughter of Philip, although not the child of his principal wife.

in Asia. In 305 B. C. like the rest of the Successors he assumed the title of king, and for seven years Thessalonice was queen of Macedon. Her husband may have loved her and he certainly honored her. The city that he built for her and named for her still is called Thessalonike, Saloniki.

Cassander died in 298 B. C. and was succeeded by his eldest son Philip, whose reign was short. At his death Thessalonice was regent, and the succession was disputed between her two surviving sons, of whom Alexander was his mother's favorite. We are told that she did nothing unjust to help him. The other son Antipater killed his mother, who, if we may believe Justin,[133] died like another, but innocent, Clytemnestra, baring the breasts that had nursed him to her murderer and beseeching him not to kill her. Alexander called in Pyrrhus of Epirus and Demetrius the Besieger to help him against the matricide Antipater, but the aid given by Pyrrhus cost the young king dear, for the Epirote demanded Tymphaea, Acarnania, Amphilochia, and Ambracia as his reward, and the calling in of Demetrius cost him his life, for he was killed by order of Demetrius at a banquet at Larissa. The Macedonian army hailed the Besieger as king. The matricide took refuge with his father-in-law Lysimachus in Thrace and was afterward killed by the order of Lysimachus,[134] who made a treaty of peace with the new king of Macedon.[135]

With the death of Thessalonice and her sons the line of Philip and Alexander came to an end. All except Alexander the Great and Philip eldest son of Thessalonice and Cassander, died by violence. Alexander killed Philip's son Caranus and the others who might have become Pretenders to the throne during his absence in Asia;[136] Olympias killed

---

[133] Justin. XVI, 1, 1.

[134] Diodorus (XXI, 7) says that Demetrius killed Antipater because he did not wish to have him share the kingdom with him.

[135] Plut. *Dem.* XXXVI, *Pyrrh.* VI; Justin, XVI, 1, 2; Pausan. IX, 7, 3.

[136] Beloch, III², p. 72.

his daughter Europa, child of Cleopatra, his son Philip
Arrhidaeus, and his grand-daughter Eurydice; Philip's
daughter Cynane was killed by Alcetas, brother of Perdiccas,
and his daughter Thessalonice by her son Antipater; Cassander killed Olympias, wife of Philip, and the two sons of
Alexander the Great, Alexander and Heracles; Cassander's
sons Antipater and Alexander were killed by Lysimachus and
by Demetrius respectively.

> Sin is the child of Sin, the impious act
> Begets a new brood of impiety;
> Old wickedness brings forth new wickedness
> When the appointed hour for that birth comes.
> Bad angel of the house and strong for ill,
> Accursed Lawlessness, black with the doom
> And fate of all the race, works on and on
> Forever, like the sin that gave it birth.[137]

EURYDICE III AND LYSANDRA

Wives of Antipater and Alexander, the Sons of Cassander 298-294 B. C.

Philip, son of Cassander, who succeeded him in 298 B. C.,
lived to reign only a few months, and no marriage of his is
mentioned. He was the eldest of the three sons of Cassander
and could not have been more than seventeen at his death.
His brothers were probably close to him in age, and the matricide Antipater was hardly more than a boy when he committed his monstrous crime. He and his brother Alexander
both married daughters of their father's sisters, Antipater
marrying Eurydice, the daughter of his aunt Nicaea, wife of
Lysimachus, and Alexander marrying the daughter of Eurydice, queen of Egypt. His wife was named Lysandra. Cassander doubtless arranged the marriages for his youthful sons
before his death. Eurydice, according to Justin,[138] fled to
her father's court with her young husband when Demetrius

---

[137] Aeschylus, *Ag.* 763 ff.   [138] Justin, XVI, 2, 4.

was proclaimed king of Macedon after killing Alexander. Lysimachus made peace with Demetrius, put his son-in-law to death when the latter accused him of treachery in abandoning his cause, and imprisoned his daughter Eurydice for supporting her husband. " Il était de ceux pour qui la raison d'État répond à tout ",[139] a practical politician. Very likely his young wife Arsinoe encouraged him in this conduct toward claimants to the throne of Macedon.

The case of Lysandra constitutes a great puzzle. Were there two Lysandras, as Niese [140] thinks, one the wife of the young Macedonian Alexander and one the wife of Agathocles, son of Lysimachus, who fled after her husband's murder to Seleucus at Antioch? Plutarch's account [141] of the motives of Seleucus for asking the hand of Demetrius' daughter in 300 B. C., or a little after, is that he " saw Lysimachus taking one daughter of Ptolemy for himself and one for his son Agathocles ". And it is well attested that Agathocles' wife was named Lysandra. Plutarch's Greek is usually interpreted to mean that in 300 B. C. the marriages of father and son to the two daughters of Ptolemy had taken place. But the participle is present, not aorist, and the tense implies that the arrangements had not been completed. Pausanias [142] says that Lysimachus on his return from the war against the Getae (293 B. C.) married Agathocles to Lysandra, daughter of Ptolemy.[143] I take this, together with the passage in Plutarch, to mean that Ptolemy about 300 B. C., a time when he was disposing of his daughters, offered one to Lysimachus, and one to Agathocles, and that the latter affair was not concluded until some years later. Ptolemy about this time proffered his daughter Ptolemais to Demetrius and the pair were betrothed, but the marriage did not take place until 286 B. C., twelve or thirteen years after the betrothal. According to this

---

[139] Bouché-Leclercq, *Lagides*, I, p. 146.

[140] *Geschichte der Griechen und Makedonischen Staaten* I, pp. 354, 388, 402-404.

[141] Plut. *Dem.* XXXI.

[142] Pausan. I, 9, 7.

[143] Cf. Droysen, II, 2, p. 236.

hypothesis (based on the present participle in Plutarch, *Dem.* 31) the marriage arranged between Agathocles and Lysandra met with some setback, perhaps the opposition of Arsinoe, and Ptolemy, with an eye on the succession in Macedon, gave his daughter to the young Alexander, who if born in 313 B. C. would be perhaps eighteen at the time of the marriage. After his death by violence in 295 B. C., Lysandra will have returned to Ptolemy's court and then some two years later married Agathocles. There is still the difficulty of Pausanias' statement in I; 10, 3 that the old Lysimachus succumbed to love and married Lysandra's sister Arsinoe at a time when he had grandchildren, as Lysandra then had children by Agathocles (300 B. C.). Either there were two Lysandras, daughters of Ptolemy, or as seems more probable, this statement of Pausanias is to be treated as a carelessness on his part.

Since Lysandra was the older half-sister of Arsinoe and child of the queen Eurydice, no doubt jealousies and enmities had arisen in their girlhood in the court of Alexandria between the daughters of two rival queens. Whether or not Arsinoe had been in love with Agathocles in Thrace, she certainly now wished to remove all who could stand in the way of her ambition for her little son Ptolemy. Perhaps with the active help of Ceraunus, full brother of Lysandra and half-brother of Arsinoe, Agathocles was killed. Lysandra with her children fled to Seleucus in Antioch. Perhaps Ceraunus went with her, though Tarn [144] thinks that he stayed with Lysimachus and became his right-hand man in place of the murdered Agathocles. If he went with his sister Lysandra (as is stated by Appian), [145] and if he had no hand in killing Agathocles, one might think that his later conduct toward Arsinoe was actuated by vengeance for the sake of Lysandra. But in the case of such a cruel and wicked man there is no need to seek for any motives except his own mad

---

[144] *Antigonos Gonatas,* p. 125.
[145] Appian, *Syr.* 62; Pausan. X, 19, 7; Memnon, *F.H.G.* III, 533.

ambitions. Nothing more is known of the fate of Lysandra or
her children. We hear only that she was so enraged against
her father that it was with difficulty that his son Alexander
obtained from her the body of his father for burial after the
battle of Kouroupedion in which the old king was killed.[146]

Both of these women, who were for a brief space queens of
Macedon, were grand-daughters of Antipater the Regent, and
the little that we learn of them shows that both were women
of spirit in the Macedonian tradition. We do not know
whether Eurydice died in the prison to which her father
condemned her, or what the fortunes of Lysandra were in the
Seleucid court. Aside from the tragedy of their fates the
chief point of interest in their lives for the historian is the
fact that like Gygaea and Stratonice of old in the Macedonian
royal house of the fifth century these princesses were used
by their fathers for the making of advantageous political
alliances. It may have been the fear that Phila, wife of
Demetrius and sister of Cassander, would marry her daughter
Stratonice to one of Cassander's three sons, heirs to the throne
of Macedonia, that brought Seleucus to seek the hand of
that young girl after Ipsus, and brought Ptolemy to offering
his three daughters, Lysandra, Ptolemais, and Arsinoe, to
the young king of Macedonia, to Demetrius I, and to
Lysimachus.

PHILA, DAUGHTER OF ANTIPATER AND WIFE OF DEMETRIUS THE BESIEGER, KING OF MACEDON, 294-289 B. C.

Antipater the Regent had many sons and daughters. Of
these his son Cassander became ruler of Macedonia and
finally, after his murder of the young heir, king; three of
his daughters were married to Successors of Alexander the
Great who also became kings. Indeed two of his daughters
were each married to two Successors, Phila to both Craterus
and Demetrius, and Nicaea to Perdiccas and to Lysimachus.
His daughter Eurydice married Ptolemy, who later was king

---

[146] Pausan. I, 10, 5.

of Egypt. In 323 B. C., the year of Alexander's death, his generals were all brilliant possibilities, and it was beyond the power of prophecy to foretell which of them would gain their ambitions and whose hopes would be baffled by defeat and death. Antipater was faithful to the reigning house, but with an imbecile and a baby sharing the official throne as the "Kings" and the real power in the hands of the Commander of Europe [147] (στρατηγὸν τῶν κατὰ τὴν Εὐρώπην) (himself) and the Chiliarch of Asia (Perdiccas), it was apparent to a man of his political foresight and acuteness that anything might happen. So he made haste to put himself and his daughters into strategic positions by marrying them to the most promising. He made some mistakes. Perdiccas was obviously the *grand parti,* as he was commander of the army, Guardian of the kings,[148] and full of ambition. He married Nicaea, who was brought to him by her brother, but secretly cherished the intention of making a marriage with Cleopatra later. This proved his ruin when Antipater learned his design. Nicaea was then married to Lysimachus, and in 322 B. C. Phila was given by her father in marriage to the splendid Craterus, close friend and ally of Antipater. In 321 B. C. Eurydice was married to Ptolemy. Phila was her father's counterpart in mind and political genius; she was frequently consulted by him, even in her girlhood, about affairs of state, and he prized her judgment.[149] She was a woman of the world in which she lived, but was not brutalized by it as was her brother Cassander, who sacrificed everything for ambition, as Phila did for loyalty. Antipater distrusted his son Cassander and in his will suggested that the kingdom be left in the hands of his old friend Polyperchon, to the great anger of Cassander.

Phila had the virtues, so rare in her time, of generosity, kindness and pity; her soul was not devastated by wild

---

[147] Arrian, *Succ.* I, 1 a. Cf. Schwahn, *Klio,* 1931, pp. 324 f.

[148] Diod. XVIII, 2, 4.

[149] Diod. XIX, 59, 4-5.

gusts of passion and vengefulness such as shook the soul
of Olympias. It has been suggested on not very good evidence that she had been already married in her girlhood to
Balacrus,[150] a general of Alexander's. The authority for this
is very dubious and the argument drawn from the unlikeli-
hood of her having remained unmarried until the time of
her marriage with Craterus is not strong, since the royal
women of the Macedonian blood often made political marriages
when beyond their first youth.

Craterus was of an immense popularity among the Macedonians; " only to see his flapping hat on the battlefield and
to hear the sound of his voice would bring the soldiers
running to fight under him ".[151] Eumenes did not dare to
place any Macedonian troops opposite him in his battle
against Craterus, for he was afraid that if they recognized
the beloved man they would go over to him *en masse*. He was
loved also by Alexander and was always absolutely devoted
to him. He disliked the Persian luxury and customs which
Alexander assumed and remained in his Macedonian sim-
plicity of habit and life, as did Antipater. He was a great
sportsman and lion-hunter; the lion-hunt at Sidon in
which he took part was perpetuated in marble by Lysippus
and Leochares, and the sculpture was dedicated at Delphi by
his son Craterus.[151a] The charm of his speech and manner as
well as his majesty and beauty contrasted with the mean
presence of the little old regent, his friend Antipater. He
had been married at the great wedding ceremonies at Susa
to the Persian princess Amastris, who lived with him for two
years (324-322 B. C.), and at his marriage with Phila married with his consent Dionysius of Heracleia on the Black
Sea. When Craterus lay dying on the battlefield, Eumenes
rode to the spot where he lay and leaping from his horse
took his hand and wept for the fate that made them enemies.

From the brief marriage with Craterus Phila had a son

---

[150] Cf. Berve, II, p. 100.   [151] Plut. *Eumenes*, VI.
[151a] Cf. *B.C.H.* XXI, 1897, pp. 598 ff., *J.H.S.* XIX, 1899, pp. 213 ff.

whom she named for his father. She was then hurried by
her father and Antigonus, governor of Asia, into another
marriage so speedily that when the body of Craterus, sent to
her by Eumenes for burial, arrived, she was already married to
a youth of barely eighteen years, the son of Antigonus, and
destined to be the famous Besieger of Cities. Antigonus had
overcome his son's reluctance to wed the woman of thirty by
pointing out the advantages of marrying the daughter of the
regent and widow of Craterus, who had been the formal
" guardian of the kingship of Arrhidaeus," [152] " his guardian
in lunacy, with the custody of his person and seal." [153] Antigonus cynically parodied a verse of Euripides as follows:

> Wed against Nature, if you gain thereby.

Demetrius showed afterward, as Plutarch notes, a tendency
to fall in love with women much older than himself.[154]

Phila for the second time married a man of heroic
beauty.[155] Demetrius was so handsome that strangers followed him in the streets for the pleasure it gave them to look
at his beauty. There can be no doubt that Phila loved him,
and it may be that he had a regard for her, for although he
was the greatest libertine of his time, famous among the
Successors for his love of women, he had the great good
quality of family loyalty. He had a deep love for his father
and mother, and this regard for the family tie, remarked upon
by Plutarch as characteristic of the family of Antigonus,
was apparently extended to his older wife. She bore him
a son Antigonus, whose devotion for Demetrius was as
passionate as that of Demetrius toward his father. Phila
was doubtless always his most revered wife, and polygamy
was not unusual among the Successors. Demetrius did
not take another wife until 307 B. C., though he had of

---

[152] Arrian, *Succ.* I, 3.

[153] Tarn in *C.A.H.* VI, 461. Cf. Schwahn, *Klio*, 1931, p. 325—" die
ganze προστασία des Krateros—auch für Makedonien ist nichts als
eine Erfindung des Duris.

[154] Plut. *Dem.* XLVIII.

[155] Diod. XX, 92, 3.

course many mistresses, one of the most famous of whom, Lamia, Plutarch notes, was as much older than himself as Phila was. Phila had been trained in a hard school of practical politics, of which her father [156] was a master, but she had a genius for loving that was extraordinary at a time when most men and women of her race and rank were ready to sacrifice everyone and everything for the sake of royal power.

Her mother-in-law Stratonice lived at the court of her husband Antigonus at Celaenae in Phrygia and later at Salamis [157] in Cyprus. Phila probably went to Asia soon after her marriage and lived there until a few years before her husband became king of Macedon in 294 B. C. She appears to have been living in Cilicia at the time when Demetrius was engaged in besieging Rhodes. From there she sent him letters and beautiful gifts: [158] among them a purple and gold mantle which she had woven and embroidered for him, a cloak such as he loved to wear. The ship that carried her tokens of love was captured by Menedemus, and Phila's letters and gifts were sent to Ptolemy in Egypt.[159] It was doubtless Phila, when queen of Macedon, who had the gorgeous mantle made for Demetrius with the spangled heavens embroidered on its purple in gold thread. It was never completed, and no later king of Macedon, however great a lover of show (σοβαρός), had courage to wear the splendid thing.[160]

For some years Phila was the only wife of Demetrius, and, realist as she was in politics, was no doubt satisfied with her position as his queen and the mother of his children and did not interfere with his mistresses. She understood the temperament of her young husband and found scope for her own great gifts of diplomacy in conciliating the soldiery when they were turbulent, and intervening between her husband

---

[156] Cf. Berve, *op. cit.* II, p. 47.
[157] Diod. XIX, 16, 4; XXI, 1, 4.
[158] Diod. XX, 93, 4; Plut. *Dem.* XXII.
[159] Plut. *Dem.* XLI.
[160] *Ibid.*

and her brother Cassander. Her husband prized her ability and found her political sagacity of as much value as her father Antipater had in his important negotiations. His marriage in 307 B. C. with the Athenian lady Eurydice, who bore him a son, Corabus (cf. Beloch, IV², 135, n. 1), probably did not disturb Phila more than his affairs with dancing-women. The Athenians are said to have been pleased with the marriage, but it did not mean that Phila was repudiated or even dishonored. Eurydice was only an " occasional " wife. If Phila was disposed to feel any jealousy about her husband's affairs with women, it would be of his devotion toward Lamia, who " made him lover of her only, although beloved by all other women ", rather than of the temporary expedient of a political marrage. A Macedonian queen would never have thought of demanding fidelity in the modern sense of the word from her husband.

The marriage in 303 B. C. with Deidameia, sister of Pyrrhus, who as a little girl had been the betrothed of the child-king Alexander, was a blow to Phila's pride because of the rank of the young princess. It was a political alliance of the highest importance, which joined Demetrius with the strong young king of Epirus and was a great step toward the gaining of Macedon. The marriage was celebrated with pomp and splendor in Argos at the time of the festival of Hera. It is not clear where Phila was at this time. It may be that she had been sent [161] by her husband to her brother Cassander to arrange a truce with him that would permit Demetrius to answer the urgent call of Antigonus to come to Asia before the fateful battle of Ipsus. Demetrius took with him his young brother-in-law Pyrrhus, who fought well at Ipsus, whereas Cassander, as soon as Demetrius had left Europe, sent his brother Pleistarchus to fight on the side of the Kings against Antigonus and Demetrius.

The year after the defeat at Ipsus Seleucus asked Demetrius for the hand of his daughter Stratonice,[162] an extraor-

---

[161] Cf. Plut. *Dem.* XXXII.   [162] Plut. *Dem.* XXXI.

dinary piece of good luck for Demetrius, who, though still commander of the seas, had lost most of his possessions on land. Phila was treated with due respect in this matter by Demetrius. He had left Deidameia in Athens, as he thought that he could count on the good will of that city, but the Athenians voted to allow none of the kings to stay in Athens and sent Deidameia to Megara with a suitable and honorable escort. The lady went on to Corinth, and Demetrius summoned his wife Phila to help him to give their daughter in marriage to the king of Syria. The bridal party came together at Rhossus on the Syrian coast, where the recent enemies, Seleucus and Demetrius, walked and talked together, unarmed and unguarded, and were the best of friends. Seleucus took his young wife up to Antioch after a splendid wedding, and Demetrius again seized Cilicia, which his brother-in-law Pleistarchus had been governing since the battle of Ipsus, and sent Phila off to explain matters to Cassander and to defend her husband against the complaints of Pleistarchus.[163] And as Phila went, Deidameia came sailing from Corinth to join her husband. Deidameia, who lived but a short time after this, bore a son, Alexander. Political marriages without regard to previous ties were fashionable among the Successors just then, and Ptolemy, who now became a friend of Demetrius through the offices of the new son-in-law Seleucus, offered him the hand of his daughter Ptolemais, a daughter of Eurydice and niece of Phila. Phila, however, did not have to suffer the indignity of seeing her own niece displace her, as the marriage took place twelve or thirteen years later, after the death of Phila.

The small son of Deidameia, Alexander, and some other little children of Demetrius, such as Corabus, son of the Athenian lady Eurydice, were put in the care of Demetrius' mother, Stratonice,[164] in Cilicia at the time of the battle of Ipsus. Phila evidently was *not* with them, when after his father's death at Ipsus he " sailed with his mother Stratonice,

---

[163] Plut. *Dem.* XXXII.   [164] Diod. XXI, 1, 4.

who was living in Cilicia, taking all her possessions to Salamis
in Cyprus since (that island) was then in the power of
Demetrius." Cyprus was captured by Ptolemy in 297 B. C.,
but Salamis held out. The account given in Plutarch, *Dem.*
35 and 38 is often misunderstood by historians.[165] For example Bevan says,[166] " The defence of the island was energe-
tically conducted by Demetrius' brave wife, Phila, but she
had ultimately to surrender in Salamis. Ptolemy returned
the chivalry shown by Demetrius in 306 by sending Phila
and her children to Demetrius in Macedonia ' loaded with
presents and honours ' ". But at the time Phila's son Antigonus was serving with his father in Greece or Macedonia, and
no doubt her elder son, Craterus (son of Craterus), was there
too, and her daughter Stratonice was queen in Syria. Phila
had no small children and was at the time between fifty and
sixty years old. Moreover the expression τοὺς παῖδας αὐτοῦ
καὶ τὴν μητέρα in *Dem.* 35 and περὶ τῶν τέκνων, καὶ τῆς μητρός in
Dem. 38 can only mean " his children and his mother ". If
" *their* " mother were meant the Greek would read τὴν μητέρα
αὐτῶν. Demetrius had small children at the time, but Antigonus and Stratonice were his only children by Phila. The last
mention of Phila after the marriage of Seleucus and Stratonice, at which she was present, tells of her going to Cassander
in Macedonia, sent to him by her husband to defend him for
having taken Cilicia from Pleistarchus, brother of Phila and of
Cassander. Since Deidameia came straight to Demetrius as
soon as Phila departed for Macedon, and since after the death
of Deidameia Demetrius agreed to marry the niece of Phila,
Ptolemais, daughter of Ptolemy, as a pledge of friendship between the two kings, it seems unlikely that Phila returned to
Demetrius. She probably remained in Macedonia, where she

---

[165] Beloch (IV¹, p. 219) understands Plutarch correctly:—" Nach
längerer Belagerung fiel auch diese (i. e. Salamis) in seine Hand,
wobei Demetrios' Mutter Stratonike und seine Kinder in Gefangen-
schaft kamen."

[166] Following Bouché-Leclercq, *Lagides*, I, p. 88; Bevan, *Egypt*,
p. 37.

6

was beloved; Plutarch states that it was greatly in Demetrius'
favour with the Macedonians when he came from Larissa to be
their king that his wife was Phila, daughter of Antipater, who
had dealt so honorably with them, and that Demetrius had a
son, then serving under him, who was also son of Phila.[167] This
was after Demetrius had gone to Greece to besiege and conquer Athens and to intervene in the affairs of Macedon, whose
young king Alexander was killed at a banquet in Larissa in
Thessaly, probably by order of Demetrius. There the Macedonian army proclaimed him king and escorted him to Macedonia. While still at Larissa he heard the news of the release of
Stratonice, his mother, and of his small children by Ptolemy,
and also that his daughter Stratonice had been given by her
old husband Seleucus to his eldest son, Antiochus, who was
desperately in love with this young step-mother, and that
she had been proclaimed queen of Upper Syria.

Phila was now queen of Macedon and had nothing to fear
from any rival. Her son Antigonus, who had her virtues and
strength, was his father's second-in-command, and her son
Craterus was the loyal aid of his half-brother, who later made
him governor in Greece. She was queen in the land in which
her father and brother had long ruled as regent and as king,
and her prestige and popularity meant much in his new kingdom to Demetrius, who had been reared in Asia. Macedonia
had never before had a queen of such fineness and wisdom.
The praise given her by Diodorus, whose source is the contemporary Hieronymus, very likely refers to this period of
her power especially. She strove to see that justice was
done and she was generous with her wealth. She might have
had a serene old age and happy death in her own country,
where Demetrius reaped the fruit of the old Antipater's
right dealing with his people because he had Antipater's
daughter for his queen. One would not expect that he
would risk his popularity with the Macedonians by a new
marriage, but in 292-1 B. C. he [168] did accept the offer of

---

[167] Plut. *Dem.* XXXVII.
[168] For this date cf. Beloch, IV², pp. 248 ff.

marriage made to him by Lanassa, the wife of Pyrrhus, whom she had left in anger when he married the Illyrian princess Bircenna.[169] She brought Demetrius Corcyra as her dower, and neither Demetrius nor any other of the Kings would refuse a lady with that island as her wedding-gift to him.

The marriage with Lanassa and the entrance of the pair into Athens [170] as Demeter and Demetrius (if it actually occurred) must have alienated the Macedonians from him. He thought himself, with his personal beauty and genius for warfare, a better man than Philip or Alexander had been, and declared that they were but kings while he was " King of Kings ", and he delighted to have his soldiers at their drinking-bouts drink the health of " Demetrius the King, Seleucus Lord of Elephants, Ptolemy the Captain of Ships, Lysimachus the Keeper of the Treasury, and Agathocles Lord of the Isles ". After five years as king of Macedon there came one of those changes of fortune which throughout his life alternately lifted him high and dashed him down. He was defeated by Pyrrhus and lost Macedonia at a time when he was preparing to invade Asia with a fleet and army that surpassed in its great ships the fleet of Alexander. The kings were all against him; his Macedonians turned to Pyrrhus, who appeared to them to be the better man, and told Demetrius that they were sick of a spendthrift king and that he would better be off to save his life. Always dramatic, he went to his tent, changed his purple and gold for a black cloak, and then slipped away to Cassandreia, the old Pydna, once the refuge of Olympias, where Phila was now staying. Pyrrhus appeared in Macedon with his troops and " all was over but the shouting", Plutarch says—(Pyrrhus) ἐκράτησεν αὐτοβοεί.[171]

---

[169] Athen. VI, 253 (Demochares and Duris). Beloch (IV¹, p. 207, n. 1) distrusts the story of the intimate relations between Demetrius and Lanassa, remarking that Demetrius could not make Lanassa queen of Macedonia because of the high regard of the Macedonians for Phila. Cf. Ferguson, *Hellenistic Athens*, pp. 141-145.

[170] This entrance of Lanassa with Demetrius is a conjecture of Reinach, followed by Tarn. Cf. *Antigonos Gonatas*, p. 49 and n. 25.

[171] Plut. *Dem.* XLIV.

Phila could not endure the loss of her country and the sight of the dazzling king in flight, most miserable of kings and without a kingdom. She did not realize the power of recovery possessed by her astonishing husband, and did not know that fate would yet put upon the throne of Macedon her son, so like her and her father in his virtues, and that he would have a long reign in her land. She took poison. If she had not lost heart, she would have seen her husband's splendor breaking out again for a short while. In this period he married her niece, the Egyptian Ptolemais, to whom he had been betrothed so long before. But in the end he was conquered by his quondam son-in-law Seleucus, who kept him in a kind of honorable imprisonment in Syria, where he became the complete prey of the gluttony and drunkenness which always got the better of him in idleness. He lingered for three years, cherishing the vain hope that his daughter, queen Stratonice, and her husband Antiochus would come and set him free.

Phila would have been comforted for her grief at seeing Demetrius beggared of all his possessions, if she could have seen the stately procession of ships [172] that escorted the ashes of the splendid king home across the Aegaean—a fitting and impressive funeral train for the king of the sea, dramatic in life and in death. The gold vase that held his ashes and the purple and gold robe and diadem that he loved gleamed from the ship's prow as the fleet sailed into the harbor at Corinth. All the cities at which Antigonus touched to do honor to his father brought wreaths for the urn and sent men dressed in black to join the escort of the king. Hymns of mourning were sung to the sound of the flute, and the sight of Antigonus, as he stood weeping by the side of the urn that held all that remained of the fiery spirit that for more than twenty years had kept the world in a tumult, made the crowd on the shore

---

[172] "A dramatic and spectacular burial" Plutarch calls it—Ἔσχε μέντοι καὶ τὰ περὶ τὴν ταφὴν αὐτοῦ τραγικήν τινα καὶ θεατρικὴν διάθεσιν, *Dem.* LIII.

weep too, for Antigonus and for Demetrius.[173] Phila would have rejoiced to see that her glamorous husband, who had brought her much sorrow and much gladness, was buried with the pomp and splendor that he loved and in the city that bore his name. She was a woman of great magnanimity and devoid of selfish ambition, but she was also a woman of active mind and of great political gifts, and it may be that her life as wife of Demetrius was not the bitter and tragic lot that most historians [174] suppose it to have been, but one that gave scope for her great energy and her talent for diplomacy and service.

In spite of her tragic death she may be accounted the most fortunate, and was assuredly the best of the great Macedonian queens. The good she did lived after her and blossomed in her sons, Antigonus, the great king, and Craterus, his faithful lieutenant, both men of character, like Antipater and her husband Craterus in their loyalties. Plutarch in his essay on Brotherly Love cites the service of Craterus to Antigonus as an example of his theme. All her children rose up and called her blessed.

QUEENS OF MACEDON FROM PHILA, WIFE OF ANTIGONUS GONATAS, TO LAODICE, WIFE OF PERSEUS

The wives of the later kings of Macedon appear to have taken small part in political affairs and comparatively little is known of their lives. Not even the name of the second wife of Philip V, the mother of his son Demetrius, is known. The wife of Antigonus was Phila, the daughter of his sister Stratonice and her first husband, the old king Seleucus. The second Phila was her husband's much younger niece. She would be about twenty-one years old at the time when she came from Asia to be married at Pella in 276 B. C. The marriage sealed a treaty between Antiochus, her half-brother and step-father, and Antigonus, who was now

---

[173] Plut. *Dem.* LII, LIII.

[174] Cf. Tarn, *Antigonos*, p. 97; Beloch IV[1], p. 231.

firmly seated on the Macedonian throne. Philosophers and
poets came to the wedding, among them the astronomer and
physician Aratus, who afterward wrote his celebrated poem
Phaenomena at the suggestion of Antigonus. He now wrote
the wedding-hymn for the royal pair, and it has been suggested that his poems " Treaty-bringers " and " Hymn to
Pan " were both composed for this occasion. He remained at
court and wrote poems for Phila as well as for her husband.
What part the new queen took among the learned men of her
Stoic husband's *entourage* is not related. She very likely inherited quietude from her mother Stratonice, of whom Tarn
writes, " Practically all that is known of her character besides
the usual Macedonian interest in literature is that she was
devoted to religion and to the memory of her father Demetrius ".[175] Antigonus had had no earlier wife, though an *hetaira*
had borne him a son, Halkyoneus, whom he loved and with
Antigonid loyalty brought up as a prince, establishing a festival in his honor after his death. Phila bore him a son Demetrius. No doubt Antigonus held her in affection and honor—
Plutarch says that his dissolute father Demetrius held all
his wives in honor—and he must have thanked the fate that
gave him a quiet wife in the same year in which Ptolemy II
was marrying that firebrand, his sister Arsinoe II. No such
honors were Phila's as those which Arsinoe attained.[176] She
had a statue at Delos [177] and doubtless elsewhere. Arsinoe
II had perhaps five years of glory as wife of Ptolemy Philadelphus and then an " immortality " as apotheosized queen.
Phila had a long, perhaps happy, life as queen of Macedon's
philosopher-king.[178]

Her son Demetrius married her half-sister Stratonice while

---

[175] Tarn, *Antigonos*, p. 349. For marriage of Phila see Westermann, *Aratus*, pp. 53, 60.

[176] Beloch, IV[1], p. 372, comments on the Macedonian opposition to
a worship of royalties, such as prevailed in Egypt.

[177] *O.G.I.* 216.

[178] Cf. Tarn, *Antigonos*, p. 389, n. 60, for the length of her life.

he was still crown prince. Stratonice must have been considerably older than he, but perhaps his father remembered that his own mother had been much older than his father Demetrius. It was a political marriage arranged by Antigonus and Antiochus II, brother of Stratonice. No male [179] children were born of this marriage, and when Demetrius came to the throne in 239 B. C. he accepted the invitation of queen Olympias II of Epirus to marry her daughter Phthia.[180] Stratonice had left her husband [181] before the new marriage, and is next heard of in Syria stirring up trouble for Demetrius and seeking a new marriage alliance with another nephew, Seleucus II. The account of this is given in Josephus against Apion, I, 22 (*F.H.G.* III, 196). He quotes Agatharcides as follows:—

"He is telling the story of Stratonice, how she deserted her husband Demetrius and came from Macedonia to Syria and how when Seleucus refused to marry her as she had expected him to, she stirred up a revolt in Antioch, while he was engaged with the Babylonian campaign; how when the king returned and captured Antioch, she fled to Seleuceia and instead of setting sail as she might have done, was deterred by a dream and was captured and put to death."

She evidently had the spirit of the fourth-century Macedonian queens, but it was entirely ineffective at that time to gain her ends, either in Macedon or in Syria.

Of the Epirote princess, daughter of Olympias II, whom Demetrius married, nothing further is known. Eusebius [182] states that Philip was the son of Chryseis, a Thessalian

---

[179] Perhaps there was a daughter, Apame, who was married to king Prusias of Bithynia. Cf. Beloch, IV², p. 137.

[180] Justin, XXXVIII, 1, 1-2.

[181] Perhaps at the time when Antigonus was arranging a marriage between his son Demetrius and Nicaea, widow of his nephew Alexander, son of Craterus, in order to get possession of Corinth, then in Nicaea's possession. Beloch thinks that Nicaea became the wife of Demetrius. Cf. Beloch, IV², p. 137; Plut. *Aratus*, XVII.

[182] Euseb. I, 237; Plut. *Aem. Paul.* VIII; Justin, XXVIII, 3.

captive, but Tarn [183] has shown by the evidence of inscriptions
that he was the son of Phthia, whose Epirot blood accounts
for the violence of his nature and his murder of his son.
Tarn suggests that the third wife of Demetrius, who is
generally regarded as Philip's mother, may have adopted
him. After her husband's death this lady married Antigonus
Doson, who was the guardian of his nephew Philip. She
bore him several children, whom Eusebius says he did not
rear, because of his desire to keep the kingdom for Philip.

WIVES OF PHILIP V

With regard to Plutarch's statement that the wife of Philip
adopted the child of an Argive sewing-woman named Gnathae-
nium and gave out that the infant was the son of herself and
Philip,[184] Beloch [185] says that though only a scandalous invention, it has the value of indicating that Perseus did pass for
the child of Philip and his wife and also that his mother was an
Argive woman. He has recovered her name, Polycrateia, from
Livy XXVII, 31 and some details of her history from this passage and from Livy XXXII, 21. She was the wife of Aratus,
son of the great Aratus of Sicyon, and a member, as her name
shows, of an important and ancient Argive house, to which
Polycrates, who was such a power in Egypt under Ptolemy
Philopator and Ptolemy Epiphanes, belonged. Livy says that
Philip took her from her husband and carried her off to Macedon, promising to marry her (*spe regiarum nuptiarum*).
Beloch argues that this promise must have been fulfilled,
since Perseus, whose age would bear out the supposition that
he was her son, was actually considered the heir to the throne
and inherited it. She probably died before Philip's marriage
to the mother of Demetrius, whose name has not been preserved. Beloch says that this second wife could not have
been a member of any of the various reigning houses, as such

[183] *C.Q.* XVIII, 1924, pp. 17-23. Cf. Jacoby, *F. Gr. Hist.* II, p. 862.
[184] Plut. *Aem. Paul.* VIII; *Aratus* LIV.
[185] Beloch, IV², p. 140.

a royal alliance would hardly have escaped mention. He thinks that she was probably a daughter of some Macedonian or Thessalian noble, like Chryseis, and would count in the eyes of the Macedonians as of better birth than an Argive lady, such as Polycrateia. This would account for the epithet *pellex* applied to the latter and the stressing of Demetrius' resemblance to his father and the fact that Perseus bore no likeness to Philip. (Nam etsi minor aetate quam Perseus esset, hunc tamen iusta matre familiae, illum paellice ortum esse: illum ut ex vulgato corpore genitum nullam certi patris notam habere; hunc insignem Philippi similitudinem prae se ferre.)[186]

Niese said [187] " Ich bemerke hier dass wir von den Frauen Philipps nichts wissen ". Beloch's investigation has probably brought to light the name of the first wife and some facts of interest in her life.

LAODICE, WIFE OF PERSEUS

Perseus, the last king of Macedon, son of Philip and the Argive woman Polycrateia, is said by Livy [188] to have killed his first wife, whose name is not mentioned, with his own hand. His second wife, the last queen of Macedon, was Laodice, daughter of Seleucus IV. The marriage with Laodice was celebrated with the greatest splendor; [189] the Rhodians incurred the anger of the Romans for the magnificent escort which they gave the bride, bringing her home to Macedonia with their fine ships, the timber for building which had been given them by Perseus, who also gave a gold body-scraper to every member of the crew of the ships that brought his bride to Macedon. He married the Seleucid princess at the request of her father, " not seeking, but sought ", says Livy. His prestige as a bulwark against Rome was high in Asia, and at the same time that he himself married he gave his sister as a wife to Prusias II of Bithynia, who " begged and

---

[186] Livy, XXXIX, 53. [188] Livy, XLII, 5.
[187] Niese, III, p. 31, n. 3. [189] Polyb. XXV, 4, 8-10.

besought him " for her: *sororem dedisse Prusiae precanti atque oranti* (Liv. XLII, 12).

After Laodice's gorgeous homecoming, attended by the Rhodian fleet, our next notice of her is the inscription from Delos, now at Oxford, dated about 177 B. C., in which the people of Delos honor queen Laodice, daughter of king Seleucus and wife of king Perseus, for her goodness and her piety toward the temple and her good will toward the people of Delos.[190]   After this we hear no more of her during her husband's ten years of reigning until the disastrous end, when, as Plutarch tells, she went with him and their children on that miserable flight to the island of Samothrace, where they took refuge in the temple of the Dioskouroi.[191]   As suppliants they were safe there, but Perseus was lured from the sanctuary by a Cretan, who promised him a safe conveyance by sea to Thrace, where his sister was wife of king Teres, for himself, his family, and his treasures.   It is in this passage, which describes the difficulty of escaping from the temple, that his wife is mentioned, and again in the same chapter it is said that he and his wife escaped to the wall of the precinct, when his hopes of taking ship were dashed.   His children he had given in charge to Ion, a false friend, and because of them Perseus came and yielded himself to the Roman conqueror.   In the great triumph of Aemilius Paullus these little children, two boys and a girl, so young that all who looked on them were filled with pity, walked behind the chariot of their father which bore his armor and his diadem.   Behind them walked their father, clad in black, wearing the heavy boots that marked the Macedonian.   His wife was not in that procession.   How she escaped to the court of her uncle Antiochus we do not know, but in a few years we hear that her brother Demetrius Soter offered her in marriage to Ariarathes V of Cappadocia,[192] who rejected the offer to marry

---

[190] Ditt. *Syll.*[2] I, 294.
[191] Plut. *Aem. Paul.* XXIII.
[192] Diod. XXXI, 28; Justin, XXXV, 1.

the widow of Perseus. As Bouché-Leclercq [193] says, he was not anxious to marry a prospective quarrel with Rome. Moreover he acquired much merit with Rome for his refusal, of which he sent word to the Senate together with a crown, worth ten thousand pieces of gold. The Senate was pleased with his renunciation of the alliance with Demetrius and his friendship, and accepted the gold crown, acknowledging it with the customary Roman gifts.

It seems not improbable that Laodice was then married by her brother Demetrius Soter in perhaps 162 B. C. His wife Laodice bore him three sons, Demetrius II, Antiochus VII, and Antigonus, who was killed with his mother by Ammonius,[194] the prime minister of Alexander Balas, after the death of Demetrius Soter in 150 B. C. It is generally held that this Laodice is the widow of Perseus, rejected by Ariarathes V of Cappadocia, and then married by her brother Demetrius; but as Bouché-Leclercq says,[195] " L'identité d'une Laodice prête trop souvent aux discussions ". However, since Livy gives the name of Demetrius' queen as Laodice, he may have married his sister Laodice after her rejection by the Cappadocian king.

Kahrstedt [196] discusses silver and copper coins of Demetrius Soter which have on the obverse jugate heads of Demetrius and Laodice. Head [197] considers that these are coins of Demetrius and his sister-wife. The *Cambridge Ancient History* [198] in the *stemma* of the Seleucids cautiously puts a mark of interrogation in place of the name of the wife of Demetrius I, Soter.

We know nothing of any political action on the part of

---

[193] Bouché-Leclercq, *Seleucides*, I, p. 324.

[194] Livy, *Epit.* 50, per quem et amici omnes regis et Laodice regina et Antigonus Demetrii filius, occisi.

[195] Bouché-Leclercq, *Séleucides*, II, p. 589.

[196] *Klio*, X, p. 278.

[197] *Hist. Num.* 764.

[198] *C.A.H.* VII, table IV.

Laodice while she was a Macedonian queen, nor of any of the queens of that country after the stormy times of Olympias and the young queen Eurydice. The power for which the fourth-century queens strove was theirs only by force of circumstances and because of their own strong will and determination to secure it. With the queens beginning with Thessalonice the normal condition of the Macedonian monarchy reasserts itself, in which the people will suffer no woman to be their king.

CHAPTER II

THE SELEUCID QUEENS

APAME

The first Seleucid queen was one of the brides at the great wedding at Susa in 324 B. C., when Alexander himself took one or perhaps two Persian wives and gave his generals each a Persian princess. Apame was the only one of the ladies married at that wedding-feast to become the ancestress of a line of Hellenistic kings. Seleucus and Ptolemy alone of the bridegrooms mentioned by Arrian[1] survived to found a kingdom, and nothing further is heard of the wife whom Ptolemy took at Susa. She would have been of no political value to him in Egypt. Apame is said by Arrian to have been the daughter of the Bactrian Spitamenes; Strabo[2] is confused about her genealogy and states that her father was Artabazus. Livy[3] in speaking of Apamea says that that city got its name from Apame, a "sister" of king Seleucus; but this is without doubt a mistake originating in the later Seleucid use of "Sister" as a dynastic title for the wife of the king. Tarn[4] thinks that the mother of Apame must have been an Achaemenid princess, whose royal blood was an asset to Seleucus in maintaining his rule over Iranians.

With the exception of a marriage[5] of Seleucus with a daughter of the Hindoo king Sandracottus in 303 B. C. to seal a treaty with him, Apame was his only wife until in 298 B. C. he followed the example of Lysimachus in taking a wife much younger than himself when he made a treaty of alliance with her father, Demetrius the Besieger. The Hindoo

---

[1] Arrian, VII, 4, 5-6.

[2] Strabo, 578.

[3] Livy, XXXVIII, 13, novaeque urbi Apameae nomen inditum ab Apama sorore Seleuci regis.

[4] Tarn, C.Q. XXIII, 1929, pp. 138 ff.

[5] Strabo, XV, 724; Appian, Syr. 55.

would have been only a subordinate wife and no rival to
Apame, but when her husband married Stratonice with great
pomp at Rhossus on the coast of Syria, it meant that Apame
was put away from her position as chief queen of Seleucus.
Aside from the question of Seleucus' affection for Apame it
had been a wise policy for him as successor of Alexander the
Great in the East to continue his idea of racial union between
the Macedonian and Persian stocks and to set the example
of it in his family, an example that was followed by few of
his successors. His son Antiochus, who was made viceroy of
the provinces beyond the Euphrates after the battle of Ipsus,[6]
had the advantage of being half-Iranian in blood.

Other sons of Seleucus and Apame are mentioned by implication by Appian,[7] Justin, and in the inscription *OGI*
213. Rehm has shown that Apame was still queen in the
year in which her husband married Stratonice. The people
of Miletus in that year honored her with a bronze statue.[8] She
was an honored wife of Seleucus, who called three cities [9]
by her name, but there is nothing to show that she had any
power or influence in the government. Whether she came
back to her husband and her queenship when Seleucus gave
his new wife to his son is not known. The Persian blood
brought by her into the Macedonian family of the Seleucids
continued down to the last Seleucid and also to the last
Ptolemy, since the Persian strain was introduced into the
Ptolemaic family by the marriage of Cleopatra "the Syrian"
to Ptolemy V of Egypt in 198 B. C. after the battle of Panium.

STRATONICE I

The Seleucid dynasty did not introduce the custom of
brother-and-sister marriage as early as did the Ptolemaic,

---

[6] Appian, *Syr.* 62.

[7] *Ibid.* 61; Justin, XV, 4, 9.

[8] Rehm, *Milet*, I³, p. 262.

[9] Appian, *Syr.* 57; Strabo, XVI, 749.

whose second representative married his full sister. But the
Seleucids in the second generation had a marriage almost as
shocking to modern conceptions of morality as the other form
of incest. Seleucus in 293 B. C. gave to his son by Apame
his young wife Stratonice, who had already borne him a
daughter. Appian [10] tells at length of the way in which
Seleucus was brought to give his wife to his son. Erasis-
tratus, the king's physician, told the old king the reason for
the apparent ill-health of his son, who was sick with love for
his step-mother. Seleucus preferred his son's happiness to
his young wife; he was very likely glad enough to return to
his old wife Apame. At the same time he solved the problem
of the government of the eastern provinces of the empire by
sending his son and Stratonice as king and queen of the east.
Appian uses for their title the plural βασιλέας, kings;
Plutarch [11] says that he appointed Antiochus king and
Stratonice queen. Seleucus bade the pair remember that
" what the King holds as right *is* right ".[12]

Demetrius was much pleased at hearing that his daughter
was given by Seleucus to Antiochus and that she had been
proclaimed queen of the East. The news came to him at a
happy moment and a high point in his fortunes after he had
been received by the Macedonian army and proclaimed king
of Macedonia.

Stratonice, who had borne a daughter Phila to Seleucus,
bore to Antiochus four children, namely Seleucus, who after
being associated with his father in the kingship was put to
death by him on the charge of conspiracy in 268 B. C.;
Antiochus II, called God, who reigned from 261 to 246 B. C.;
Apame, who married Magas of Cyrene and was the mother
of Berenice II of Egypt; and Stratonice, who married her

---

[10] Appian, *Syr.* 59-61.

[11] Plut. *Dem.* XXXVIII.

[12] Cf. Hdt. III, 31. The Persian Councillors discover a law that
permits the monarch to do what he likes. Cambyses takes advantage
of it to marry his sister, a procedure that was against the old
Persian custom.

cousin Demetrius II of Macedonia. Little is known of her life except that it is clear from inscriptions that she was zealous in the observance of religious rites and made many offerings at Delos to Leto, Artemis, and Apollo, a god whom the Seleucids regarded as their ancestor. The people of Delos also honored her with a statue in the precinct.[13]

A marble statue-basis, once in private possession in Naples and now lost, had the following inscription: [14]

βασίλισσαν ᾿Αρσινόην βασιλέως
Πτολεμαίου καὶ βασιλίσσης Βερενίκης
Στρατονίκη βασιλέως Δημητρίου.

" Stratonice, daughter of king Demetrius, dedicates (a statue of) Arsinoe, daughter of king Ptolemy and queen Berenice."

It is not known where the statue-base was found and the date of it is quite uncertain. A close friendship between Arsinoe II of Egypt and Stratonice has been inferred from it; [15] it is, however, possible that the statue of Arsinoe was dedicated by Stratonice on some purely formal occasion and that it does not signify intimacy.

Stratonice died in 254 B. C.,[16] outliving her husband by seven years. She is referred to in the Ilian decree [17] as sister of her husband, and as queen. This appellation of sister has caused much discussion. It may be that Seleucus adopted her when he gave her to his son, but it is more likely that the title is used as in the Ptolemaic dynasty.[18] Stratonice kept the title of queen during the time when her son [19] Antiochus was co-regent with her husband; in the Ionian

---

[13] Homolle, *B.C.H.* XIV, 1890, p. 509, n. 3.

[14] *O.G.I.* 14.

[15] Tarn, *Antigonus*, pp. 123, 350.

[16] Beloch, IV², pp. 199-200. Kugler, *Von Moses bis Paulus*, pp. 317 ff.

[17] *O.G.I.* 219.

[18] See discussion in Beloch, IV², pp. 200 f. Cf. Stein, P. W. *s. v.* " Stratonike ", sp. 320.

FIGURE 2.

COMBAT BETWEEN GREEK AND PERSIAN, SHOWING THE περισκελίδες OF A
PERSIAN WARRIOR. CF. FIGURE 4b.

decree of 268 B. C.[19] her name with the title follows that of her husband and her son.

It is strange that in her many dedications at Delos she never calls herself wife of Antiochus, but either " daughter of king Demetrius and queen Phila," or " daughter of king Demetrius." Whether this habit indicates her great devotion for her father,[20] or whether it was the result of her having had two men who were father and son for her husbands, which might cause confusion between early and later dedications, is not clear. Wilhelm [21] thinks that Stratonice followed third century usage in omitting her husband's name. It was perhaps love for her father and perhaps remorse that she let him die in the Syrian Chersonese in the constantly disappointed expectation that she would come with Antiochus and set him free, that led her to dedicate jewelry that had belonged to him [22] in the temple at Delos.[23]

In 276 B. C. Stratonice sent her daughter Phila to Macedonia to marry her brother Antigonus Gonatas, and the son of this marriage, Demetrius II, married her daughter Stratonice II in 255 B. C. or a little later.

---

[19] *O.G.I.* 22, 34.

[20] Tarn, *Antigonos*, 350.

[21] Wilhelm, *Berl. Phil. Woch.* 1912, p. 314.

[22] *I.G.* XI, 199 B, l. 51.

[23] Referring to several entries in the Delian inventories which catalogue offerings made by queen Stratonice, daughter of Demetrius the Besieger and queen Phila of Macedon, Tarn (*Antigonos Gonatas*, pp. 349-50) says, " and she had marked the occasion of the marriage of her daughter Phila to Antigonus in 277 or 276 by the dedication to Apollo of Demetrius' necklace which she had preserved, and her daughter's ankle-rings." The inventory of Antigonus (I. 274) *I.G.* XI², 199 B, l. 51, mentions these as follows: περιδέραια τὰ Δημητρίου καὶ φιάλια καὶ περισκελίδα ἀνέθηκε Στρατονίκη. This notice leaves the ownership of the περισκελίς in doubt, but from later inventories it appears that the bracelets for the legs are a part of the decoration, κόσμος, of Demetrius as well as the necklace. Cf. *I.G.* XI, 287, B, l. 2, and restorations in 296 B, 37 and 298, 142. He was, like the Persians (Hdt. VIII, 113), στρεπτοφόρος and ψελιοφόρος, and was the most extravagant in his dress of any of the kings, surpassing even Alexander in the luxury of his Persian dress (Athenaeus, 535; Plut. *Dem.* 2). (For περισκελίδες see Figure 2.)

7

Stratonice seems to have inherited the tact and good sense of her mother Phila, who knew so well how to make the best out of life's bad bargains. Both mother and daughter had husbands forced upon them and both appear to have shown loyalty and kindness in all the relations of life. After the death of Stratonice in the year 254 B. C.[24] a vase-foundation was established at Delos in her memory by her brother Antigonus [25] or by her son Antiochus.[26]

Her offerings at Delos show her to have been a woman of great wealth. She had the title of *basilissa,* was worshipped at Smyrna as Aphrodite Stratonikis,[27] and is mentioned with her husband and son in honorific decrees, but she had no independent power. Her husband is said to have loved her greatly and he took no other wife. Her three daughters were queens, two queens of Macedon and one queen of Cyrene; two of them came to an unhappy end. One of her sons was put to death by his father, and the other, Antiochus II, was perhaps poisoned by his repudiated wife after he had recalled her to live with him. Only her daughter Phila had a life of quiet and happiness at the court of her husband, Antigonus Gonatas.

LAODICE I

Laodice I, wife of Antiochus II, was the first woman of the Seleucid dynasty to show the masterful and managing traits which are regarded as especially marking the Macedonian woman of the ruling houses. The question of her origin and her exact relation to the royal family is not settled. Polyaenus [28] says that she was a sister of her husband, having the same father, i. e., that both were children of Antiochus I. This statement is accepted by many historians as giving the first instance of brother-and-sister marriage among the

---

[24] For the date cf. Beloch, IV², p. 514; Kugler, *Von Moses bis Paulus*, pp. 317 ff.

[25] Tarn, *Antigonos*, p. 351.

[26] Cf. Beloch, IV², pp. 514 f.

[27] *O.G.I.* 228, 229; *Syll*³. 990. Cf. *O.G.I.* 222.

[28] Polyaen. VIII, 50.

Seleucids, and Bouché-Leclercq [29] is inclined to believe that Laodice was her husband's full sister. Against it is the passage of Porphyry [30] in which Laodice is said to be the daughter of Achaeus. Beloch [31] holds that she was certainly a member of the royal family and most probably a cousin of her husband, that is, a child of a brother of her husband's father. The dates of her birth and her marriage are not known. Her husband was forty years old at his death [32] and was probably in the neighborhood of twenty-five when he became king in 261 B. C. Laodice bore him four children, Seleucus Callinicus, Antiochus Hierax, Stratonice, married about 240 to king Ariarathes of Cappadocia, and another daughter, probably named Laodice, who became the wife of Mithradates II of Pontus in 245 B. C. From the age of the eldest son (cf. Beloch, *l. c.*), it is likely that Laodice became the wife of Antiochus soon after he was made co-regent with his father in 267 B. C.

In 252 B. C. Antiochus II after a long period of war made peace with Ptolemy Philadelphus, and the Egyptian king gave Antiochus his daughter Berenice with such a rich dowry that she was known as Φερνοφόρος, the Dowerbringer.[33] This marriage meant that Laodice was divorced by Antiochus and that Berenice's children would inherit instead of the sons of Laodice. The date of the marriage to Berenice is given by a letter of Artemidorus, the Egyptian house-steward of the *dioiketes* Apollonius, to the *oikonomos* Zeno, written on the thirteenth of April, 252 B. C.: "When I was writing you, we were approaching Sidon, accompanying the queen as far as the border." [34] Laodice had been put aside, as her grandmother Apame had been, because of the political arrange-

---

[29] Bouché-Leclercq, *Séleucides*, II, p. 546.

[30] Porphyry, *F.H.G.* III, 707; Euseb. I, 251.

[31] Beloch, IV^2, pp. 200 f.

[32] Porphyry, *loc. cit.*

[33] Jerome on Daniel, XI.

[34] Edgar, *Zeno Pap.* 42, *Annales*, XIX, 1920, p. 93.

ments of two kings and their ambitions. Ptolemy sent [35] his daughter jars of Nile water to make her fruitful and hasten the birth of an heir to the Seleucid kingdom who should also be his own grandson. That child was born, but was not to live long. Laodice had been recompensed for the repudiation of her as queen by estates in the neighborhood of Babylon and Borsippa, given to her and to her two sons, Seleucus and Antiochus. This is recorded in a cuneiform inscription from Babylon.[36] Another inscription [37] records the sale of lands in the neighborhood of Zeleia by Antiochus to Laodice. In this inscription, which belongs to the year 253-252 B. C., Laodice has neither the title of queen nor that of sister. Antiochus had probably already divorced her, or was on the point of so doing, preparatory to his reconciliation with Ptolemy and his marriage with Berenice. Laodice, who, like all the Hellenistic queens, was a woman of great wealth, retired with her sons to Ephesus. After some years Antiochus tired of his new life, returned to Laodice, and on his death-bed in 247 B. C. named his eldest son by her, Seleucus, his heir. It was said that she poisoned him in the fear that he might change his mind and return to Berenice,[38] but this story is probably the Egyptian version of the event.

Laodice was again queen and co-regent with her son, who was not yet twenty; but there was another queen in Antioch, the Egyptian Berenice, with her little son. Her father Philadelphus had died in 247 B. C., and her brother Ptolemy III was king. Laodice succeeded in getting adherents of hers in Antioch, where she had so long been queen, to kill first the little son and then Berenice herself, who had fled to the temple of Apollo in Daphne. Berenice was killed before her brother Ptolemy, who had marched from Egypt to save her,

---

[35] Polyb. *ap.* Athen. II, 45 c.

[36] Lehmann-Haupt, *Zeitschrift für Assyriologie*, VII, p. 33, n. 2.

[37] *O.G.I.* 225.

[38] Appian, *Syr.* 65; Pliny, *N.H.* VII, 53; Jerome on Daniel, XI, 6; Valerius Maximus, IX, 10; Polyaenus, VIII, 50.

arrived with his army. Beloch [39] believes that the famous
Gurob [40] papyrus was written by the nauarch of Ptolemy's
fleet, who after conquering Cilicia arrived in Antioch amid
great rejoicings on the part of the inhabitants and had
an audience with the " Sister ", that is, queen Berenice,
who would naturally be called the " Sister " by an Egyptian
admiral. She was in any case killed before the arrival of
her brother. It may be that Polyaenus is right in saying
that her death was concealed by Ptolemy in order that he
might gain time and the advantage of sending out decrees in
her name.[41]

Laodice is condemned by all historians ancient and modern,
with the exception of Beloch, who calls their judgment
unjust [42] and declares that she only supported the rights of
her sons, and for that end it was, of course, necessary to
remove the rival queen and her son, the usual procedure at
this time in such cases. Without wishing to condone the
crimes of Laodice, I find it a refreshing change from the sen-
timents of other historians that Beloch actually mentions the
fact that "Alexander at the time when he became king committed much worse deeds, or let them occur ".

Beloch also defends the execution of Laodice's lady-in-
waiting, Danae, as deserved punishment for high treason.
The story of Danae is quoted from Phylarchus by Athenaeus.[43]
Her lover Sophron was in command of Ephesus under Laodice, who, suspicious of his loyalty to her, summoned him to
her presence. Danae, the daughter of a *hetaera* who had
studied with Epicurus, was present at the interview, and
knowing her mistress' intention to put Sophron to death,
gave him some hint by a gesture when Laodice was suggesting
something to him. He understood and dissimulated, asking
Laodice for two days to consider the matter, and fled in that

---

[39] Beloch, IV¹, pp. 675-6.
[40] Wilcken, *Papyruskunde*, I², 1.
[41] Cf. Wilamowitz, *Hermes*, XLIX, 1914, p. 447.
[42] Beloch, IV¹, p. 676.
[43] Athen. XIII, 593; *F.H.G.* I, 339.

night to Ephesus, which he later surrendered to Ptolemy.
Laodice condemned Danae to be flung down from a high cliff,
though they had been great friends up to that time. Danae
refused to answer any questions of Laodice about her lover,
and when standing on the cliff she said, " No wonder men
despise the gods. I have saved my lover, who has been a
husband to me, and this is my reward from heaven. Laodice
has killed the man who was her husband and she receives all
this glory ". It is difficult to be objective enough to praise
Laodice for this murder.

After this " Laodicean War " (Λαοδίκειος πόλεμος, *Inschriften von Priene*, 37, 134) little more is heard of Laodice. It
appears from a passage in Plutarch [44] that in the war between
her two sons she stirred up the younger one, Antiochus, who
was only fourteen, against Seleucus. It seems probable that
she was jealous of the power and prestige of her elder son
and thought that she could better control her younger one,
Antiochus the " Hawk ", who is said by Justin to have received that name because of his rapacity and greed. Appian [45]
says that Ptolemy killed her, but it is difficult to see when
she could have fallen into his hands, and this statement is
generally discredited. In 236 B. C. her two sons appear
reconciled, after the war which every one agrees she must
have stirred up, and they together restore to the Babylonian
temples the estates once given Laodice and her children by
Antiochus.[46]

History has recorded no good of Laodice. She was an
energetic woman who owed her power to the facts that she
was the mother of heirs to the throne who were minors at
the time of their father's death, and that she was strong and
unscrupulous in defending their rights. She appears to have
had her own power in mind rather than theirs if it is true,
as it seems to be, that she set them against one another and so

---

[44] Plut. *Frat. Am.* p. 489 A.

[45] Appian, *Syr.* 65.

[46] Rostovtzeff, *Klio*, I, p. 299, n. 1. *Zeitschrift für Assyriologie*,
VII, p. 330. Cf. Beloch IV², p. 543; *C.A.H.* VII, p. 720.

brought about the War of the Brothers. Her prestige was so great that she established, to the great confusion of history, the name Laodice, which had been the name of the mother of the first Seleucus, as the dynastic name of princesses in the Seleucid line, and it was also taken over into the Pontic royal house. An important example of the uncertainty caused by this name is that offered by *O.G.I.* 224 in the πρόσταγμα of king Antiochus in which he ordains, in his desire to increase the honors of his sister-wife Laodice, because of her affection and devotion in their life together, that besides the chief-priests of the king in all the satrapies there shall be chief-priestesses of the queen. It is impossible to decide whether the queen Laodice of this inscription is Laodice, wife of Antiochus II, or her grand-daughter Laodice, the wife of her grandson Antiochus III.

BERENICE, SISTER OF PTOLEMY EUERGETES, WIFE OF ANTIOCHUS II OF SYRIA

Berenice, daughter of Ptolemy II and Arsinoe I, and named for Ptolemy's mother, must have been close to thirty years of age when she was married to Antiochus of Syria in 251 B. C. It is possible that she may have been betrothed in her childhood to the son of Arsinoe II and that intrigues connected with the succession may have kept her single so long. It was perhaps to procure her fertility at the somewhat late age for having children at which she married that her father had the jars of Nile water sent her continually " so that his daughter might drink the water of no other river ".[47] Berenice was given such an enormous dowry by her father that she was called Phernephoros, the Dower-bringer.[48] Antiochus, " called God ", her husband, was already married to his half-sister Laodice, by whom he had two sons. He was attached to Laodice and his children, and married Berenice for the substantial advantages offered him by Philadelphus along with the bride.[49] In a

---

[47] Athen. II, 45 c.   [48] Jerome on *Daniel*, XI, 5.
[49] Appian, *Syr.* 65.

year he was weary of Berenice, though she bore him a son,
and returned to Laodice at Ephesus while Berenice remained
with her son at Antioch.　To ensure his not turning back to
Berenice and her son under threats which were sure to come
from Ptolemy in Egypt, Laodice is said to have poisoned him.
She had her son Seleucus proclaimed king in Ephesus and
Asia Minor.[50]　To prevent Berenice's baby from being proclaimed king in Antioch she sent kidnappers to that city
who carried off the child.　Berenice pursued them in a chariot
and struck the chief magistrate of Antioch, who had been
bribed in this business by Laodice, with her spear and then
with a stone which killed him.　She then appealed to the
crowd as suppliant[51] for the life of her child, which had
apparently been secretly killed by the magistrates whom Laodice had bribed.　A child was exhibited to her as her own,
but kept in the possession of the officials.　Justin[52] says
that she shut herself up in Daphne with her child and that
when the news of the treatment which she was receiving
spread abroad in the cities of Asia, help was sent to her from
various sides.　Her brother Ptolemy, leaving his newly-mar-
ried wife, was rushing all his troops to his sister.　He did not
succeed in saving her and her child from Laodice, and it does
not seem possible that he saw Berenice alive. She could surely
not have been killed *after* his arrival.　Yet the Gurob papyrus, which is now regarded as a letter or memorandum composed either by Ptolemy himself or by one of his[53] officers,
speaks of " Sister ", of her sending messages to the com-

---

[50] Val. Max. IX, 10.

[51] Polyaen. VIII, 50.

[52] Justin, XXVII, 1. 4.

[53] Roos, *Mnemosyne*, LI, 1923, pp. 262 ff., suggests that the officer
in command of the fleet was Lysimachus, brother of both Ptolemy
and of Berenice.　This would account for the word " sister." Beloch
(IV², pp. 200 f.) follows Wilcken in holding that the letter is the
report of an officer belonging to the staff of the admiral of Ptolemy's
fleet.　Cf. Wilcken, *Papyruskunde*, I², p. 2. " Der siegreich Feldherr
is ein anderer als der Erzähler."

manders asking for help, and further of a visit of the writer to
the Sister after an enthusiastic reception by the priests, magistrates, and citizens of the city of Antioch. The " Sister " was
once held to be Laodice. The title is now referred to Berenice,
and if she is the " Sister ", it appears from the letter that she
was living after Ptolemy's arrival and actually was seen by
him. Bevan [54] points out how incredible this is, and suggests
that the sister is Ptolemy's queen, his bride Berenice, who in
her eagerness to see him has braved the journey to Antioch in
time of war. This also seems only less incredible, and the
truth is apparently told in Polyaenus' tale which has been
condemned as unhistorical romance. He says that Berenice
and her child were killed before Ptolemy arrived ; her ladies-
in-waiting concealed her body and dressed up one of themselves in the queen's robes and crown in order that Ptolemy
might send out letters in the name of the young king and
Berenice. The papyrus is, then, an official *communiqué,*
written by an officer while Ptolemy was still keeping from
public knowledge the fact that he had arrived too late to save
his sister. This would explain the summary reference to the
sister and the immediate necessity of dealing with " business ",
possibly a euphemism for vengeance on Laodice. Polyaenus
appears to be confirmed by the papyrus. At any rate he offers
a reasonable explanation, whereas all the other interpretations
land us in inextricable difficulties.[55]

We know that Berenice died bravely in the manner of the
Macedonian women, defending the rights of her little son,
and that Ptolemy, who came too late to save her, overran with
his army a great part of the Seleucid kingdom, and brought
home (245 B. C.) vast treasures, among them images of
Egyptian gods and other sacred things that had been carried
off by Cambyses and the Persians after him. The book of
Daniel, prophesying eighty years after the event, says that
" the king of the south shall come with an army and shall

---

[54] Bevan, *Egypt,* p. 202.

[55] See, however, Beloch, IV[1], p. 675, n. 1.

enter into the fortress of the king of the north and shall prevail, and shall also carry captive into Egypt their goods with
their princes and with their precious vessels of silver and of
gold, and he shall continue more years than the king of the
north." [56] For the images of the gods brought back by him
it is said that the Egyptians called Ptolemy *Euergetes,* the
king who does good to his people.

So Ptolemy had glory and honor from the campaign, but
his sister Berenice died a victim to the political ambitions of
kings, her father, Ptolemy Philadelphus, and her husband,
Antiochus called God.

Three Laodices, Wives of Seleucus Callinicus, Antiochus Hierax, and Antiochus III Called The Great

The wife of Seleucus II (246-226) was another Laodice,
perhaps the niece of his mother. Her brother Andromachus
is twice mentioned by Polybius [57] as "brother of Laodice,
wife of Seleucus". Beloch believes that her father's name
was Andromachus and that he was son of Achaeus, father of
Laodice I. Nothing more is known of the history of the wife
of Seleucus II except that she was the mother of Seleucus
III [58] and of Antiochus III.

It is not certain that the wife of Antiochus Hierax was
named Laodice. She was the daughter of Ziaëlas of Bithynia
and was given to Hierax during the "War of the Brothers"
when her father made a treaty with him. It is disputed
whether the Laodice mentioned in Polybius, V, 74, 5, is the
daughter of Hierax and his Bithynian wife, or the niece of
Hierax, and daughter of his sister Laodice, wife of Mithra-

---

[56] *O.G.I.* 54, 56; Polyaen. VIII, 50; Jerome on Daniel 11; Justin
XXVII, 1. 8-9; Catullus, LXVI, 35.

[57] Polyb. IV, 51, 4; VIII, 22, 11.

[58] Seleucus III (226-5 to 224-3 B. C.), Soter (*O.G.I.* 245), who was
killed in Phrygia not long after he became king, apparently was not
married. There is no mention of a wife of his.

dates II. Beloch,[59] who believes that this Laodice is the daughter of Hierax, discusses the complicated question in detail.

There is greater certainty about Laodice, wife of Antiochus III (223-187). She was his cousin and daughter of Laodice, sister of Seleucus II, her husband's father, and of Mithradates II of Pontus. Polybius [60] describes her coming, escorted by the admiral Diognetus, to Seleuceia-at-Zeugma to meet her bridegroom. She is called by Polybius " a virgin, now designated wife to the king ". Her father Mithradates boasted that he was descended from one of the seven Persians who had slain the Magi and that he had under his sway a kingdom along the Euxine which had been bestowed upon his ancestors by Darius. Antiochus met his bride with the pomp and ceremony due her rank and celebrated the marriage with royal magnificence. He took her to Antioch and proclaimed her queen and then turned back to preparations for war against Ptolemy Philopator of Egypt, for the purpose of recovering Coele-Syria and Palestine. This marriage took place in 221 B. C. and a son Antiochus was born the following year. Other children of the king and queen were Seleucus IV, Cleopatra " the Syrian ", who was married to Ptolemy V of Egypt in 198 B. C., Antiochus IV, Laodice, and Antiochis, later queen of Cappadocia. In 195 B. C. Antiochus joined in marriage his eldest son Antiochus and his daughter Laodice,[61] the first instance of brother-and-sister marriage in the Seleucid house. It appears from Babylonian [62] cuneiform records that the son was associated with the father in the kingship from 208 B. C., when the names of the two kings Antiochus and Antiochus occur. The son Antiochus, who had given an audience to Hannibal at Daphne in 195 B. C.,

---

[59] Beloch IV², pp. 202. Against his view, Stähelin, P. W. XII, sp. 706 ff.; Bouché-Leclercq, *Séleucides*, I, pp. 567-568.

[60] Polyb. V, 43.

[61] Appian, *Syr.* 4.

[62] Clay, *Babylonian Records in the Library of Pierpont Morgan*, II, p. 13; *Morgan Library Collection*, 2171; Beloch, IV², p. 192.

died suddenly in 192. It is possible that his widow married
her brother Seleucus IV, the name of whose wife is unknown,
and she may have married her younger brother Antiochus IV,
whose wife Laodice is mentioned in the Inscription from
Dyme.[63]   But these later marriages of Laodice, who was
married in 195 B. C. to her eldest brother, are merely doubtful conjectures.

Laodice, daughter of Mithradates, who was married at
Zeugma-on-the-Euphrates in 221 with pomp and splendor to
Antiochus III, is mentioned in an inscription, now in the
British Museum,[64] in which the people of Iasus express the
loyalty they feel toward the Great King Antiochus, and
toward queen Laodice and their children. It is probably this
Laodice whose honors are increased by her husband because
of her affection and devotion to him in their life together,
and because of her piety.[65]   He perhaps took no other wife
during her life time; in 191 B. C. in the midst of the war
with Rome and having, as the historians say, reached the age
of fifty, he fell in love with a Greek girl in Euboea, when he
had on hand two most important undertakings, the freeing
of the Greeks and the war with Rome.[66]   He had a great
wedding-feast in Chalcis and called his young bride, who was
very beautiful and of good Chalcidian family, Euboea from
her native island. Polybius says that the king passed the
winter in Euboea in feasting and riotous living, being (Polybius states) a hard drinker, who took delight in revelry.[67]
But this charge of frivolous inactivity has been disproved by
Kromayer [68] in his analysis of the campaign of Antiochus.
When he was forced to retreat from Greece to Ephesus he
took his young wife with him, and we learn from Livy [69] that

[63] *O.G.I.* 252.

[64] *O.G.I.* 237.

[65] *O.G.I.* 224.

[66] Polyb. XX, 8; Appian, *Syr.* 16.

[67] Polybius, XX, 8; Livy, XXXVI, 11.

[68] Kromayer, *Antike Schlachtfelder*, II, p. 135.

[69] Livy, XXXVII, 44, 5.

FIGURE 3.

BRONZE HEAD OF CLEOPATRA THEA. NAPLES.

Cf. Pfuhl, *Jahrbuch*, XLV, 1930, pp. 43 ff.

after the battle of Magnesia the king fled to Apamea with his wife and infant daughter. Antiochus was killed in the East in 188 B. C. It is not certain that his wife Laodice was dead at the time, but nothing more is heard of her nor of the young wife Euboea. His daughters, " chiefly anonymous ", as Bouché-Leclercq [70] says, " appear only on the occasion of diplomatic marriages ", except for Cleopatra " the Syrian," who married Ptolemy V of Egypt.

The names of these Laodices, after the first one who played an important part in affairs from 252 B. C. until her death, appear only when historians mention the marriage of the reigning king or of the crown-prince, or else in an honorific decree of some Greek state. It is not possible to get any idea of their character or of their lives. Laodice, wife of Antiochus III, if it is she who is mentioned in *O.G.I.* 224, is praised by her husband for her exemplary conduct as wife and for her piety toward the gods.

From this time on the wives of the Seleucid kings are either puzzling Laodices, such as the wife of Demetrius I, who may have been his sister, widow of the last king of Macedonia, or else Cleopatras from Egypt, two of whom had previously been married to a Ptolemy.

CLEOPATRA THEA (Figs. 3 and 5a)

Cleopatra Thea was the wife of three Seleucid kings, Alexander Balas, Demetrius II, and Antiochus VII, called Sidetes. Until she was over forty, nothing is recorded of her actions except in the usual accounts of diplomatic marriages. After that time, when all her husbands are dead, she steps forth for a few years as queen, issuing her own coinage and acting as guardian of her minor son Antiochus VIII, Grypus. But for these last years of her life (125-121 B. C.) she would not rank as she does, as one of the most energetic and murderous of the queens. As it is she competes with Laodice I and with her own sister, Cleopatra III of Egypt, for the bad

[70] Bouché-Leclercq, *Séleucides*, I, p. 226 and note.

eminence of being regarded by historians as the most wicked and most detestable of the Hellenistic queens.

She was the daughter of Cleopatra II of Egypt and her brother Philometor, children of Cleopatra " the Syrian ". She was perhaps the eldest child, though the date of her birth is not known,[71] and was perhaps the daughter whom Philometor betrothed to his brother Euergetes II on their reconciliation in 151 B. C., though it was her younger sister Cleopatra III who later became the wife of Euergetes. In 150 B. C. Philometor gave her in marriage to a protegé of Attalus of Pergamum, Alexander Balas, who pretended to be a son of Antiochus IV, to whom he bore a striking resemblance. After Alexander had conquered Demetrius I, " Ptolemy went out of Egypt with his daughter Cleopatra and celebrated her marriage at Ptolemais, with great glory, as the manner of kings is." [72] With the help furnished by Attalus and Ariarathes as well as by the Jews and by Ptolemy of Egypt,[73] Alexander gained a victory over Demetrius I in a battle in which the king was killed; the Pretender was received at Antioch with great rejoicing. He had the blessing of Rome in his usurpation, for the arch-plotter, Heraclides, had taken him and an alleged sister, of course called Laodice, before the Roman Senate, which recognized the two as children of Antiochus in the decree, " Alexander and Laodice, children of a king who has been our friend and ally have come before the Senate with their plea. And the Senate gives them permission to return to their ancestral kingdom and votes to assist them as they request ".[74] Among the first acts of the impostor as king was to put to death Laodice, wife of Demetrius I (who was perhaps his sister and widow of Perseus of Macedon), and Antigonus, little son of Demetrius.[75]

---

[71] Strack, *Dynastie*, p. 198, n. 24.

[72] *I Maccabees*, X, 58.

[73] Appian, *Syr.* 67.

[74] Polyb. XXXIII, 16 ff.

[75] Livy, *Epit.* L.

The young interloper with the hungry greed of a parvenu now gave himself up to a life of debauchery such as he had dreamed of, but never hoped to attain in the days of his sordid origins.[76] "Because of the weakness of his soul", says Diodorus,[77] "he proved useless in the rank of king", and the government at Antioch was given over to Hierax and Diodotus. Cleopatra Thea bore Alexander a son who was destined to be called king for a brief time and to die a child, victim of the plots of Diodotus. Before long Alexander was roused from his drunken pleasures by the advent of the young son of the late king Demetrius and his sister Laodice [78] with an army of Cretan mercenaries under a brigand chief called Lasthenes. The Jews whom Balas had favored stood by him, but Ptolemy Philometor arrived with fleet and army, and before long had renounced his son-in-law, and after securing possession of his daughter the queen, gave her to the young Demetrius (146 B. C.) and supported his claims to the kingdom. The little Antiochus was placed in the care of some Arab chieftains by his father, who fled from Antioch. Ptolemy Philometor might himself have been king of Syria, but deemed it wiser to persuade the people of Antioch to receive Demetrius, who was as yet hardly grown to manhood, and Cleopatra married the young king, who was several years younger than herself. In a battle of the next year between Alexander Balas and Ptolemy, the Egyptian king was mortally wounded; the head of Alexander Balas, who had been assassinated by some of his own officers, was brought for the dying Ptolemy to look upon.[79]

There ensued in Syria a time of anarchy and misrule by the Cretan ruffians, who pillaged and murdered at will. Demetrius was too young and too weak to govern,[80] and Cleopatra

---

[76] Justin, XXXV, 1—pristinarum sordium oblitus.

[77] Diod. XXXIII, 3.

[78] It is probable, though not certain that Demetrius I married his sister Laodice, widow of Perseus of Macedonia.

[79] Josephus, *A.J.* XIII, 4, 8.

[80] Diod. XXXIII, 4.

Thea had not yet begun to show her strong will. It was a
time of terror and civil war. Diodotus took advantage of the
hatred which the natives of Antioch felt for Demetrius to
fetch the little son of Cleopatra Thea and Balas from his
hiding-place among the Arabs. He drove Demetrius out of
Antioch and made himself master after establishing the little
Antiochus as nominal king. In a year or two the little king
died; it was said afterward that Diodotus, who had taken the
name Tryphon, had killed him. He now called himself king
and αὐτοκράτωρ and sent to Rome to ask for recognition,
which he did not get.[81] Demetrius went off to conquer the
Parthians and after winning some victories was captured
and kept a prisoner by Mithradates.

And now the next Seleucid king and the third husband
of Cleopatra Thea appears. This was the younger brother of
Demetrius, Antiochus VII, who had grown up in Pamphylia
in the coastal city of Side and had the name Sidetes from this
fact. Cleopatra had been staying at Seleuceia-in-Pieria while
her husband Demetrius was absent on the Parthian campaign.
She sent to Antiochus (138 B. C.), who was in Rhodes, and
invited him to marry her and claim the kingdom. This was
done by advice of her friends, and she herself was afraid that
the people of Seleuceia would surrender the city to Tryphon.[82]
The coming of Antiochus, a king of the old royal line, proved
immensely popular. He fought a battle with Tryphon and
chased him to Dora in Phoenicia, where the usurper finally
committed suicide. Tryphon had reigned three years. The
new king proved a vigorous ruler and established order in the
various parts of the country that had been disorganized by the
misrule of the last years. Cleopatra had by her second husband
two sons, Seleucus V and Antiochus Grypus, and now by
Antiochus Sidetes another son, Antiochus Cyzicenus. Demetrius had remained at the Parthian court, where he became

---

[81] Diod. XXXIII, 17; Josephus, *A.J.* XIII, 5-7; Head, *H.N.* 767.
[82] Josephus, *A.J.* XIII, 7, 2.

such a favorite that the king Mithradates gave him his daughter Rhodogune in marriage.

Antiochus proved a strong and energetic king, beloved by his people, and he treated the Jews in his dealings with them with so much good sense and uprightness that they called him "Pious".[83] In 130 B. C. he undertook a campaign against the Parthians to recover the provinces of the east and also to free his brother from captivity.[84] He perhaps intended to allow his brother to rule in the east with his Parthian wife while he remained with Cleopatra Thea in the western part of the empire. Successful in his first battles, he demanded of the Parthian king Phraates that he should let Demetrius go free. Though Phraates refused the other conditions imposed and continued the war, he did free Demetrius, probably in the hope that he would seize the Syrian kingship in the absence of Antiochus. Antiochus died fighting in Parthia, the last of the Seleucids to retain anything of the splendid strength and vigor of the Founder of the dynasty.

Of Cleopatra Thea during these years of warfare nothing is heard. But now that Demetrius II, her former husband, returns to his old kingdom, disliked by his subjects and hated by his wife, she begins to take action. She had already sent her son Antiochus Grypus to Athens, and the son by her last husband she now sent to Cyzicus, whence his nick-name of Cyzicenus. It is said that she was intensely indignant with Demetrius because he had married Rhodogune at the Parthian court.[85]

The mother of Cleopatra Thea, Cleopatra II of Egypt, at war with her husband Euergetes II, came to Syria to seek the help of her daughter's husband against him. In revenge for the aid which Demetrius attempted to give her, Euergetes set up as king of Syria an impostor called Alexander Zebinas, who held the power at Antioch for five years (128-123 B. C.).

---

[83] Josephus, XIII, 8, 2.

[84] Appian, *Syr.* 68.

[85] Appian, *Syr.* 68.

8

Cleopatra Thea and her children were in Ptolemais at the time when Demetrius was defeated in battle by the usurping king; and when her husband came to Ptolemais Cleopatra refused him admittance, and he was killed soon afterward at Tyre by the governor of that city, it was said by the order of his wife. In *Epitome* 60 Livy says, " Disturbances in Syria are also related, in which Cleopatra destroyed Demetrius, her husband, and her son Seleucus, in rage because after she had killed his father, Seleucus assumed the diadem against her order." Appian says that she killed with her own hand this son who had been sent back from the Parthian court. He had accompanied his uncle Sidetes on the Parthian campaign. A sister of his, Laodice, who also was taken on that adventure, was captured by Phraates II, who fell in love with her beauty and married her.

Cleopatra Thea now assumed the queenship, and in the year 125 B. C. had silver tetradrachms struck bearing her veiled and diademed head on the obverse, on the reverse the double horn of Abundance, with the inscription " of queen Cleopatra, goddess of Plenty ".[86] The face on the one extant coin is handsome and wilful.[87] On other coins her head is jugate with that of her son Grypus, but hers is in front. She is the first and almost the only Hellenistic queen to strike coins in her own name only.[88] Kahrstedt believes that this silver coinage with her head and legend alone was restricted to the year 125 B. C. or soon after and that she was soon obliged to put the head of her son on the coins as well as her own. The fact that

---

[86] βασιλίσσης Κλεοπάτρας, θεᾶς Εὐετηρίας. The only extant example is in the British Museum. Cf. Fig. 5a.

[87] Pfuhl (*Jahrbuch*, XLV, 1930, pp. 43 f.) compares the " Libyan locks " of the coins of Cleopatra Thea, both the one just noted and those which show her head jugate with her son, and concludes that the well-known bronze head from Herculaneum in Naples with these locks is a bust of Cleopatra Thea, showing her in massive form in middle life, with the ugly nose of her earliest coins made more classical. Cf. Fig. 3.

[88] Kahrstedt, *Klio*, X, pp. 279 f. Cf. pp. 276 f.

he conquered the usurper Zebinas in 123 B. C. would give him a prestige that would not be agreeable to his mother, and in that year Ptolemy Euergetes II gave him his daughter Tryphaena. This, too, would arouse the jealous apprehension of the older queen, and if we may believe the testimony of Appian and Justin, she had learned the dynastic lesson that he who wishes at all costs to rule should not scruple to kill whoever stands in the way. Appian says that she killed her son Seleucus either because she feared his vengeance on her for his father's death or else she was possessed by a frantic hatred of all the world. Justin tells of her meeting her son Antiochus Grypus, when he came in heated from hunting, with a cool drink of poisoned wine. He, "velut pietate cum matre certaret"—"as though vying with his mother in politeness", bade her drink the cup. She refused. He insisted, and after some protestations on her part and the production by him of evidence of her bad intention in offering the wine, she drank it and died.[89] Her death came two years after her son had expelled his rival and had married her niece, the Egyptian princess, and her attempt to kill Grypus doubtless had its motive in her dislike to relinquish her position of queen-regent, which she would naturally give up now that her son had reached his majority, secured his kingdom, and married a wife. Her sister Cleopatra III of Egypt was more successful in bullying her troublesome son and his wives and in retaining her power.

Her children were Antiochus VI Dionysus by Alexander Balas; Seleucus V, Antiochus VIII Grypus, and a daughter Laodice, wife of Phraates II, by Demetrius, and a son Antiochus IX Cyzicenus by Antiochus Sidetes. Eusebius appears to confuse them in his statement that she bore five children to Sidetes.[90]

---

[89] Appian, *Syr.* 69; Justin, XXXIX, 2.

[90] Bouché-Leclercq, *Séleucides*, II, p. 600. Tarn, accepting the statement of Eusebius, gives Cleopatra Thea a family of eight children and says that this is the largest known Hellenistic family (*Hellenistic Civilisation*, p. 23).

Her crimes seem to be confined to the last years of her life. She had passed from one king of Syria to another, and her life had trained her to be exactly what she appears to have become—an egotist, mad for power and stopping at nothing to get it. Her eldest child had been taken from her. She killed one son and attempted to kill another, and the death of her husband Demetrius is charged to her account. It is always possible that stories about her were invented by her son Grypus, who himself had a considerable knowledge of poisons and administered the poison-cup to his mother. In commenting on the description which Diodorus gives of the vices of his brother Antiochus IX Cyzicenus,[91] Bouché-Leclercq [92] well says, " In this *mélange* of intemperance, versatile puerility, and ill-employed energy, it is easy to recognize the hereditary traits of the Seleucid temperament." Cleopatra Thea's sons were worthless kings and by their quarrels for the kingship destroyed the little that was left of Seleucid power and prestige. She herself must be put in the list of the Hellenistic queens who, " Seleucid or Lagid, recoiled before no obstacle that would transform their distaff into a sceptre ".[93]

Her name appears joined with that of her husband Antiochus, here called the Great, in a Delian inscription [94] in honor of her son Antiochus IX Cyzicenus. The title " Great " added to the name of Antiochus confirms Justin,[95] who says Antiochus began to be called Great after his three victories which enabled him to occupy Babylon. In Delian inscriptions [96] her son Grypus, son of Demetrius, has among his titles that of Philometor, Mother-Loving. When the manner of Cleopatra Thea's death is considered, this title has an ironic flavor.[97]

---

[91] Diod. XXXIV, 34.

[92] Bouché-Leclercq, *Séleucides*, I, p. 407.

[93] *Ibid.* 397.

[94] *O.G.I.* 255-256.

[95] Justin, XXXVIII, 10, 6.

[96] *O.G.I.* 258-260.

[97] The title Philometor appears sometimes to be given to rulers

The Last Seleucid Queens

The Seleucid dynasty, as it dies, becomes economical of queens. Cleopatra Thea was the wife of three kings; her son Grypus married first Tryphaena, daughter of Ptolemy VII, Euergetes II, and after that her sister Cleopatra Selene, who had been the wife of her brother Ptolemy VIII. Antiochus IX Cyzicenus married in succession two ex-wives of Ptolemy VIII, Cleopatra IV of Egypt and Cleopatra Selene, ex-wife of Ptolemy VIII and of Antiochus Grypus. Cleopatra Selene is the last Seleucid queen of whom history relates anything. She lived to marry the son of her last husband, who was known as Antiochus X, " the Pious ", a name given to him in Appian's opinion in jest because of his piety in marrying the lady. These queens will be discussed among the queens of Egypt. The last to be called Seleucid kings, Philip II and Antiochus XIII, were descended respectively from Cleopatra Tryphaena, wife of Grypus, and from Cleopatra Selene, wife of Cyzicenus. The wealth and the royal blood of these last queens made them desirable matches for the Seleucid kings in the final death-throes of that dynasty.

Apame, Stratonice, the Laodices, the Cleopatras of the Seleucid line, queens whose names are recorded from the occasion of the great wedding at Susa in 324 B. C. to the death of Cleopatra Selene, murdered by Tigranes in Mesopotamia in 68 B. C., have among them some women of unusual courage and energy, but none so resplendent in history as the Arsinoes, Berenices, and Cleopatras of Egypt. The two most famous are Laodice, wife of Antiochus II called God, and Cleopatra Thea. The last of them, Cleopatra Selene, outdid the rest in the adventurous character of her life and the number of kings whom she married.

---

whose mothers have acted as their guardians and co-regents, such as Ptolemy VI, Ptolemy VIII, and Cleopatra II. Cf. Strack, *Dynastie*, pp. 132 ff.

CHAPTER III

PTOLEMAIC QUEENS

Eurydice and Berenice, Wives of Ptolemy I

Eurydice, fourth daughter of Antipater the Regent, was married to Ptolemy in the years in which Antipater married his daughters to Successors, as though he foresaw that he would be the ancestor of kings. Phila was given to Craterus and to Demetrius, Nicaea to Perdiccas and to Lysimachus, and Eurydice to Ptolemy. This marriage very likely took place in 322 B. C.[1]

Eurydice's husband, like the other Successors, was fond of women and had various mistresses, among them the famous Thais, who bore him two children. He had married at the great wedding in Susa in 324 B. C. a Persian lady Artacama, or Apama,[2] whose fate is not known. Tarn has suggested[3] that soon after his arrival in Egypt he married an Egyptian princess. He infers this marriage from the existence of a princess Ptolemais,[4] " daughter of Ptolemy Kheper-ka-ri ", that is, Ptolemy with the solar name of Nectanebo. Bouché-Leclercq[5] thought that this daughter might be Arsinoe II. The daughter had the name of Ptolemais and so must have been legitimate, as the Ptolemies did not give the dynastic name to illegitimate children.[6] If it is true that he allied himself in this way with the old line of the country on arriving in his satrapy, he soon relinquished the idea of the advantages of such a marriage, for in 322 B. C., most probably, or a little later he married Antipater's daughter.

---

[1] Beloch, IV², p. 178.
[2] Arrian, VII, 4, 6.
[3] Tarn, *C.Q.* XXIII, 1929, pp. 138-141.
[4] Sethe, *Hieroglyphische Urkunden*, p. 27, n. 12.
[5] Bouché-Leclercq, *Lagides*, III, p. 88, n. 1.
[6] Tarn, *loc. cit.*

He was apparently content with Eurydice for some years, in which four children were born to them, Ptolemy called Ceraunus, another son, and two daughters, Ptolemais and Lysandra. Several years after the marriage Ptolemy fell deeply in love with a young widow, who had come from Macedonia as a lady-in-waiting to Eurydice, to whom she was related; her mother Antigone was a daughter of Antipater's brother Cassander. Whether both ladies, Eurydice and Berenice, remained at the court in Alexandria is not known, but it is probable that Eurydice left it as soon as she saw that her son's claims for inheriting were to be disregarded in favor of Berenice's son. In 286 B. C. she was living in Miletus, and there she gave her daughter Ptolemais in marriage to Demetrius, widower of her own sister Phila. She doubtless hoped that this alliance with the king of the sea would help her son Ceraunus in his ambitions. Ptolemy preferred Ptolemy, Berenice's son, whom in 285-4 B. C. he associated with himself in the kingdom. Eurydice's son Ptolemy was a violent and vicious man whose life was stained with horrid crime. He had none of the good qualities of his ancestors except a fiery energy which made him ruler of Macedon for a brief time and brought him to defeat and death at the hands of the Gauls.

His mother was a rich heiress, and as such might have married again even late in life. She evidently preferred to remain queen of Egypt, though repudiated, and to give her energy to the interests of her children. She was apparently established in Cassandreia by her son during his reign in Macedon, and the last mention that we have of her tells of her there, ruling by the support of her mercenary troops. Polyaenus says that she " restored liberty to Cassandreia ", and was honored by a festival called Eurydicaea established by an Apollodorus who got control of the government in that city. The further fate of Eurydice is unknown.[7]

Her daughter Lysandra was first married to the young

---

[7] Polyaen. VI, 7, 2.

Alexander, son of Cassander, for a short time king of Macedon, and after his death to Agathocles, son of Lysimachus.
Ptolemais was married to Demetrius the Besieger and had a
son, Demetrius the Fair, who was the father of Antigonus III
of Macedon, called Antigonus Doson. Another son of Eurydice was put to death at the instance of Arsinoe II on the
charge of plotting against his half-brother Ptolemy Philadelphus.

BERENICE I (Fig. 4c)

The statement that Berenice, who succeeded her cousin
Eurydice as wife of Ptolemy I, was Ptolemy's half-sister rests
on a wrong emendation of a scholium on Theocritus. It is
said, for example, that " A scholiast on Theocritus (XVII.
61) says that Berenice was a half-sister of Ptolemy's,
daughter of Lagus by another wife ".[8] But as a matter of
fact the very corrupt scholium gives the name of Berenice's
father in the genitive as Γάμου or Γαμάου. Since this can
be easily emended to Μάγου, the dynastic name for Berenice's
male descendants by her Macedonian husband Philip, it can
be only a fixed idea of the prevalence of brother-and-sister
marriage in the Ptolemaic dynasty that induces historians to
prefer the emendation to Λάγου. That emendation has been
shown to be wrong by Buecheler and Hoffmann,[9] and it is a
strange case of the perpetuation of an error by succeeding
historical writers without verification of the fact, that the
statement still persists. Berenice named her son Magas for
her father, who married a niece of Antipater, and was probably of more distinguished family than her husband Philip,
who is said by Pausanias [10] to have been of simple origin.

---

[8] Bevan, *Egypt*, p. 52, n. 2.

[9] Hoffmann, *Makedonen*, pp. 222-223; Buecheler, *Rhein. Mus.* XXX,
1875, p. 59; Wendel, *Scholia in Theocritum, ad. loc.*; Stähelin, P. W.
XI, sp. 462. Bouché-Leclercq also (*Lagides*, I, p. 42) distrusts the
story that Berenice was a half-sister of Ptolemy and says that it was
probably invented to make the custom of brother-and-sister marriage
go back to the Founder of the dynasty.

[10] Paus. I, 7, 1.

(a) Hyacinth Gem with Portrait
of a Ptolemaic Queen, perhaps
Arsinoe Philadelphus.
Boston Museum of Fine Arts

(b) Lecythus in the possession
of Grace H. Macurdy.

(c) Chalcedony Gem with Portrait
of a Ptolemaic Queen as Isis,
perhaps Berenice I.
Boston Museum of Fine Arts
But cf. Pfuhl *Jahrbuch*, XLV, 1930, pp. 44 f.

Figure 4.

She was a widow with two children when she came with her cousin (once removed) Eurydice, to Egypt. Her son and daughter were named for her own father and mother, Magas and Antigone. Theocritus calls Berenice herself " Daughter of Antigone ", emphasizing the connection with the house of Antipater.

Some historians believe that Berenice was not the wife, but the mistress of Ptolemy from 316 B. C. on, and that he did not marry her until 287 B. C. or a little earlier. " Ptolemy had married Antipater's daughter Eurydice, and her long struggle with her maid-of-honor Berenice, who was Ptolemy's mistress, had ended before 287 in Ptolemy repudiating Eurydice and marrying Berenice." [11] Beloch argues from her presence in Greece with Ptolemy in 309 B. C. that she must then have been only his mistress; he says " Greek commanders took their mistresses, but not their wives with them on campaigns ".[12] But Ptolemy was not a Greek general, but a Macedonian brought up in the tradition of queens on the battlefield. Arsinoe II later accompanied her husband to Suez in the Syrian War, and Arsinoe III was with her brother, whose wife she soon became, at the battle of Raphia and ran before the troops, encouraging them before the fighting began. Since Macedonian custom allowed women of royal rank to appear on the battlefield (Olympias, Cynane, and Eurydice, for well-known earlier examples) and to associate freely with men, it does not seem plausible that Ptolemy should take up with the Greek prejudice, which ran counter to the whole tradition of his race.

Beloch cites also the fact that Pyrrhus on going to Alexandria in 298 B. C. found that Berenice " had the greatest influence of Ptolemy's wives and surpassed the others in character and intellectual power," [13] and so paid most of his attentions to her, making such a good impression that he

---

[11] Tarn, *Hellenistic Civilisation*, p. 11.
[12] Beloch, IV[2], pp. 180-181.
[13] Plut. *Pyrrhus*, IV.

was given Berenice's daughter Antigone as a wife. Beloch thinks that the passage implies that Berenice was not queen in 298 B. C., and holds that at the earliest she was elevated to the throne about 290 B. C., and that because of this formal elevation Eurydice and Ceraunus left Egypt.

Matrimonial arrangements were somewhat irregular among the Macedonian Successors to Alexander the Great. Polygamy was a custom in old Macedonia and the Successors did what they liked. In Egypt after the first two generations marriages were regularized by the deification of the king and queen together in their lifetime.[14] It may be that Berenice was queen in some sort from 316 B. C. until she was given the position of Ptolemy's only queen and mother of the heir to the throne. That she, the widow of an undistinguished Macedonian, should have held the heart of the ambitious Ptolemy for so many years reveals her as a woman of extraordinary charm and good sense. It was a time when the Successors married avowedly for political reasons and Ptolemy appears to have considered marrying Cleopatra in 308 B. C., and it is possible that the famous beauty and politically-minded lady, Cratesipolis,[15] who commanded important Greek cities and an army of mercenaries, was favorably regarded by him at the time when she put Corinth in his power. She would hardly have done this if she had not expected a great reward, and the most natural reward was that she should become his queen. But Berenice bore him a son about this time, and whatever her status was before the repudiation of Eurydice, there can be no doubt that she was always tenderly loved by Ptolemy. That love is celebrated by Theocritus in the seventeenth idyll:—

" They say that no woman ever won such love from a husband as that with which Ptolemy loved his wife, and still greater love did he receive from her."

Theocritus praises her for her wisdom and Plutarch speaks

---

[14] Cf. Beloch, IV¹, p. 371.
[15] Macurdy, *A.J.P.* L, 1929, pp. 273 ff.

of her intellectual power. The scholiast[16] on Theocritus 17, 34 says that she was the most chaste of wives. Her daughter Antigone became the wife of Pyrrhus in 298 B. C., and her son Magas was viceroy and later king of Cyrene. Her eldest child by Ptolemy, Arsinoe, was given in marriage in 300-299 B. C. to the old king Lysimachus of Thrace, who put away a wife who was dear to him, the Persian princess Amastris, widow of Craterus and of Dionysius of Heracleia, to marry Ptolemy's daughter. These royal marriages of her children suggest that Berenice was considered a lawful wife of Ptolemy, if not his chief queen, for Lysimachus would hardly have given up the wealthy and beloved Amastris to marry a bastard daughter of Ptolemy.

It is not clear whether Berenice lived to see her son Ptolemy proclaimed king in 284 B. C. If she was born, as Beloch reckons, in 340 B. C., she was considerably younger than her husband, who died in 282 B. C. at the age of eighty-four.

Her son built temples for his father and mother in which their statues made of gold and ivory stood " to succor mortals ", Theocritus says. That poet speaks of Ptolemy II as the first to build temples to his parents, and in this poem of laudation of Ptolemy II he describes the deification of the old Ptolemy, whom Zeus has given honors like those of the immortals and a golden house in heaven, where he sits between Alexander and Hercules, while Berenice has been placed in a shrine by Aphrodite, where she listens to the prayers of lovers.

A procession in a festival instituted by Ptolemy II and described by Callixenus[17] is often ascribed to a celebration, perhaps the second, of the Ptolemaea, a penteteric festival probably celebrated on the birthday of the dead king.[18] The extravagant splendor and incredible luxury of this πομπή make

---

[16] Βερενίκην λέγει τὴν Μάγα μὲν θυγατέρα γυναῖκα δὲ Πτολεμαίου τοῦ Σωτῆρος, αὕτη ἐν ταῖς σώφροσι γυναιξὶν εὔδηλος ἦν. (Μάγα Buecheler, Rhein. Mus. XXX, 1875, p. 59.)

[17] Callixenus in F.H.G. III, pp. 58 ff.; Athen. V, 196.

[18] Bouché-Leclercq, Lagides, I, pp. 155-159. Cf. Meyer, Untersuchungen, pp. 67-68.

it an effective baroque Hellenistic contrast to the Periclean
example of Athenian " love of Beauty with thrift ", the Pana-
thenaic procession of the Parthenon frieze. After the chariots
bearing images of gods and kings, the mummers of every
kind, men, women, and children carrying crowns and vases
of gold and silver and all kinds of offerings, Sileni, Satyrs,
Victories, Bacchanalian figures, elephants, giraffes, ostriches,
antelopes, parrots, peacocks, negroes, Indian women, camels,
and innumerable other participants in this fantastic procession, which blazed with gold, had all passed, games were held
in which Ptolemy I and Berenice were given gold statues of
themselves standing on gold chariots, and their son Ptolemy
also received the like.

The procession and festival formed a notable tribute to
his parents and was also an intimation to Antiochus,[19] of the
wealth and power of the king who was " of all the kings the
shrewdest amasser of wealth, the most splendid spendthrift,
and the most magnificent in all his works ".[20]

Berenice later shared the title of Saviour, by which Ptolemy
had been worshipped, and they were put in the official list of
deified royalties next to Alexander. She appears in no public capacity in the government; her influence must have been
great, nevertheless, as it was her son who succeeded her
husband, and not his first-born, Ptolemy, son of Eurydice.
Her eldest child Arsinoe, a " thrice-married woman ", finally
married her brother and practically governed Egypt through
him during the five years of their marriage. A third daughter,
Philotera, remained unmarried. She too received great honors
from her brother and from the Egyptians. Berenice had her
own temple in Alexandria, the Bereniceum,[21] near the temple
of the Saviour Gods in which she and Ptolemy her husband
were worshipped together.[22] Two towns were named in her

---

[19] Bouché-Leclercq, *Lagides*, I, p. 159.
[20] Appian, *Praefat.* 10.
[21] Callixenus ap. Athen. V, 202 D.
[22] Von Prott, *Rhein. Mus.* LIII, 1898, pp. 460 ff.

honor, one in Epirus, founded by her son-in-law Pyrrhus,[23] and one on the Red Sea, founded by her son Ptolemy.[24]

Arsinoe I (Fig. 4a)

Arsinoe I is a vague figure, of whom history has recorded little beyond the facts of her marriage to the second Ptolemy, the birth of her children, and her banishment to Koptos in the Thebaid soon after the arrival in Egypt of Ptolemy's sister Arsinoe, who superseded Arsinoe I and became Ptolemy's wife and queen. As the two queens have the same name, also the name of the mother of the first Ptolemy, it has been suggested that Arsinoe I was the daughter of Arsinoe II [25] and her first husband Lysimachus, father of Arsinoe I. This relationship between the two Arsinoes is chronologically barely possible, and if it really existed, it is remarkable that no ancient writer has added to the charges against Arsinoe II the enormity of dispossessing her own daughter by marrying that daughter's husband. It is probable that Arsinoe I was the daughter of Nicaea, daughter of Antipater, who was married to Lysimachus in 322 B. C. or a little later. The eldest daughter in the Macedonian families was generally named for her grandmother. The names Phila and Stratonice alternate in the Antigonid family, and Arsinoe and Berenice in the early Ptolemaic, for the eldest daughters. If Arsinoe I was a daughter of Arsinoe II, she must have been the eldest daughter and in that case would have in all probability been named Berenice. It is possible that the wife of Antipater, whose name is not known, was an Arsinoe and that her granddaughter, the daughter of Nicaea, was named for her.

The date of the marriage between Ptolemy II and Arsinoe I is uncertain; it probably lay between 285 B. C.,[26] and 281 B. C. As three children were born in the few years in which

---

[23] Stephen of Byzantium, s. v. Βερενίκαι.

[24] Plin. VI, 16; Stephen of Byzantium, loc. cit.

[25] Rohde, Der Griechische Roman, 2nd ed. p. 81, n.

[26] Beloch, IV², p. 130.

the marriage lasted, a date nearer 285 B. C. seems reasonable.
Perhaps the marriage took place about the time (285 B. C.)
when the old Ptolemy took his son as co-regent, or shortly
after.   The children of the marriage were Ptolemy, Lysimachus, and Berenice, the daughter named according to the custom just mentioned, for her paternal grandmother.   Our
chief knowledge of Arsinoe after her marriage comes from the
well known scholium on Theocritus XVII, 129, in which
the names of her children are given and the statement is made
that Ptolemy discovered that she was conspiring against him
in concert with Amyntas and the Rhodian physician Chrysip-
pus, and sent her to Koptos in the Thebaid, whereupon he
married his own sister Arsinoe, and when the latter died without bearing him children, he had the children of the first
Arsinoe called the children of Arsinoe II.   This interpretation of this frequently misunderstood scholium will be discussed in connection with the second Arsinoe.

It cannot be doubted that Arsinoe I was the victim of her
successor's determination to be queen of Egypt, as the discovery of the alleged plot immediately followed when that
lady sought refuge and a new queenship at her brother's
court.[27]

The first Arsinoe's son Ptolemy became king of Egypt at his
father's death, her daughter Berenice was for a short period
queen of Syria, and her son Lysimachus outlived the other two
and was murdered by his nephew, king Ptolemy Philopator.[28]

It was doubtless Ptolemy I who had arranged the marriage
between Lysimachus' daughter and his son Ptolemy at a time
when Lysimachus was the most powerful of all the monarchs.[29]   After the death of her father and the old Ptolemy
Arsinoe had no one left to defend her rights.

That she lived in state in her retirement at Koptos has
been indicated by a hieroglyphic inscription on a thin slab of

---

[27] Beloch, IV¹, pp. 582 ff.

[28] Polyb. XV, 25.

[29] Beloch, IV¹, pp. 241 f.

basalt discovered by Sir Flinders Petrie.[30] The office of the writer was that of major-domo in the house of queen Arsinoe. He describes himself as " chief officer of his majesty and chief of the servants of the princess, the great favorite, mistress of two lands, pleasing the heart, gracious, and sweet of love, fair of crowns, receiving the two diadems, filling the palace with her beauties, the principal royal wife, pacifying the heart of the king, of Upper and Lower Egypt lord of both lands," etc.[31] Petrie remarks from the rendering of her name in the hieroglyphics that this must refer to the first Arsinoe, who was in exile in Koptos when the inscription was written. He infers from her flowery titles and the fact that statues of her were erected by her major-domo side by side with those of her husband that she might have had something like absolute authority in the petty kingdom assigned her.[32]

She was doubtless protected by the sacred character of the queenship as well as because she was of high descent and was the mother of Ptolemy's heirs. There is no instance after her of the actual exiling of any queen of Egypt. Cleopatra II, whose husband Euergetes II married her daughter, kept her place beside them as Cleopatra the Sister and though set aside from her position as wife of the king she retained her place as reigning queen.

How long Arsinoe I lived at Koptos is not known. No historian tells anything further about her, nor does her name recur on any document so far discovered.

ARSINOE II (Fig. 5b)

If the three most famous and extraordinary princesses of Macedonian blood of the centuries from the fourth to the latter part of the first before Christ should be selected, the obvious choices would be Olympias of Macedonia, Arsinoe, sister and

---

[30] *Koptos*, pl. XX, pp. 20-21.
[31] Quoted from *Koptos*, p. 20.
[32] *Ibid.* p. 21.

wife of Ptolemy Philadelphus of Egypt, and Cleopatra the
Seventh of Egypt, who bore children to the Romans, Julius
Caesar and Mark Antony. Of the three, Arsinoe was the greatest politically. Unscrupulous as the other two, she had more
common-sense than Olympias and was not hampered by the
tempestuous and wild nature which was the ruin of that queen,
and she appears not to have been given to pleasure and sensu-
ous delights as was Cleopatra, the "Inimitable Liver". Arsinoe
was more like the men of the line in her power of planning and
the definiteness of her political aims. She was clearly the true
daughter of the astute Ptolemy and much more his intellectual heir than the madman Ceraunus or the sensualist
Philadelphus.

Her beauty is greatly extolled by numismatists, and if coins
and busts represent her fairly she must have been lovely.
Tarn has a beautiful description of her head as shown upon
a coin. " It shows a finely chiselled face of purest Greek
type, pensive, remote, and austere, the nunlike effect only en-
hanced by the usual long heavy veil; nothing can be less like
the Arsinoe of tradition, and no lovelier face has come down
to us from the Greek world." He says that there is no doubt
that it is idealized. She belonged to a handsome race, and
inherited from her mother Berenice the charm that enabled
that lady of rather obscure position compared with that of
her rivals to win and keep the heart of one of the most
ambitious and scheming of the Successors, at a time when the
Generals expected to make marriages that would help them on
to the throne of Macedon.

Arsinoe was married when only fifteen or sixteen to the
king of Thrace, Lysimachus, old companion-in-arms of her
father Ptolemy, who, though himself in the end marrying for
love, had no such foolish thought for his children, but married
them all " where profit could be got ". It does not seem possible that Arsinoe's mother was not regarded as Ptolemy's
wife, if not his chief queen, at the time of her daughter's
marriage to so distinguished a king as Lysimachus. He gave

FIGURE 5a.

UNIQUE COIN OF CLEOPATRA THEA, DATING FROM THE YEAR 125 B. C.

British Museum.

FIGURE 5b.

BRONZE HEAD OF ARSINOE II OF EGYPT.

Boston Museum of Fine Arts.

up, it is said reluctantly, his Persian wife Amastris, to whom
he had been married for two years, in the course of which
she bore a son Alexander. Amastris,[33] a woman of character,
went back to her kingdom of Heracleia on the Pontus and
gave her energies to government and to rearing her children.
She founded a city named for herself and issued coinage.[34]
Lysimachus later gave Arsinoe the cities which had belonged
to Amastris.

Lysimachus had a son Agathocles whose mother was Nicaea,
Antipater's daughter (for whom Lysimachus had named
Nicaea, the city in Bithynia so famous later for the Council
of Nicaea. This son was twenty years old when the young
bride came to the court of his father. Here was material for
a drama with a familiar theme, and the possibility of the
girl's falling in love with the young son and heir is so obvious
that the story that she did so may equally well be a romantic
invention, as most historians declare, or the historical fact,
since historical facts are often very romantic. Her friend [35]
Stratonice, Phila's daughter, married her husband's young
son, with her husband's consent, and Arsinoe with her
political sense for what was practical may have felt that
Agathocles as future king might be worth consideration as a
lover. The old Lysimachus might have been the victim of
her poison instead of Agathocles, if her alleged advances to
the latter had not been rejected.[36] When Lysimachus made
a jest about a mistress of Demetrius, that king [37] remarked
that his own harlot was more chaste than the " Penelope "
of Lysimachus. When the young wife had become a woman

---

[33] Diod. XX, 109, 7; Polyaen. VI, 12; Arrian, *Anab.* VII, 4, 5;
Memnon in *F.H.G.* III, p. 539; Strabo, XII, 541.

[34] Kahrstedt, *Klio*, X, pp. 280 f.

[35] Tarn's idea that they were friends is based on the inscription,
O.G.I. 14, now lost.

[36] Justin, XVII, 1, 4—ministra Arsinoe noverca veneno interfecit;
Pausan. I, 10, 3.

[37] Plut. *Dem.* XXV.

9

of thirty [38] and more (283 B. C.) and had borne three sons
to Lysimachus, she accused Agathocles, who was now a successful general and husband of her half-sister Lysandra, of dis-
loyalty to his father, and it is said gave her old husband
(he was now not far from eighty) the poison with which he
destroyed his son.   According to another version Agathocles
was imprisoned, and Ptolemy Ceraunus, who had come from
Egypt with his mother Eurydice, killed him in prison.   The
young wife fled to Seleucus to ask him to take vengeance on
Lysimachus.   Whether Ceraunus went with her is uncertain
and is both affirmed and denied by historians.[39]   Tarn believes that Ceraunus remained with Lysimachus and became
his righthand man.

In the war that broke out between the two old kings who in
their glorious youth had marched with Alexander as fine
young captains, the armies met in Lydia at Kouroupedion.[40]
Arsinoe had gone to the city of Ephesus, the name of which
her husband in her honor had changed to Arsinoea.   But
after the defeat and death of Lysimachus and the deserting
of his troops to Seleucus, Arsinoe was not safe in her city
and escaped the men who would murder her by the unscrupulous ruse of dressing a maid in her royal robes and leaving her
to be slain as queen.   She blacked her own face, put on rags,
and looking the part of a dirty beggar, slipped through to the
shore where ships were waiting to convey her to Macedon.[41]
There her late husband had been king for about four years
after his defeat of Pyrrhus.   In Cassandreia, where he had
been worshipped with divine honors, Arsinoe entrenched herself and her three children.   She had immense wealth and

---

[38] Bevan is wrong in saying that Arsinoe was a young woman of
twenty-one at this time (*Egypt*, p. 54) and "little more than a
girl" (*ibid.* p. 57).   She was born in 315 B. C. and must have been
thirty-four.

[39] Cf. Tarn, *Antigonus*, 125, n. 261.

[40] Memnon *F.H.G.* III, p. 532, 8; Justin, XVII, 1. 4; Strabo, XIII,
628; App. *Syr.* 64; Porphyr. *F.H.G.* III, p. 698, 4.

[41] Polyaen. VIII, 57.

could support an army of mercenaries. Ceraunus was now for the moment heir to Lysimachus, since he had stabbed Seleucus, his aged benefactor, near Lysimacheia on the Thracian Chersonese, as the old king was looking at an altar,[42] an alleged memorial of the expedition of the Argonauts or of the Trojan War. Ceraunus then put the royal diadem on his head and appeared in the camp of soldiers at Lysimacheia with a *fait accompli* and a body-guard. The incredible villain was chosen king by the army, which, like armies before and since, was dazzled by the " strong man " and overawed by the coolness and sureness of his crimes. Now Ceraunus was king of Macedonia and of Thrace, but he very well knew the spirit of his half-sister Arsinoe, who was in Cassandreia with her sons, the rightful heirs of Lysimachus. Arsinoe hoped that her eldest son Ptolemy might get the kingdom of Macedonia with the help of her own brother, the king of Egypt. Ceraunus, knowing how she loved queenship, sent a message to her that he would make her queen of Macedon and would adopt her children, making her eldest, Ptolemy, his heir.[43] For one moment her cunning matched his, for she demanded marriage before the assembled army outside her city gates. Ceraunus consented, and Arsinoe in overflowing joy heard herself hailed queen of Macedon and threw wide her gates. He marched into the town and killed the two younger children of his new wife, who vainly strove to save them, in her arms.[44] Her eldest son had warned his mother against the murderer and had escaped to Illyria.[45] Arsinoe probably owed her life to Ceraunus' fear of vengeance from Egypt; the soldiers appear to have been poor hirelings or ruffians who did not raise a sword to prevent his crimes. The next year he came to an end suitable to his life. He was defeated by Gauls and killed and his head affixed to a spear point which they carried with them as they pillaged Macedonia.

---

[42] App. *Syr.* 63.
[43] Justin, XVII, 2, 7 ff.

[44] Justin, XXIV, 2 and 3.
[45] Trogus, *Prolog.* XXIV, 5.

Arsinoe fled to Samothrace and thence to Egypt, where all
her ambitions were destined to a fulfillment beyond the dreams
of any Macedonian woman of her time and before it. She had
cried out with joy to hear herself proclaimed queen before
the gates of Cassandreia; she was destined in Egypt to be a
queen exercising the power of a king and to be worshipped as
a goddess with cults in many parts of the Greek world.[46]
She received honors such as no Greek or Macedonian woman
had ever received before. The Gods gave her all that her
heart desired except that her son Ptolemy should sit upon the
throne of Macedon or of Egypt.

In Egypt she soon spread in the household of her brother
Ptolemy the same confusion that she had brought into the
court of Lysimachus, this time without disaster to herself.
She accused her step-daughter, Arsinoe, daughter of Nicaea
and niece of Eurydice, of a plot against her husband, Ptolemy,
who exiled his wife to Koptos in the Thebaid and married
his full sister, Arsinoe, child as he also was of Ptolemy and
Berenice. This marriage of sister to brother was an age-long
custom in Egypt, but had never been known in Macedonia
or in Greece, where it was considered an outrage to civilized
morality. Yet Theocritus had been so influenced by the
Alexandrian atmosphere and his desire to keep the court
patronage that in his eulogy of Ptolemy Philadelphus he pro-
claims the royal incest as a beautiful and divine thing, pat-
terning after that of Zeus and Hera. Bury (*Hellenistic Age,*
p. 11) states that " the marriage of brother and sister, in-
cestuous in the eyes of the Hellenes, was practised in Macedonia and the hellenized Macedonian monarchs never learned
to consider it abominable ". I think that there is no ground
for this statement, as there is no case of such a marriage in
the Macedonian dynasty, and very few certain instances
among the Seleucids. The Macedonians accepted the custom

---

[46] If it is true that she was deified a short time before her death
(Bevan, *Egypt*, pp. 129 and 386; but cf. Beloch, IV¹, 371), she
was the first Macedonian woman to be deified in her life-time. Her
mother Berenice received divine honors after her death. Meyer, E.,
op. cit., p. 65.

in the kingdoms in which it already existed in eastern lands.[46a]
In both Greece and Macedonia the marriage of non-uterine
brother and sister was permitted. Herodotus tells of
Cambyses' asking the Persian elders whether there was a law[47]
which permitted him to marry his full sister with whom he
was in love. Such marriage was not permitted by the Persian
code, but the councillors discovered a law that permitted the
monarch to do whatever he chose. Cambyses therefore married first one sister and afterward another.

Arsinoe was married to her brother for five years more or
less. She died in July 270 B. C., or 269 B. C. (See Tarn in
C. R. XL, 1926, p. 87) ; the date of her marriage is still in
dispute. Theocritus was evidently engaged by Ptolemy at
some time after the event to celebrate his victories in the
Syrian War and also to make the new kind of marriage look
better in the eyes of the Greeks and Macedonians by showing
that it was an affair of the gods.

" Upon the crimson altars Ptolemy and his noble spouse
set burning the flesh of many an ox. No more splendid wife
than she ever clasped in bridal chamber her bridegroom,
loving him from her heart, her brother and her lord. In
this fashion was the marriage of Immortal Gods fulfilled, of
the children that Rhea bore the rulers of Olympus, and Iris
strews one bed for the sleep of Zeus and Hera."

Her time for rule was short when compared with that of
some of the later queens, such as Cleopatra II and Cleopatra
III, but the years were crowded with honors and glory. Her
motive for marrying her brother is so evident that it needs
no discussion. Historians have written much on his motive
in marrying her, and diverse reasons are alleged, ranging from
love (this is not the favorite explanation, as she was so much
older) to the advantages to be got from the rights she may
have kept in the cities presented to her by her old husband
Lysimachus, those of his second wife Amastris, of which he

[46a] Kornemann, *Klio*, XIX, p. 355.
[47] Hdt. III, 31.

had got possession after her death,[48] Heracleia, Amastrios, and Tios, on the Black Sea, and also Ephesus and Cassandreia. She could put in the claims of the young Ptolemy, her own son by Lysimachus, for these places if opportunity should offer. She may have used these cities for an argument when urging the marriage on her brother, for she doubtless left no stone unturned, but her trump card may very well have been the fact that in Egypt it would be an excellent plan politically to do what the Egyptians did in the way of marriage. Osiris and Isis were a good precedent in that land, whereas the Greeks and Macedonians were not greatly edified by the two children of Ptolemy Soter following the example of Zeus and Hera. It seems likely that it was the scheming brain of Arsinoe, not that of the invalidish and slothful Philadelphus, that saw the point of the value of the brother-and-sister marriage in this respect and the enormous popularity it would bring them with the Egyptian priests.

Arsinoe was, of course, absolutely a managing woman; she was the directing power in the government after she married him, not so much because she stepped into the shoes of a long line of queens who had held sway in old Egypt, but rather because of her character and that of her husband. Memnon [49] has painted her in his phrase, " Arsinoe was one to get her own way ". Her husband is described in the fourteenth idyll of Theocritus in this way:— [50]

" The very best sort for a free man to serve under; a good head, fond of the arts; given to love of women; with an eye for a friend and an eye for a foe still keener; a generous giver who does not refuse when asked, but do not keep asking him for everything."

A man like that would be easily managed by a woman who had inherited from her father far more of his strong character than he. She followed a time-honored Macedonian custom in having all the possible claimants to the throne, such as his

---

[48] Memnon, *F.H.G.* III, p. 530.
[49] Memnon, *F.H.G.* III, p. 531.
[50] Theocritus, XIV, vv. 59 ff.

brother Argaeus and another half-brother, son of Eurydice, killed on the charge of plotting, a charge that it was always easy to bring against such close relatives.

Tarn [51] gives as a likely reason for her marriage (putting it, conjecturally, in 276-5 B. C.)—"Ptolemy married her after his defeat in Syria, because things were going badly for him and he needed her strength and brains to manage the war, which he was going to lose, as he lost the second Syrian war, when she was not there to help him." It was admittedly the brains of Arsinoe that made a success of the reign of the lazy though clever Ptolemy II up to the time of her death. To quote Tarn [52] again, "The way she pulled round the lost war against Antiochus I and turned it into a sweeping Egyptian triumph might rank, if we knew the details, as one of the biggest things a woman ever did." Beloch [53] on the other hand says that Arsinoe alone had something to win by this marriage and that without a doubt it was she who brought influence to bear on her brother to bring him to marry her.

It is known from the Pithom stele that she went with Ptolemy in January of 273 B. C. to Heroönpolis on the Isthmus of Suez to inspect the defences of Egypt against foreign attack. In the decree of Chremonides [54] of 266 B. C., four years after her death, her husband is said to have followed the policy, προαίρεσις, of his ancestors and of his sister in his zeal for the freedom of the Greeks. This is the first instance in the history of the rulers of Macedonian blood in which a woman's policy finds mention in a public document as influencing affairs of state. The reason for her eagerness in promoting Greek freedom may be found in her hostility to Antigonus, who had what she regarded as her son's heritage from Lysimachus, the throne of Macedon. The good feeling

---

[51] *J.H.S.* XLVI, 1926, p. 161.

[52] *Hellenistic Civilisation*, p. 51.

[53] Beloch, IV[1], p. 583.

[54] *I.G.* II, 332, 333. Ditt. *Syll.*[3] 434. ὅ τε βασιλεὺς Πτολεμαῖος ἀκολούθως τῇ τ[ῶν] προγόνων καὶ τῇ τῆς ἀδελφῆς προ[α]ιρέσει φανερός ἐστιν σπουδάζων ὑπὲρ τῆς κοινῆς τῶν Ἑλλήνων ἐλευθερίας.

between Egypt and Athens brought about by her activity is reflected in a fragment ascribed to Alexis (perhaps inserted in a play of his, since he would have been nearly a hundred years old at the time to which the verses refer) in which the poet drinks the health of Ptolemy and of the Sister of the King and of the *entente cordiale*.[55]

The results of the Syrian war of 276-274 B. C. are glowingly described by Theocritus, who naturally gives the credit of it to Ptolemy. After telling of the cities in Egypt of which Ptolemy is lord the poet says—" He cuts off a slice of Phoenicia and part of Arabia and Syria and Libya and black Aethiopia; he gives his orders to Pamphylia and the spearmen of Cilicia, and the warriors of Caria, and the Lycians, and the islanders of the Cyclades. His navy is the best that sails the seas. Every sea and every land and all the roaring rivers are under the sway of Ptolemy and he is the richest of all the kings by far." [56]

Whether the greater share of the glory for all this belongs to Arsinoe or not—and in the dearth of information that cannot be known—it is certain that she acted as a spur in all the action, political and military, of her indolent and pleasure-loving brother. His brain may have been equal to hers, but Arsinoe was not hampered by the sensuality which was such a strong part of the king's character, and she had a flaming energy, and a motive to direct it in her desire to advance the interests of her own son Ptolemaeus, son of Lysimachus. She would have him, if it lay within her power, sit on the throne of Macedonia, and of Egypt. The statement is generally made that she in her lifetime adopted the children of the first Arsinoe, but Beloch has shown the incorrectness of this misunderstanding of the highly compressed Greek of the scholium on Theocritus 17, 128, on which this inference rests. It is strange that no one of those who make the

---

[55] Kock (*F.C.A. II Alexis*, 244) denies that the verses can belong to Alexis.

[56] XVII, vv. 85 ff.

statement have noticed that Ptolemy is the subject of the verb εἰσεποιήσατο and not Arsinoe.

The scholium reads as follows: Καὶ εἰσεποιήσατο αὐτῇ τοὺς ἐκ τῆς προτέρας Ἀρσινόης γεννηθέντας παῖδας. ἡ γὰρ ἀδελφὴ καὶ γυνὴ αὐτοῦ ἄτεκνος ἀπέθανεν.

"He married his sister Arsinoe and he had the children of the first Arsinoe legally called those of his sister, for the latter died without bearing him children."

The word ἄτεκνος is often taken to mean that Arsinoe had no living children at all at the time of her death. But the word means "barren," "not having borne children", and refers here to the fact that the marriage between Philadelphus and his sister produced no offspring. She is admitted [57] to have had at least one child who, as Bevan thinks, was killed in her arms at Cassandreia by her half-brother. We infer from Justin [58] and Trogus [59] that she had three sons, two of whom were killed by Ceraunus, while the third evidently escaped to Illyria.

The statement of the scholiast is highly compressed, but it is clear, as Beloch notes, that it is Ptolemy's action that is stated and not Arsinoe's, and the point of bringing in her "dying barren" is that she had borne *him* no children.[60]

This scholium is the great support of those who deny that the co-regent of Philadelphus from 267 B. C. to 259 B. C. is the son of Arsinoe and Lysimachus. Two or three years after the death of Arsinoe her husband took a co-regent who is called Ptolemy son of Ptolemy; mention of him continues in the papyri from 267 B. C. to 259 B. C. and in the Revenue papyrus his name is stricken out, in the year 259 B. C., and does not recur. I believe that Beloch and Tarn have shown convincingly that this Ptolemy was the son of Arsinoe who escaped the murderous hands of Ceraunus in 282 B. C. and

---

[57] Bevan, *Egypt*, p. 57.

[58] Justin, XXIV, 3, 5-7.

[59] Trogus, *Prol.* XXIV.

[60] Beloch, IV², pp. 183-184. Cf. Tarn, *C.A.H.* VII, p. 703—"She adopted his eldest son by Arsinoe I."

that Philadelphus adopted him "after Arsinoe's death as a sort of replacement of his mother, who had been most emphatically co-regent herself ".[61] The chief arguments against this identification [62] shatter both on the word εἰσεποιήσατο of which Ptolemy is the subject, and on ἄτεκνος.[63] Bevan's statements that "Arsinoe died childless and adopted the children of the other Arsinoe" and that the theory that the co-regent of 267-259 was Ptolemaeus, son of Lysimachus, is "incompatible with the statement of the Scholiast" cannot stand before Beloch's clarification of the meaning of the scholium.

Tarn shows further that this son of Arsinoe after his co-regency was made governor of Ionia by his adoptive father when the heart of the old Philadelphus turned back to his own son, and further that Arsinoe's son died in 260-259 B. C. in the attempt to make himself independent of the old Ptolemy. Bouché-Leclercq and others call the governor of Ephesus mentioned by Athenaeus [64] Ptolemy the Bastard, but, as Beloch says, the dynastic name Ptolemy would not be given to a bastard. Since we have facts, meagre though they are, establishing the existence of Ptolemaeus, son of Arsinoe, which all the other data fit, and since there is no record of a bastard Ptolemaeus, it seems unnecessary to invent the bastard.

It is strange that nothing is heard of Arsinoe's son during

---

[61] Tarn, *Antigonos*, pp. 445 f.

[62] Bevan, *Egypt*, pp. 63, 65.

[63] The words ἄτεκνος and ἀτεκνία are used by Aristotle as the technical words for sterility in human beings and in animals. See the Index of Bonitz who gives all the cases. Since the young Arsinoe *had* borne children, the word must refer only to her marriage with her brother (as argued above), and it is his children who are discussed by the Scholiast and *his* disposition of them, not *her* adoption of them.

See also Bouché-Leclercq, *Lagides*, I, p. 162, n. 3. Cf. Eur., *Ion*, 1463, where Creusa says:

"I am no longer childless, nor a barren woman."

ἄπαιδες οὐκέτ' ἐσμὲν οὐδ' ἄτεκνοι.

[64] Athen. XIII, 593. Meyer, E., *op. cit.*, p. 66.

the time of his mother's influence and rule in Egypt. One would expect to hear of his marriage, or of a plan for his marriage to some princess. I suggest that Arsinoe, who spared the lives of the children of her predecessor, intended to have the little Berenice marry her son when the girl should be old enough. If Arsinoe's son was adopted by his uncle and step-father, the marriage would have the effect of continuing the brother-and-sister marriage, the ἱερὸς γάμος, after the Egyptian manner, which had proved so acceptable to the Egyptians. There appears to have been no talk of a marriage between Ptolemy Euergetes and his sister. This may have been due to a persistence of the old Macedonian and Greek repugnance to incest, or to an intention on the part of Arsinoe to marry Berenice to her own son. Berenice was in the neighborhood of thirty when she was given in marriage by her father in 247 B. C. to Antiochus of Syria. The plan of Arsinoe suggested above may have been the cause of the lateness of her marriage, and there may have been some connection here with the deferred marriage of Berenice of Cyrene to Ptolemy the Third. She was betrothed to him before 259 B. C. by the arrangement of Magas, her father, and Philadelphus, but the marriage was deferred until 246 B. C. After the death of Ptolemaeus, governor of Ionia, in revolt against Philadelphus, there may have been a question of a marriage between the two children of Philadelphus, Ptolemy and his sister Berenice.

The honors that were showered upon Arsinoe by Greeks and Egyptians and by her husband, Ptolemy, are evidences of the extraordinary character of this " thrice-married woman ", as Theocritus calls her in *Id.* 12, 5, when he is no longer enjoying the favor of the Alexandrian court. She must have employed the greatest tact and good sense in managing her self-indulgent husband. Her " gift for getting her own way ", which Memnon notes, in part rested on her ability to let other people have their own way when it did not interfere with her plans. Wilcken [65] says that no happiness could be

---

[65] Wilcken, P. W. 11, sp. 1284.

expected from this marriage of Philadelphus with his older
sister, and he points to the king's many mistresses in proof
of this. But Arsinoe had a very different definition of happiness from the one here suggested, and her husband's mistresses did not count at all in her scheme of things. She was
quite willing that her husband should divert himself with
them to his heart's content, for what she desired, and got,
was power in her hands and the adoption of her son Ptolemy
as her husband's heir in part or whole. So long as she could
gratify her ambition and had free scope for her natural gifts
she would be far from troubling herself about Bilistiche and
Cleino, Myrto and Pothine, and the rest of her husband's
fancies. She had won an impregnable position in the government of Egypt and had a mind and political sense far above
that of the usual woman. She infinitely preferred her part
as her husband's directing power to that of his mistress
Bilistiche. After Arsinoe's death the aging sensualist had
Bilistiche deified as Aphrodite,[66] so easy then were the honors
of deification, but that tribute counted little in comparison to
those given to Arsinoe by Greeks, Egyptians, and by Macedonians in Egypt. In Macedonia itself the " Sister " was not
so highly regarded. Antigonus was her enemy, and the kind
of marriage which she inaugurated was not adopted in the
homeland of her ancestors, though the Seleucids following
Anatolian ancient custom [67] occasionally married their sisters.
She established the word " Sister " in the dynastic sense in
which it appears in Egypt and in Syria even in cases in
which the king and his wife are not brother and sister. The
use of the title in the famous decree of Chremonides is striking and significant. The words καὶ τῆς ἀδελφῆς (προαιρέσει)
mark a new era in the history of the power of queens of

---

[66] Plut. *Amator.* 9. Cleino, according to Athenaeus X, 425 f., bore
also the attribute of the double horn of plenty, which was the
especial token of Arsinoe. Bouché-Leclercq says that in all this
"Arsinoe was not forgotten. She served as original for the copies."
Lagides, I, p. 185.

[67] Kornemann, *Klio,* XIX, p. 355.

FIGURE 6.

BLUE ENAMEL OENOCHOE INSCRIBED WITH NAME OF ARSINOE PHILADELPHUS.

British Museum.

Macedonian blood. Olympias with all that she had to do in making Epirote and Macedonian history never achieved definite and lasting recognition as did Arsinoe. Her husband renamed for her the whole of the Fayûm, calling it instead of the " Lake " the " nome Arsinoites ", and many cities throughout the Egyptian realm also had her name. The Egyptian priests gave her a special throne-name, and her husband had statues made of her with the horn of abundance in her left hand.[68] " There is also upon Helicon a statue of Arsinoe, whom her brother Ptolemy took to wife. She is carried upon a bronze ostrich," says Pausanias.[69] In his first book he tells of her statue which stood with those of the kings of Egypt before the Odeum. She was the one queen among them all, and her statue was doubtless a monument of her policy of good will for the freedom of the Greeks. There was also a statue of her at Olympia among the statues of the Egyptian kings. The growth of the Egyptian sea-power under her policy is reflected by the offerings of gilded shells made by sailors in the temple of Agathé Tyche in Delos.[70] M. Vallois calls attention to a series of enamelled faience oenochoae (an example in the British Museum, Figure 6) representing a woman carrying in her left arm a horn of plenty and holding in the other hand a phiale with which she is about to pour a libation beside an altar. The oldest of the series bear the names of Arsinoe Philadelphus and of Berenice II, with Agathé Tyche as an associated deity. Since Athenaeus [71] tells of εἰκόνων, portraits which Ptolemy had made of his wife holding the double horn of plenty, a device which is also found on the reverse of the coins bearing the head of Arsinoe, M. Vallois suggests that the king " wished to suggest without imposing it the assimilation of Arsinoe with the Goddess of Good Fortune ". Callimachus

---

[68] *Athenaeus*, XI, p. 497.

[69] IX, 3, 1.

[70] M. Vallois in *Comptes Rendus Acad. Inscr.* Jan.-March, 1929, pp. 32-40.

[71] XI, 497 B.

wrote a poem on such a shell as those given as votive offerings [72] in this temple,—I quote the translation of A. W.
Mair:

"An old shell am I, O Lady of Zephyrium, but now, Cypris,
I am thine, a first offering from Selenaea: I the nautilus that
used to sail upon the sea, if there were wind, stretching my
sail on my own forestays, if Calm, that bright goddess, prevailed, rowing strongly with my feet—so that my name befits
my deed!—till I fell on the shores of Iulis, that I might become thy admired toy, Arsinoe, and that in my chambers may
no more be laid, as erstwhile—for I am dead—the eggs of the
water-haunting kingfisher. But give thou grace to the
daughter of Cleinias; for she knows how to do good deeds and
she is from Aeolian Smyrna." [73]

The temple in which Arsinoe was worshipped at Zephyrium,
a promontory between Alexandria and the Canopic mouth of
the Nile, was built by the admiral Callicrates. Athenaeus
quotes an epigram by Posidippus on this shrine and another
has been found on a papyrus in the Fayûm. This last is given
by Blass in *Rhein. Mus.*, XXXV, 1880, p. 90, and also by
Mahaffy, *Empire of the Ptolemies,* pp. 160 and 161, n. 5. In
the former of the two the poet says that the nauarch Callicrates has established Arsinoe Philadelphus in the temple as
sovereign over the Western Shore in thankfulness for safety.
"And she will give fair voyages and will smooth the sea even
in mid-winter in answer to prayer." In the newer poem
the Temple speaking says. "I have a place midway between
the shore of Pharos and the Canopic mouth . . . , where Callicrates had me built and named me shrine of queen Arsinoe
Cypris. But come, ye maidens of the Greeks, to Aphrodite
of the Western Shore who will hear your prayers, and ye
men who have your business in the waters, for the admiral
has built this shrine a fair haven from all the waves."

---

[72] They were perhaps mounted in gold as cups. Cf. the two
nautilus-shell goblets of seventeenth-century Dutch work in the
Victoria and Albert Museum, South Kensington.

[73] Mair, *Callimachus,* pp. 140-143.

Callimachus wrote a poem of which the opening line remains on the celebration of the marriage of Arsinoe to her brother:

" Stranger, I lift my voice in song to celebrate the marriage of Arsinoe ". Beloch [74] suggests that the poem was designed for the cult of the queen when she was made a goddess.

Another hymn of extraordinary interest, composed by Callimachus on the occasion of Arsinoe's death has been recovered from a papyrus now in Berlin.[75] The poem is amazingly vivid and dramatic in the part that can be read; most of it is badly mutilated. Arsinoe is addressed as she passes beyond the moon to her place in the heavens beneath the Starry Wain, while her people lament. The bitter cry is heard—" Our Queen is gone ", ἡμετέρα βασίλεια φροῦδα. Her " Great Spouse " is mentioned and his ordainment for the burning of funeral fires for her who has shared his couch. Of what follows little can be made out until we come to the remarkable and imaginative passage in which Philotera, the deified sister of Philadelphus and Arsinoe, who is flying from Sicilian Enna, where she has been with Demeter, to Lemnos, sees clouds of smoke arising from the funeral fires and entreats Charis, wife of the Fire-God, to fly to the topmost peak of Athos and to look abroad to see whence comes this smoke that fills her with foreboding. " Who is it that has died? What city is burning holocausts? The wind is from the South. The southwind is blowing fresh and strong. Is it Libya that is in distress, I pray you? " From the snowy height of Athos Charis sees that the smoke is coming from the burning sacrifices in Alexandria. She tells Philotera, " Lamentations fill your city. For no lowly one, but for one of high degree, for your only sister, child of your own mother, they beat their breasts and mourn. Everywhere the cities of the earth have put on black."

---

[74] Beloch, IV², p. 586.

[75] *Pap. Berlin*, 13417 A; Pfeiffer, R., *Callimachi Fragmenta Nuper Reperta* (1923), pp. 3 ff.

Koerte [76] points out the startlingly novel appearance of the baroque in poetry in this hymn in the grandiose and supernatural character of its personages and incidents, in a manner familiar in the sculpture of the Hellenistic period. The word ὁμάδελφον incidentally settles the disputed question of the relationship of Philotera to Arsinoe and indicates that Philotera too was the daughter of Berenice and full sister of Philadelphus and Arsinoe.

Arsinoe Philadelphus died in July, 270 B. C.[77] (according to the dating of Ernst Meyer, 269 B. C.). The Mendes stele says that "this goddess departed to the sky, she joined the company of Ra" in the month Pachon of the fifteenth year of Ptolemy. Apparently shortly before she died she became the goddess Philadelphus deified by her brother, and he shared with her the cult of Brother and Sister Gods. In history he is known by her title Philadelphus, which distinguishes him from the other Ptolemies. He may have been relieved when his indolence was no longer incessantly spurred by her restless energy and glad to turn back to his own son Ptolemy, whom he finally betrothed (in 261 B. C.?) to the daughter of his half-brother Magas of Cyrene; but Arsinoe was a tower of strength to him in death as she had been in life. The diversion of the *apomoira* or tax of one-sixth on wines and fruits [78] from the Egyptian priests to the cult of Arsinoe Philadelphus in the year 262 B. C. gave the royal government the control of the sacred revenues. It is no wonder that he contented himself with mistresses and took no other wife [79] when his departed goddess was such a source of income and was worshipped in every temple in Egypt beside the gods of the country. The fact that her frivolous husband deified one

---

[76] Koerte, *Hellenistische Dichtung*, p. 92.

[77] Bissing, as quoted by Von Prott, *Rhein. Mus.* LIII, 1898, p. 464, n. 1. Meyer, *op. cit.*, pp. 65-66.

[78] Mahaffy, *The Revenue Laws of Ptolemy Philadelphus*, Columns 23-27.

[79] Bouché-Leclercq, I, p. 185, n. 1.

of his harem [80] as Aphrodite did not detract from the solemn worship of Arsinoe Aphrodite by land and sea wherever the Ptolemaic influence prevailed. Pliny tells of splendid yellow topaz brought from the Topaz Island in the Red Sea for Berenice, mother of Ptolemy, which so pleased the king that he had a statue of Arsinoe, six feet in height, carved from it and set up in the Arsinoeum in Alexandria which he had built in her honor.[81] He had an obelisk one hundred and twenty feet high brought with great labor and expense to place in her precinct.[82] Another honor which this king, who loved to spend money on something new, devised for his goddess-wife was a magnetized chapel in the Arsinoeum in which an iron statue of Arsinoe was to float in air. This plan was cut short by the death of the architect Timochares and by that of Ptolemy himself. Pliny calls the placing of the obelisk a service of love (*munus amoris*) and we need not deny that Ptolemy Philadelphus had some measure of affection for his sister, though we recognize that she was supremely useful to him.

On the matter of her husband's devotion Bouché-Leclercq [83] says that if by chance the great piety of Philadelphus toward her memory was only a premeditated attitude, one might say that the astute and criminal Arsinoe was regretted by no one. Tarn adduces dedications on the vases of the foundation called Philadelpheia at Delos with her name preceding that even of Apollo which show that her men who served under her thought well of her.[84]

About the character of Arsinoe, Tarn, who has a more favorable opinion of her than other historians (such as Bouché-Leclercq, who calls her " cette terrible Arsinoe ") says this: [85] " The flaw in Arsinoe was not perhaps immorality but ambition, an overmastering ambition to which she was ready to sacrifice most things; and it is not necessary to suppose her

---

[80] Bouché-Leclercq, I, p. 184, n. 3.

[81] Pliny, *N.H.* XXXVII, 108.

[82] Pliny, *N.H.* XXXVI, 68.

[83] Bouché-Leclercq, I, p. 217.

[84] Tarn, *Antigonos*, p. 292.

[85] *Ibid.* p. 123.

10

a bad woman merely because she became a great ruler." This judgment implies that a woman can have but one vice and that breaking the moral law for her means breaking her marriage vows. There is unfortunately little doubt that Arsinoe, if not a murderess by her own hand, yet frequently was an instigator to murder, and she effectively ruined the lives of a number of men and women who stood in her way. Of course such murder was a recognized procedure in her time. The murdering of rivals in power was regarded as only a safe, natural, and essential precaution for any king, ἀσφαλείας ἕνεκα, in the interest of his security on the throne. It can only be said for Arsinoe that her murders were like those which are so often condoned by historians in the case of Philip, Alexander, Cassander, and other great men.

Arsinoe had beauty and intellect. She appears to have been one of the greatest administrative women who have ever lived and she had all conceivable honors. It is difficult to call her a good woman. I believe that no record of a single good deed on her part has been handed down to us. In her energy, political foresight, and utter unscrupulousness the Gods made her to match the men of her time.

BERENICE II

The lives of the two Berenices, respectively the sister and the wife of Ptolemy Euergetes, must have run parallel to each other (if we accept the earlier date for the birth of Berenice of Cyrene), as they were contemporary Egyptian princesses and cousins. Moreover their lives touched at the crises of the Syrian Berenice's fate. What there was of friendship and intercourse between them when one was princess and youthful queen of Cyrene and the other was at her father's court in Alexandria has not been noted in any of the extant accounts of them.

Berenice II, like her grandmother Berenice I, had a reputation for virtue, and no such reproach attached to her name as to her grandmother's in her early relation with Ptolemy I.

Like her she was greatly beloved by her husband. The quality
of bravery is hers in the first and in the last tale that is told
of her life. Her father was Magas, son of Berenice I by her
first husband, the Macedonian Philip, and her mother
Apame, daughter of Antiochus I of Syria and of Stratonice,
Phila's daughter. Her father had rebelled against the
Egyptian overlordship of Cyrene in the first Syrian war and
at the end of the war had been recognized as king of Cyrene
under the nominal overlordship of his brother. Before his
death he had betrothed Berenice to Ptolemy's son Ptolemy,
following the Greek custom of marrying the heiress to the
nearest male relative, not her brother.[86] The old king had
recalled his son from banishment and acknowledged him as
his successor. The betrothal was however opposed by the
queen mother Apame and by sentiment in Cyrene against
losing independence by the union which would come about
by the marriage of the heiress of Cyrene and the heir of
Egypt. Preferring the friendship of Macedon, Apame offered
the hand of Berenice to a son of Demetrius the Besieger,
who was also a grandson of Ptolemy I, as his mother was
Ptolemais, whom Demetrius married in 286 B. C. shortly
before his death. This son, Demetrius the Fair, was as famous
for his beauty as his father had been. He came at once to
Cyrene and became king, marrying Berenice, who was still
very young.[87] His good looks, unfortunately, made such an
impression on Apame that she took him for a lover. This
so outraged Berenice and the courtiers that Demetrius was
killed in her mother's bed-chamber, Berenice standing at the
door while the soldiers dispatched him. She warned the
slayers not to kill her mother, who attempted to shield her

---

[86] Beloch, IV¹, p. 599.

[87] Beloch, IV¹, pp. 615 ff. Beloch (IV², p. 189) does not believe
that a long time intervened between the slaying of Demetrius and the
composition of Callimachus' poem, Βερενίκης πλόκαμος. Tillyard and
Wace, B.S.A. XI, 1904, p. 119, hold that Berenice was not married
to Demetrius.

lover with her own body.[88]   The testimony of Justin, who tells this dramatic tale, is not highly regarded, but the testimony of Callimachus, who knew Berenice when she became queen of Egypt, cannot be doubted.   We have his evidence in the Latin version of "Berenice's Hair", by Catullus.   In this poem Berenice is praised for a brave deed of her girlhood by which she got a king for a husband.   The Tress of Hair says to Berenice in the poem of Catullus,[89] "I have known you valiant when you were but a little maid.   Have you forgotten the brave deed that won you a king for a husband?   Braver deed could no other dare."

Beloch infers from this passage that the husband was won by the brave little girl soon after the deed, and by this and some other arguments which seem to me to leave his cause not proven he does away with the puzzling wait usually assumed between the betrothal of Berenice and Ptolemy and their marriage.   He puts the death of Magas in 250 B. C. and the death of Demetrius the Fair and the marriage of Berenice in the same year.   I find Tarn's discussion more convincing, although the troubling questions of the long betrothal and the rule of Ptolemy in Cyrene side-by-side with Berenice, but not married to her (assumed from the coins) are left in an unsatisfactory state.[90]

If my suggestion that Ptolemy's sister Berenice was destined by Arsinoe to be the wife of her son, the co-regent with Ptolemy and later governor of Ionia, is tenable, it is possible that on his death in 259 B. C. Philadelphus may have played with the idea of a brother-and-sister marriage between his two children.   He may have cherished some distrust of the son whom he had neglected so long and have feared to make him king of Cyrene independently.

Both Berenice and her husband had suffered, and adversity had hardened the character of the young Ptolemy.   Perhaps from this compulsion of circumstance he harked back to the

---

[88] Justin, XXVI, 3, 8.

[89] Catullus, LXVI, pp. 25 ff.

[90] Beloch, IV[1], p. 615, IV[2], p. 189; Tarn, *Antigonos*, pp. 449 ff.

old strong Macedonian type instead of resembling his elegant, voluptuous father. Callimachus has left in the version of Catullus a picture of the love of Berenice and her husband which, court-poetry though it is and far-fetched in its conceits, has a sincerity that contrasts with the nauseous flattery of Theocritus when that poet praises the married love of Ptolemy II and his sister. The occasion of the original poem was the dedication by Berenice of a tress of her hair in the temple of Arsinoe Aphrodite in Alexandria as an offering to bring her bridegroom safely back from Syria, whither he had marched to save his sister Berenice, wife of Antiochus, from the vengeance of that monarch's former wife Laodice.

> qua rex tempestate novo auctus hymenaeo
> vastatum finis iverat Assyrios.[91]

It has been suggested that in her eagerness to see her bridegroom she even braved all the dangers of the journey from Egypt to Antioch to join him there in the city in which his sister Berenice had been defending herself and her infant son. Bevan [92] thus interprets "the Sister" of the Gurob papyrus to mean Berenice queen of Egypt. This interpretation has been considered in connection with the fate of Berenice of Syria.

The marriage of these two cousins belonging to the House of Ptolemy, both of whom had endured hardship from a parent in their youth, appears to have been an exceptionally happy one and a contrast to the scandals and horrors that were rife in the family history of most of the Ptolemies. No tales of mistresses of Ptolemy III nor of baseness in the court-life have come down.

A gold plate in the British Museum given by Mehetmet Ali to Sidney Smith was one of those laid between the foundation stones of a temple of Osiris at Canopus, built by Ptolemy. The inscription on it reads—" King Ptolemy, son of Ptolemy and Arsinoe, Brother and Sister Gods, and queen Berenice,

---

[91] Catullus, LXVI, 11-12.
[92] Bevan, *Egypt*, p. 202.

his Sister and Wife, dedicate the precinct to Osiris." [93]
Berenice shares her husband's title of Benefactor on the
marble block from Cyprus, also in the British Museum, and
in other dedications, and in the Decree of Canopus. They
had four children, Ptolemy, Arsinoe, Magas, and Berenice.
The death of the little Berenice is mentioned in the Decree of
Canopus, where it is decreed that since she has gone over to
the Eternal World suddenly while still a maiden, she shall
have a boat procession and a feast in all the temples of the
land in the month Tybi, and an image made of gold and
precious stones shall be placed in the temples to be worshipped as the image of Berenice, Lady of Virgins; a crown is
to be placed on its head, differing from that on the head of
her mother Berenice and made of two ears of corn with an
asp-crown between them and behind a papyrus-shaped sceptre
such as the goddesses hold in their hands, and about this the
tail of the asp-crown shall be woven. She is to receive various
other honors, and the bread given to the wives of the priests
is to have a special shape and is to be called the "Loaf of
Berenice ".[94]

The Decree, passed in 237 B. C., increases the honors paid
to the Benefactor Gods in all the Egyptian temples and gives
these magnificent divine honors to their dead child. Of their
other children, Ptolemy became king after his father's death,
Arsinoe was married to her brother some time after the battle
of Raphia, 217 B. C., Magas was scalded to death in his bath
by order of his brother Ptolemy, who also permitted the
murder of his uncle Lysimachus, son of Philadelphus, and
finally the murder of his mother Berenice,[95] who was sus-
pected of preferring her son Magas to Ptolemy.

The gallant and good pair, the "Gods Benefactors", had
in Ptolemy a son most despicably wicked, given to vices of

---

[93] *C.I.G.* 4694; *O.G.I.* 60.

[94] *O.G.I.* 56.

[95] Polyb. V. 34, 36, XV, 25; Justin, XXIX, 1, 7; Strack, *Dynastie
der Ptolemäer*, p. 194.

every kind and a drunkard. The national failing of the Macedonians, who were a hard-drinking people, became more deadly in the soft and enervating Egyptian climate. Polybius [96] gives an appalling account of the young Ptolemy, whose evil propensities were unredeemed by any quality of strength or intellect. He was a debauched aesthete, with literary tastes and a passion for the orgiastic cult of Dionysus. He was completely under the domination of a corrupt man, Sosibius, who is described by Polybius [97] as a quick-witted and inveterate scoundrel with a criminal nature. This man persuaded the young king to connive at the murders of his mother, his brother, and his uncle. Berenice at the time of her death, if she was born in 273 B. C., would be over fifty, and forty-five if born in 266 B. C., a date advocated by Beloch. Her daughter Arsinoe, the next queen of Egypt, was also murdered later by the gang of Sosibius, Agathocles, the king's favorite, and his sister Agathocleia, the king's mistress, and their mother Oenanthe. The bold spirit of Berenice, shown when she was a *parva virgo,* stayed with her until the last, for Polybius [98] says that her murderers were afraid that Berenice's spirit (τόλμα) would foil them in their plot. She had evidently used her great influence in favor of her good son Magas to make him strong with the troops.[99]

The plotters endeavored to secure on their side the Spartan king Cleomenes, who had fled to Ptolemy Euergetes with his army. Cleomenes stood out against them, saying that the king would be better off with still more brothers like Magas to defend and secure his kingship. The upright conduct of the Spartan made him feared by the courtiers of the degenerate young king. They said of him, " He is a lion going up and down among sheep ". Plutarch says that is a good picture of Cleomenes in the palace with his fierce, intrepid eyes that took in all that they saw.

---

[96] Polyb. V, 35.
[97] *Ibid.* XV, 25.
[98] *Ibid.* V, 36.
[99] Plut. *Cleomenes,* XXXIII; Polyb. XV, 25.

Berenice's end was like her beginning. She knew how to live dangerously and how to die bravely. She loved perfume [100] made of roses and encouraged the rose-growers of Cyrene, and she had a pitiful heart. Her husband was once playing dice and kept on with his throws while a page at his side read the list of men condemned to death and got the king's sanction and seal for the death-penalty. Berenice, taking the roll from the page, bade him stop reading the names, for, she said, it was right to give one's whole mind to the decision whether a man should live or die and not be throwing dice while deciding, for one should not dice with the lives of men. Ptolemy looked at her with pleasure and never after that decided the fate of a man while he was himself engaged in playing dice.[101] John Shirley's famous "Song of Calchas" is an antidote to Theocritus' eulogy of Ptolemy Philadelphus. The last lines of it apply to but few of that House, but it can be truly said of Berenice that her actions of bravery and justice have "blossomed in the dust".

In the dissolute and weak young Ptolemy IV Aeschylus would have seen the *Alastor,* the Evil Genius of the race, glutting himself with blood. He is accounted one of the worst of the Ptolemies by Strabo, who calls him in the list in which he gives distinctive epithets of the Ptolemaic kings, "Philopator, he of Agathocleia", naming him by his base mistress.[102] Strabo says that after the third Ptolemy the others degenerated because of voluptuous living and that the three most evil were the fourth, the seventh, and the last. Such was the son of the good and brave Berenice the Second.

Arsinoe III, Sister and Wife of Ptolemy Philopator

The first appearance of this princess in history is on the battlefield of Raphia in Coele-Syria where her brother met and conquered Antiochus of Syria. In the account given in

---

[100] Athen. XV, 689 a.

[101] Aelian, *V.H.* XIV, 43.

[102] Strabo, XVII, 795; Polyb. XIV, 11; Plut. *Cleomenes,* XXXIII.

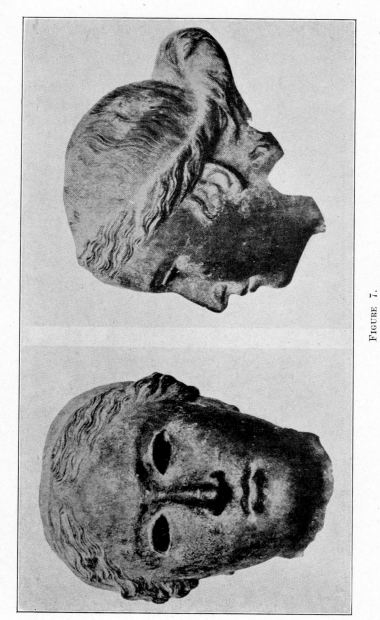

FIGURE 7.

BRONZE HEAD OF ARSINOE III.

In the Ducal Palace at Mantua.

third Maccabees [103] Arsinoe, when at first defeat threatened the Egyptians, went again and again to the army and encouraged the soldiers, standing before them with hair flying, and weeping as she begged them to fight bravely for their wives and children and for their own safety. Polybius gives no such picturesque detail, but confirms the fact that the girl-princess was brought to the battle by her brother and that she exhorted the troops, especially those of the phalanx, on whom their hopes depended. After this vivid picture of a true daughter of Berenice the brave the outlines of her life become misty, and though we learn of the misery of her marriage to one of the worst of the Ptolemies, the mentions of her in decrees and inscriptions supply most of the meagre whole. After the defeat of Antiochus, who was driven back to Gaza with all of Coele-Syria lost to him, Ptolemy and his sister spent three months in Syria and in Phoenicia, where the king re-established the Ptolemaic power in the newly recovered cities. According to the story given in third Maccabees he came to Jerusalem and sacrificed to the most High God and then desired to enter the Holy of Holies, after he had admired the beauty and order of the rest of the temple, declaring that whoever might be debarred from this honor, he must not be. And when he was for forcing his way in, " God scourged him who was greatly uplifted with violence and insolence, shaking him to and fro as a reed by the wind, so that lying on the ground, powerless and paralysed in body, he could not so much as speak, being smitten by a righteous judgment." [104] It is not beyond the limit of possibilities that some such fit may have come upon the superstitious king, who was given to orgiastic and " mystic " cults, especially that of the god Dionysus; he may well have been stricken with some paralysis of fear and terror when he felt the horror that his act inspired in the Jews. " So incessant and vehement was the united cry of the multitude that an indescribable

---

[103] *Maccabees*, III, 1-4; Polyb. V, 83.

[104] Charles, *Apocrypha*, I, pp. 163 ff.

uproar arose. For it might have been thought that not only
the people but even the walls and the whole pavement were
crying out, since all preferred death to the profanation of the
holy place." [105]

After the three months of political activity and sight-seeing
in the Levant he returned to Alexandria in company with
Arsinoe " after ending the war ", says Polybius,[106] " in a way
that surprised the courtiers, considering the general conduct
of his life." Arsinoe was probably very much younger than
her brother and only a slip of a girl when she encouraged the
soldiers at the battle of Raphia. Her son was not born until
209 B. C., and the youth of the young queen was very likely
the reason for the fact that she did not have a child for so
many years after her marriage.

We can only guess at the suffering of the queen, living in
the palace in which the basest of creatures held sway, the pair
Agathocleia and Agathocles and their horrible mother.[107]
They completely governed the drunken Philopator, who
" spent his nights in debauchery and his days in gluttony ".[108]
A book was written about Arsinoe after her death by the
distinguished scholar, Eratosthenes, who had been the king's
tutor. Had it survived it would have been a most precious
historical and human document, but by a whim of fortune
only a scrap has been kept of it by Athenaeus [109] in a discussion of festivals rarely mentioned—one of these was the
Λαγυνοφόρια, which existed in Alexandria in the time of Ptolemy Philopator. The context from which the anecdote in
Athenaeus has been taken evidently said something to the
effect that Arsinoe in company with Eratosthenes and others
somewhere in Alexandria met a man who was carrying green
boughs. " Since Ptolemy was in the habit of founding all
kinds of sacrifices and festivals, Arsinoe asked the man what
day he was celebrating and what the festival was. He replied

---

[105] *Ibid.* 164.
[106] Polyb. V, 87, 6.
[107] Plut. *Cleomenes*, XXXIII.

[108] Justin, XXX, 1, 8.
[109] Athen. VII, 276 b.

FIGURE 8.
MARBLE HEAD OF ARSINOE III.
Boston Museum of Fine Arts.

that it was the lagynophoria (Feast of Bottle-bringing) and that the participants ate food that they had brought themselves, and lying on beds of green boughs each drank from his own flask, that he had brought with him.

"Then the man went his way. Arsinoe looking at us said, ' This is a sordid kind of arrangement. It means the gathering of a promiscuous crowd of people, victuals left over from yesterday and not decently served '. Now if the festival had been pleasing, the queen would have spared no pains in making the same preparations as in the Feast of Pitchers, for in that feast the guests feast by themselves, but the one who has invited them provides the entertainment of food, etc."

The story is assigned by Mahaffy [110] to Arsinoe Second, and the last part of it is misunderstood to indicate " a contemptuous neglect on her part of the masses in Alexandria and at the same time, a perhaps equally contemptuous liberality ". Eratosthenes was only five years old at the time of Arsinoe Second's death, so that rules her out from the anecdote. Bevan,[111] too, seems to read too much into the Greek when he says that Arsinoe " broke out into bitter words at the shame of the royal house and the abasement of the royal dignity ". He also thinks that " each drinking from his own bottle " means that the feast " ended up with every one, court and people, getting gloriously drunk out of doors." This is not said or implied in the Greek, for the point of the man's story is the furnishing by each man of his own food and drink. Arsinoe is disgusted with the cheapness of the entertainment and its promiscuity.[112] Drunkenness was usual in the festivals of Dionysus which Ptolemy so loved that he had the ivy-leaf of that god tattooed on his body. Intoxication in itself, inside the palace or out of doors, could not have so shocked the queen, who was so often the witness of her

---

[110] Mahaffy, *Empire of the Ptolemies*, pp. 161 f.

[111] Bevan, *Egypt*, 236.

[112] Bouché-Leclercq, *Lagides*, I, p. 328. Cf. n. 2.

husband's vice. It is a pity that something of more moment about Arsinoe was not quoted by Athenaeus. But we at least know that the old librarian and scholar wrote lovingly about her in his book " Arsinoe ".

Of her husband Philopator no good word has come down to us. But he was a builder of monuments, and Mahaffy declares that " Had Polybius and Plutarch been lost and inscriptions only been preserved we should have formed quite another picture of Philopator ". Bevan points out in answer to this the utter worthlessness of the official language of inscriptions as evidence regarding character. No amount of building can offset his crime of matricide and his other murders.[113]

Arsinoe's son Ptolemy, born probably in 209 B. C., was soon declared king with his father. He succeeded to the throne when he was six years old, after his father's mysterious death, which Justin [114] says was concealed for a time. Arsinoe was not permitted by Sosibius and his gang to survive long.[115] Polybius gives an astonishing picture [116] of the scenes in the palace when Sosibius and Agathocles crowned the little king before the phalanx of Macedonian soldiers and displayed the two silver urns which Agathocles said contained the ashes of Ptolemy and of Arsinoe, now to be given public burial. The soldiers disbelieved their false tales, and though they prevailed for the moment, the mystery of Arsinoe's death aroused suspicion of the wretches who now had the little king in their power. Polybius tells of the vengeance taken upon the arch-sinners who had ruled the palace so long and met an end as awful as that which they had inflicted upon Arsinoe. This lady, whom life appears to have

---

[113] Bevan, *Egypt*, pp. 250 f.

[114] Justin, XXX, 2, 6.

[115] Müller, *F.H.G.* IV, p. 558 (n. on Joann. Antioch. frag. 54) suggests that the queen perished in a conflagration kindled near her apartment expressly for the purpose of killing her. John of Antioch says that she was treacherously killed by Agathocleia. *F.H.G. loc. cit.*

[116] Polyb. XV, 25, a and b.

FIGURE 9.

MARBLE HEAD OF ARSINOE III.

Boston Museum of Fine Arts.

brought little but evil, had after her death the honor of an eponymous priestess.[117] Her husband had given one to the mother whom he had killed, and the great queen Arsinoe the Second was the first to have had that honor. So on the Rosetta Stone (*OGI* 90) we read, " Pyrrha, daughter of Philinus, being the athlophoros of Berenice Euergetis, Areia, daughter of Diogenes, being Kanephoros of Arsinoe Philadelphus and Eirene, daughter of Ptolemaeus, being priestess of Arsinoe Philopator ". Her son Ptolemy Fifth, called Epiphanes and Eucharistos, the God Manifest and Blessed, was the first child in the Ptolemaic dynasty born of a marriage between a full brother and sister.

" She endured insult throughout her life," says Polybius. Her marble bust in Boston (Figs. 8-9) shows a handsome Macedonian face with an expression of brooding sadness, as of one who has known the bitterness of life. Of the beautiful head in Mantua (Fig. 7), Pfuhl (*Jahrbuch,* XLV, 1930, pp. 39 f.) says that it is the perfect representation of fine and noble womanhood, with the strong spirit of the old Macedonian nobility alive in it.

THE CLEOPATRAS OF EGYPT

1. Cleopatra I of Egypt, called " The Syrian "

Antiochus the Great had three daughters. Before beginning war with Rome he decided to bind the neighboring kings to his cause by giving his daughters in marriage to the most powerful of them. Cleopatra, his eldest, was betrothed to Ptolemy V of Egypt, afterward given the title of Epiphanes. Antiochis was assigned to Ariarathes, king of Cappadocia, and the third, whose name is not mentioned, was offered to Eumenes of Pergamum, but rejected by him.[118] The betrothal of Ptolemy and Cleopatra took place when both were children after the defeat of the boy Ptolemy's forces by her father at

---

[117] Bouché-Leclercq thinks that this cult of Arsinoe instituted after her death, was expiatory. Cf. *Lagides*, I, p. 328, n. 2 and p. 349, n. 2.

[118] Appian, *Syr.* 5.

Panium [119] in 200 B. C., by which battle Antiochus won back
Coele-Syria, which he had lost to the father of Ptolemy at
Raphia in 218.   Appian says that he was courting the little
Ptolemy to make himself safe from attack from that quarter
in his war with Rome.   The Jewish version is that he wished
to secure the kingdom of Egypt eventually for himself.[120]
Probably with the mixture of motives to be found in such
kings both purposes were hovering in his brain, though the
first contingency, that of war with Rome, was the more imminent.   The young pair, when old enough, were married at
Raphia, the scene of the old battle, in 193 B. C., and it was
said that the bone of contention, Coele-Syria, was given by
Antiochus, who had recently won it back, to his daughter for
a part of her dowry.   Ptolemy had come of age in 197 at the
early age of twelve years, and in the decree on the Rosetta
Stone, which was passed the following year on the occasion
of the festival to celebrate the " reception of sovereignty " by
him, all sorts of Egyptian honors are heaped upon him.
Instead of a Macedonian monarch ruling in Egypt like his
predecessors the young king has become a Pharaoh, laden with
sacred titles and with gold asp-crowns for his shrines in the
Egyptian temples.   Like a Pharaoh he was crowned in Memphis, the old capital.   All the exaggerated adulation and the
Pharaonic pomp of the decree written on the Rosetta Stone
to celebrate the " reception of monarchy " by the young king
are proof of the weakening of the Macedonian power in Egypt
and the growth of the influence of the native Egyptians.   The
contempt of the Macedonians and Greeks for the ordinary
Egyptian appears in the fifteenth idyll of Theocritus in the
poet's praise of Philadelphus for checking their outrages:
  " Since your father is among the Immortals, no robber
attacks the wayfarer, creeping upon him in the Egyptian

---

[119] Holleaux (in *Études d'histoire hellénistique*, *Klio*, VIII, 1908,
pp. 267 ff.) decides that the battle of Panium took place in the
spring or summer of 200, a year or a little less than a year after the
capture of Gaza by Antiochus.
[120] *Daniel*, XI, 17.

manner. The tricks these Egyptians used to play, men dishonest in the bone, one as bad as another, base cheats, every man a knave." [121]

The split between the Macedonians and the native element, and the strength of the Egyptians and their increasing dislike of the monarchy at Alexandria had been shown in a threatening way by the rebellions that began in the reign of Ptolemy Philopator and continued in that of his son. So with uprisings in Egypt, with Antiochus the Great ready to pounce upon Egyptian possessions when it should serve his purpose, and with Rome, a new great power in the west, destined in the end to make the Mediterranean a " Roman lake ", sending ambassadors to Alexandria now and then on some polite errand, and to have a look about to see how things were going in Egypt, the prospects of the kingdom and the young king were dubious.

The Cleopatras (with the exception of the shadowy Cleopatra Tryphaena, of whom we hear little) were women of extraordinary strength of character, and much better than their husbands. The Syrian princess with her vigor and brains inaugurated the line of them well. She was undoubtedly a good wife, and a good regent for her little son after the death of her husband. Had Arsinoe survived to be regent for Epiphanes, he might have been a better king; as it was, he was a better man than his father, substituting outdoor sport in the old Macedonian manner for the sordid palace revelries and sickly orgiastic practices of Philopator. But Cleopatra had doubtless a better head. She is said in the book of Daniel [122] to have been given to Epiphanes by her father in the hope that she would destroy Egypt and exalt Syria,— " and he shall give him the daughter of women to corrupt her (better, ' to destroy Egypt '), but she shall not stand, neither be for him ".[123] She was loyal to her husband and his king-

---

[121] Theocritus, XV, 47 ff.

[122] *Daniel*, XI, 17.

[123] Charles, *Book of Daniel*, p. 125.

dom, and Livy says [124] that in the year 190 ambassadors came from Ptolemy and Cleopatra, monarchs (regibus) of Egypt, bearing a message of congratulation that the consul Acilius had driven her father Antiochus from Greece.

The fact that Livy calls Ptolemy and Cleopatra *reges Aegypti* seems to indicate that her prestige as daughter of Antiochus with an enormous dowry (embracing Coele-Syria, as the Egyptians claimed) and her strong character as well gave her a position in the state equal to that of her husband. Although, like the old Macedonians, he was so conspicuously brave in hunting and horseback riding, his physical qualities were not joined to nobility of spirit or intellectual power—the atmosphere of the court in which he had been reared was not propitious for the cultivation of the civilized virtues—and Polybius tells of the cruelties [125] on his part toward the leaders of the Egyptian revolt in 184-3 B. C. He tortured and killed his victims, though because of the policy of his prime minister Polycrates the twenty-five-year-old king had taken no part in the fighting, but had spent his time in athletics and sport. The essential badness of his nature appeared in his treatment of his former minister Aristomenes, whom he punished with death because the old man had touched his arm to awaken him when he fell asleep in the presence of foreign ambassadors. Polybius says that Epiphanes became more brutal and tyrannical in his young manhood and the Egyptians hated him. He died suddenly, perhaps poisoned by his enemies, in 182-1.[126]

Cleopatra had shared her husband's titles of Epiphanes and Eucharistos, conferred upon him when he reached his majority. The two appear together often in inscriptions, for example on a temple at Philae—[127]

---

[124] Livy, XXXVII, 3, 9.
[125] Polyb. XXI, 19.
[126] Jerome on *Daniel*, XI.
[127] *C.I.G.* 4894: Strack, *Dynastie*, p. 245, no. 70. *O.G.I.* 98.

βασιλεὺς Πτολεμαῖος καὶ βασίλισσα Κλεοπάτρα
θεοὶ Ἐπιφανεῖς καὶ Πτολεμαῖος ὁ υἱὸς
Ἀσκληπιῷ.

The title of Sister derived from Arsinoe II was hers, and
she retained after the death of her husband the title of
Goddess Manifest.[128] Her eldest child may have been her
daughter Cleopatra, the date of whose birth is not known;
her son Ptolemy, afterward called Philometor, was born in
186 B. C. and the other son, also called Ptolemy, not long
after. She governed Egypt as regent for her son Ptolemy,
who was five years old at his accession, for about eight
years, and without the aid of male ministers. Another proof
that she was equal to her task of governing and was so recognized is that she was the first of the Ptolemaic queens to coin
money in her own name.[129] Moreover in *Pap. Freib.* 12-33
she [130] is named before the young king in the dating formula
of the year 3 of the king, i. e. 179 B. C. The beginning of
the formula is, " Cleopatra the mother, Goddess Manifest,
and Ptolemy son of Ptolemy God Manifest, reigning in the
third year."

Cleopatra appears to have governed wisely and well during
the years of her regentship. Her husband had been preparing to march against her brother Seleucus IV in Syria
just before his death, but nothing more is heard of this
campaign, and she maintained peace not only with Syria and
Rome, but also with her Egyptian subjects. The date of her
death is in dispute. Livy in writing of events of the year
171 B. C. says, "Antiochus was threatening the kingdom of
Egypt, contemptuous of the tender age of the king and the
sloth of his tutors." The reference is to the eunuch Eulaeus
and to Lenaeus, who assumed direction of the government
after the sudden death of Cleopatra. Kornemann (*Klio*, IX,
138) holds that the Roman embassy of the year 173 B. C., sent

---

[128] Kornemann, *Klio*, I, 75-76.
[129] Kahrstedt, *Klio*, X, p. 274.
[130] P. W. XI¹, sp. 740.

11

to Ptolemy " renovandae amicitiae causa ", came on the occasion of the death of the queen-regent to renew the treaty of peace with the new régime, and this seems a reasonable inference. Her son [131] established in Ptolemais a priest of himself and his mother. After her death she received a special priestess in Ptolemais, corresponding to the athlophoros of Arsinoe II and the Kanephoros of Berenice II and the priestess of Arsinoe III. Appian and Josephus say that Antiochus gave her Coele-Syria for a dowry [132] and though the province remained in the possession of the Seleucids, it is probable that, as Josephus says,[133] Cleopatra (or her husband while he lived) received revenues from the taxes. As the wealthy daughter of a powerful and neighboring king she was in a far better position to maintain her rights than the last queen of Egypt had been. Arsinoe was an orphan brought up in the court of her debased older brother, whom she married when only a child, and her life could hardly have been anything else than the life of perpetual insult and shame that Polybius says it was. If she had strength of character it was of no avail in that palace ruled by degenerate men and women. Cleopatra inherited from her father those qualities of boldness, ambition, and indefatigability in carrying out a purpose which Polybius ascribes to the young Antiochus.[134] Her mother was Laodice, the daughter of Mithradates II of Cappadocia, and by this descent the original strain of Persian blood resulting from the marriage of Seleucus I with the Persian princess Apame was increased to a considerable degree in Cleopatra. She brought into the rapidly degenerating Ptolemaic stock a new vigor from the more active Seleucid blood, and the results of it are seen in her daughter Cleopatra II.

She was the first of the Ptolemaic queens to be regent for

---

[131] Otto, *Priester und Tempel*, I, pp. 162, 195.

[132] This was denied by the Seleucids of the next reign. See Polybius, XXVIII, 1.

[133] Josephus, *A.J.* XII, 4, 1.

[134] Polyb. XI, 34, 15 and XV, 37.

a son in his minority, and this opportunity placed in her hands the power that had come in the past to Macedonian queens in a similar case. Even before her regentship she appears to have had a position in the government, as already noted, that surpassed that of any other queen since Arsinoe II, who attained to such very great power through her personal ability and the clever stroke of becoming a Sister Wife after the old Egyptian custom. It is, however, hardly right to state that [135] " In these Macedonian houses, as we have seen, a woman is the equal of a man ". There was never the possibility of a woman's succeeding to the throne if she had brothers,[136] and a woman's power has heretofore in the history of these houses always come from overpowering strength of character, combined with weakness in her husband's personality (e. g. Arsinoe II, Eurydice, wife of Philip Arrhidaeus), or from the position of regent for a minor son (e. g. Eurydice, mother of Philip II of Macedon, Cleopatra of Epirus, daughter of Philip II, etc.). The queenship of Cleopatra I from her prestige as a Seleucid princess, with a claim of some sort on Coele-Syria, her wealth and the vigor of her nature, together with the fact that she was regent for a term of eight years (at least), does mark an epoch in the history of woman's power in Ptolemaic Egypt.

CLEOPATRA II

Cleopatra II was perhaps the eldest child of Cleopatra I. Her parents were married in 193 B. C. and her brother Ptolemy Philometor was not born until 186 B. C. (Strack, p. 197). She may have been born in this interval and in any case was born before 181 B. C. It seems probable that the marriage to her brother did not take place until after her mother's death in 173 B. C. From that year on Cleopatra and her brother are worshipped as Mother-loving Gods. Ptolemy was fourteen or fifteen years old at the time of his accession. Whether by

---

[135] Bevan, *Egypt*, p. 282.
[136] Strack, *Dynastie*, p. 75; Beloch, IV¹, p. 377 and n. 1.

design of the queen-regent or by accident, the control of the three children and the management of the government passed into the hands of a eunuch Eulaeus and a man from Coele-Syria, Lenaeus, who had been a slave. It may be that the queen-mother had found that eunuchs and slaves were easier for her to deal with and more amenable to her orders than men of distinction and rank were, but it proved a disaster for her children and for Egypt that such base persons stood ready to seize power. Whether appointed by her before her death or not, these two actually became regents and proceeded to plunge the country into a war with the Seleucid king in the attempt to get back the old dower-land Coele-Syria. Eulaeus, says Diodorus, had but lately laid aside his lyre and his rouge-pots, and now exchanged the works of Aphrodite for those of Ares; he and Lenaeus [137] forgot in their greed who they were and what a king they were attacking. They invaded Coele-Syria, taking all kinds of treasure with them, ostensibly as bribes for the commanders of fortresses and cities in the province. When their army was defeated by Antiochus, they persuaded the young Philometor to take what treasure he could and seek sanctuary by ship on the sacred island of Samothrace. Polybius lays this cowardice on the part of Philometor to the softening of his nature by the corrupt life in the Palace under the debasing influence of his " tutors ", the eunuch and the slave. The historian contrasts the steadfastness and energy displayed by Philometor later with his softness on this occasion; the old Macedonian blood showed its strength in him when the creatures of the Palace had had their day and were dismissed.

Philometor did not reach sanctuary, but was captured by his uncle's fleet. The Seleucid king now invaded Egypt, and reaching Memphis is said to have had himself crowned there as king of Egypt. He soon desisted from this, however, and took up the cause of his elder nephew, when he heard that the younger brother was chosen king in Alexandria in place

---

[137] Diod. XXX, 15, 16.

of the fleeing Philometor and was reigning there together with his sister Cleopatra, Philometor's wife. Antiochus retreated from Egypt in 169, leaving Philometor king in Memphis and a strong garrison in Pelusium. Philometor [138] soon came to terms with his wife and his brother, and the two kings and Cleopatra reigned together in Alexandria, to the anger of Antiochus, who had been greatly pleased at the contention between the brothers, since it weakened Egypt. When he invaded Egypt again he was checked by the Romans, who now had time to turn their attention to the condition of affairs in Egypt. Ptolemy and Cleopatra had sent an embassy to Rome to ask the Senate to send ambassadors to announce to Antiochus that it was not their pleasure that war should be waged on the now united kings (sociis regibus). The result of the Roman embassy headed by Gaius Popillius Laenas is a famous and splendid tale of the cowing of the debonair king Antiochus by the dour Roman. Popillius met Antiochus with his army in a suburb of Alexandria and handed him the decree of the Senate, ordering him to cease from the war on his nephews. When the Seleucid king demurred and asked for time to consult his friends, the Roman legate drew a circle in the sand with a stick [139] which he had in his hand and told the king that he must answer the Senate before he stepped outside that circle. Overcome by this example of the Roman temper the king after a moment of hesitation agreed to abandon his Egyptian campaign. Popillius then adjusted affairs in Alexandria and sailed to Cyprus to expel the Seleucid garrison from that island.

Livy [140] says that the ambassadors came from Ptolemy and Cleopatra, the kings, *Legati ab Ptolemaeo et Cleopatra regibus.* In the same chapter he represents the ambassadors as saying that in event of a delay on the part of Rome in the

---

[138] Livy, XLV, 11. Soror plurimum adiuvit non consilio modo sed etiam precibus.

[139] Polyb. XXIX, 11.

[140] Livy, XLIV, 19.

matter of sending an embassy, Ptolemy and Cleopatra would be exiled from their kingdom and come to Rome. So in Livy XLV, 13, legates coming from Egypt brought a message of thanks to the Senate in the common name of the king and Cleopatra: "Legati communi nomine regis et Cleopatrae grates egerunt." And in the reply sent by the Senate the answer is headed *Regibus* [141] *Aegypti Ptolemaeo et Cleopatrae*, "to the rulers of Egypt, Ptolemy and Cleopatra". The importance here given to Cleopatra indicates that she retained the prestige that her mother enjoyed, and is an evidence of the growing power of the queen in Ptolemaic Egypt. Livy's phrase is confirmed by the official dating of documents,[142] the earliest of which is of the year 163 B. C., in which the formula is changed from "in the reign of king Ptolemy" to "in the reign of king Ptolemy and queen Cleopatra".

The answer of the Roman Senate to the thanks sent by Philometor and Cleopatra for the action of the ambassadors in checking Antiochus is significant: "The Senate is greatly pleased if any help and aid has been given by them and will always endeavor to have Ptolemy and Cleopatra believe that the greatest defence of their kingdom rests in the faith of the Roman people." The interest of Rome in Ptolemaic Egypt never ceased from this time on until the last queen of the Ptolemaic line died by the asp-bite rather than walk a captive in the triumph of the Roman conqueror.

Cleopatra II was the first of the Macedonian queens in Egypt to achieve a political equality [143] with her husband. This equality probably began early in their reign, for the passages in Livy which indicate it refer to the year 168 B. C. Because of the strengthening of woman-power in her reign

---

[141] βασιλεῦσι in the same sense, *Zois pap.*, Wilcken, *Urkunden der Ptolemäerzeit*, I, pp. 527-9; *Ibid.* p. 523, on no. 113 " Die Nennung der Königin an dieser Stelle ist wichtig fur die Machtstellung der Kleopatra II."

[142] Strack, *Dynastie*, p. 33.

[143] Strack, *Dynastie*, pp. 32 f. and 75.

and those succeeding hers, it is worth while to consider in this place the various circumstances that combined to give this second Cleopatra a recognized position in the state such as no queen before her had attained.

In the first place she was the daughter, perhaps the eldest child, of the wealthy and powerful princess from Syria, Cleopatra I. While she was growing from childhood to young girlhood, her mother was queen-regent of Egypt, and this example of woman-power may have stamped itself on her young and receptive mind. Moreover her own position was unique and assured, as that of her two brothers could not be. There was always the possibility of a strife between them for the throne, whereas she was the only sister and so destined to be queen of Egypt no matter which of the two brothers might triumph. The strong will and political sense shown by her throughout her long life were hers as a girl. This is clear from the part she played in making peace between the brothers, when her husband Ptolemy was king in Memphis and her younger brother Ptolemy and she were ruling in Alexandria. Her action points strongly to her being the elder sister dealing with two younger brothers.[144] Indeed it is hardly conceivable that she should have dealt with the situation with such wisdom and insight if she was younger than the fifteen-year-old younger Ptolemy. It was on her that the elder brother, her husband, counted first and foremost in his endeavor to get back to Alexandria, and it was she who did most for the reconciliation of the two brothers and for the establishing of the triple rule for them and herself. Her brains and tact saved the situation. Her husband was ready to acknowledge the dexterity with which she had arranged matters and the fact that he owed his restoration primarily to her, the proof of which is that the embassies sent in the name of both of them were sent in the year of his return to Alexandria to reign with her and his younger brother. There is no doubt that there was a strong

---

[144] But cf. *O.G.I.* 733, where only one child is mentioned.

affection between Philometor and his sister-wife, and besides that there were the political considerations to make him exalt her prestige. While she was his wife,[145] by the brother-and-sister marriage, so dear to the Egyptians, he was fortified against his ambitious younger brother, and this fact alone placed him in the hollow of his wife's hand if she chose to demand recognition. The recognition, whether a voluntary tribute and sign of his gratitude, or a response to a demand from her, was full and clear. She was queen beside her brothers. Further, her character and that of Philometor were contributing elements to her accession to power. The rottenness of the court life under the eunuchs would not touch her so much as it touched her brothers while her mother lived, and after the death of the strong Cleopatra I, the court crew did not have a long shrift. Philometor, according to Polybius, recovered from the infection of moral corruption that weakened his boyhood and came back to the best traditions of the Macedonians [146] after his short season of degeneracy. All three children inherited brains, but the younger brother, Euergetes II, as he had himself called, " Pot-belly ", as his subjects called him, was the evil genius of the family.

These, then, were the causes of the elevation of Cleopatra to an acknowledged position on the throne: 1) the fact that her mother was a powerful Seleucid princess with Coele-Syria in some way her dower, and also regent of Egypt while Cleopatra II was growing up; 2) her own character and intellect inherited from that mother which enabled her 3) to intervene between her brothers and secure the return of her husband and an amicable arrangement for the sharing of power; 4) the fact that she had in 173 B. C. become "Sister

---

[145] The first two Ptolemies each put aside a wife. After this no queen was actually put aside, although Arsinoe III was neglected and abused, and Cleopatra II was forced to share the queenship with her daughter, but neither queen was deposed.

[146] Polyb. XXVIII, 21 and XXXIX, 7.

and Wife " of Philometor by a brother-and-sister marriage after the Egyptian fashion and so was sacred in the eyes of the Egyptians; 5) the gratitude and respect cherished for her by her brother-husband, who appears to have lived with her in affection and harmony.

Strack [147] notes that after she had gained political equality as a sovereign, the succession in Macedonian Egypt belonged thereafter legally to a queen who survived her husband, with the proviso that a male member of the family should be invited by her to take a part in the government.

Cleopatra II had royal power in various combinations of rulers. She was queen with Philometor her husband; after his attempted flight to Samothrace she was queen with her younger brother, who became king in Alexandria; she then ruled for five years with her two brothers, and thereafter with her husband until his death; she was regent for a short time with her son and after his death was the " Sister and Wife " of her brother Euergetes; in a few years she became member of another triad of rulers—Euergetes II, Cleopatra the Sister, and Cleopatra the Wife; she began to count her own regnal years in 132-1 B. C. as Thea Philometor Soteira and governed Alexandria as sole sovereign in 130 B. C. After a period of exile at the Seleucid court she again joined Euergetes II and her daughter with the old style for the three; she ruled for a few months after the death of Euergetes II with her daughter Cleopatra and Ptolemy VIII. If she had left a record of her extraordinary life it would be a priceless document, not only for the settlement of moot questions in the dates and small points of historical research, but still more for the history of morals and of civilization.

Cleopatra and Philometor were able to get rid of the younger Ptolemy after five years of trouble, in the course of which Philometor was obliged [148] to leave Alexandria and go to Rome as a suppliant. While there he avoided all Oriental luxury and ostentation and refusing the royal dress and dia-

---

[147] Strack, *Dynastie*, p. 75.   [148] Diod. XXXI, 18.

dem which his cousin Demetrius offered him, he appeared before the Senate in a humble garb and lived in Rome in poor lodgings. After the division of the Egyptian inheritance was made by the Senate's giving Philometor Egypt and Cyprus and the younger brother the Cyrenaica, the triple reign was over. The younger Ptolemy continued to beg Rome to give him Cyprus and finally invaded that island, only to be captured by Philometor, who forgave his brother and betrothed one of his daughters to him. The younger Ptolemy then went back to Cyrene. Cleopatra bore four children to Philometor, a son, Eupator, who was for a few years before his death joint-king with his father and regent of Cyprus, two daughters, both named Cleopatra, and a son Ptolemy Neos Philopator, who outlived his father and was killed by his uncle Ptolemy, who succeeded to the throne.[149]

After Philometor and Cleopatra were rid of their brother and his ambitious attempts to get the kingdom, they ruled peaceably together over Egypt while the brother reigned in Cyrenaica. Of their life together we know but little. They visited the Serapeum at Memphis twice (163 and 158 B. C.), and Philae in 158 B. C. A pronaos [150] to the temple of Antaeus at Antaeopolis was dedicated by " king Ptolemy son of Ptolemy and Cleopatra, Gods Manifest and Beneficent, and queen Cleopatra, the Sister of the King, Mother-loving Gods, to Antaeus and the gods sharing his temple ". Cleopatra is called " The Sister of the King ",[151] and " Sister and Wife ", and both she and her husband are called " Mother-loving Gods ".[152]

Philometor, like his predecessors, made political marriages for his daughters, betrothing one to his brother to ratify the reconciliation between them in 154, and giving the other

---

[149] Strack, *Dynastie*, pp. 177 ff.   Bouché-Leclercq, *Lagides*, III, p. 56, n. 2.

[150] Strack, p. 248, no. 81, p. 249, no. 87.

[151] *Ibid.* p. 245, 71; p. 249, 88; p. 251, 95.

[152] Wilcken, *Urkunden*, I, pp. 480 f.; *O.G.I.* 106, 107, 108, 109; Meyer, *Klio*, XV, p. 380.

to the Syrian Pretender Alexander Balas in 150. He "celebrated the marriage at Ptolemais with great pomp, as the
manner of kings is," says the author of the first books of
Maccabees,[153] but finding this son-in-law treacherous and impossible, he substituted the young Demetrius, son of Demetrius I, as a husband for his daughter, and entered Antioch,
where he placed upon his own head the two diadems of Egypt
and of Syria, but "being naturally a good and righteous
man", says Josephus,[154] he determined to avoid the envy of
the Romans, so he called an assembly together and persuaded
the people of Antioch to receive Demetrius as king. When
Alexander returned to burn and pillage, he was driven off
by the combined forces of Ptolemy and his new son-in-law,
but Ptolemy's horse was frightened by an elephant's trumpet-
ing and threw the king on rocky ground. Ptolemy received
a wound from which he died. He was forty-one years old
and had been king for thirty-five years. He appears, in spite
of the corruption of his early training, to have recovered
himself and to have been one of the best and bravest of the
Ptolemies. Cleopatra, who shared his power and responsi-
bilities, had a steadying influence over him, when he was
tempted by the Egyptian vices of sloth and excess which
Polybius, who admires his character, says he was prone to
when not in action. Justin's [155] account of him as a mountain
of corrupt and sinful flesh is believed to rest on a confusion
of him and some other fat Ptolemy, perhaps his brother
Euergetes II.

Cleopatra's fate was to be married to one of the best of
the Ptolemies, Philometor, and one of the worst, Euergetes
II, the younger brother. She became regent after her husband's death with her son Ptolemy Neos Philopator. To have
kept the young heir alive, Mahaffy remarks,[156] must have

---

[153] *Maccabees*, I, 10, 58; Josephus, *A.J.* XIII, 4, 2.
[154] Josephus, *A.J.* XIII, 4, 7.
[155] Justin, XXXIV, 2, 7.
[156] Mahaffy, *Empire*, p. 376.

seemed quixotic to a man of Euergetes' temper. That he
was stupid enough to kill him, as Justin says he did, in his
mother's embrace [157] at the feast of the wedding between
Cleopatra and himself is improbable. " Murder in a mother's
arms " is a stock scene with Justin and one that he can
never resist using. But the boy king was murdered, whether
before or after his mother's marriage is not known. Cleopatra had been standing out against Euergetes with the help
of the Jews, who loved Philometor and his Sister-Wife, who
according to Josephus [158] had entire confidence in them and
placed their army under the command of Jewish generals,
Onias and Dositheus. These officers, apparently, were in
command of the troops with which she had opposed Euergetes, before she was forced by the will of the Alexandrians
to marry him.

Her new husband is described by Justin [159] as a man of a
very unpleasant countenance, and of abnormal fatness of
body, which was revealed by his habit of wearing transparent
robes. He is regarded as the most cruel of all the Ptolemies,
showing a relentless energy in his wicked acts that gives him
the palm for cruelty above the competitors in this respect,
Ptolemy Philopator and Ptolemy Auletes. Some modern
historians believe that his memory has been blackened by the
Greeks [160] because of his expulsion of Greek scholars from
Egypt,[161] which is mentioned by Athenaeus, who says that
the Alexandrians called him " Malefactor " (Cacergetes)
instead of " Benefactor " (Euergetes) because of his slaying
many of them and exiling so many of his brother's con-
temporaries that the islands and foreign cities were overflowing with scholars, philosophers, mathematicians, artists,
painters, physicians, teachers of physical training, and other
professional men who had been driven from Egypt. Mahaffy

---

[157] Justin, XXXVIII, 8, 4.
[158] Josephus, c. Apion. II, 5.
[159] Justin, XXXVIII, 8, 9-10.
[160] Tarn, *Hellenistic Civilisation*, p. 162.
[161] Athen. IV, 184.

had a great admiration for his "policy". For example, he thought that a "larger policy" lay behind the murders ascribed to him and that the periodic massacres of the Alexandrians of which Polybius tells were due to "one consistent policy (which) underlies all these acts, the rehabilitation of the native population at the expense of the Hellenistic settlers and Jews." [162] And so he argues that "his so-called massacres were not random violences" but were directed solely against the imported Graeco-Macedonians, whereas he never showed harshness to the native Egyptians. There is a great deal of special pleading here, and Bevan [163] rightly says in regard to the matter: "I can see no evidence for Mahaffy's statement in regard to Euergetes II that 'his policy of fusing Greeks with natives was a reasonable and gracious one', or for the notion that he had any such policy at all." The word "gracious" applied to the methods which Polybius says he took for this so-called "fusion" seems indeed a word of "sancta simplicitas".

Cleopatra became her brother's wife and bore him a son, born at Memphis a year after the marriage when her husband was being crowned in that city as Pharaoh. He was called Memphites [164] and was the first legitimate son of Euergetes. Cleopatra evidently let ambition and love of ruling outweigh loathing for her brother. She was "Sister and Wife" and mother of the heir to the throne, and to have a son by her was a source of strength to her husband. He was a man of many mistresses, but she was his first wife. He left Cyrenaica to a son of his Cyrenaean mistress, whom he highly regarded.

After several years of marriage, in which it is possible that Cleopatra bore him another son,[165] Euergetes fulfilled the engagement to marry his niece Cleopatra, betrothed to him in 154. There were thereafter two queens in Alexandria, both married to the king. The formula in documents and

---

[162] Mahaffy, *Empire*, pp. 383, 388.
[163] Bevan, *Egypt*, p. 323.
[164] Diod. XXXIII, 13; XXXIV, 14.
[165] *O.G.I.* 130, 144.

inscriptions is "king Ptolemy and queen Cleopatra the Sister and queen Cleopatra the Wife". In some only Cleopatra "the Sister" appears with the king and sometimes only "Cleopatra the Wife".[166] The situation of the two queens, mother and daughter, married to the same man, is the most revolting of all the shames of the house of the Ptolemies. What it was actually and psychologically in the daily life of the Palace and of the government cannot be known. Cleopatra the mother was of tough and resisting fibre and would not easily let go the sovereignty which she had gained so early and exercised so long. It is not certain whether the wavering of styles between the mention of the two queens and that of the "queen sister" and the "queen wife" indicates anything except the carelessness or ignorance of various scribes,[167] but it is certain that in 130 B. C. Euergetes was driven out of Alexandria and Cleopatra the Sister [168] ruled the city. The king fled to Cyprus with his wife, the younger Cleopatra, and her children, and also took with him for a hostage his son by his sister, Memphites, who was about fourteen years old. Diodorus [169] states that when he heard that Cleopatra was thoroughly alienated from him, the king killed their son and sent his dismembered body in a birthday box to his sister, whose birthday feast it was when the box arrived.

There followed a time of warfare in Egypt between the supporters of the Sister and those of the king. There was a period τῆς ἀμειξίας, "of no dealing", between the parts of Egypt under her control and the part that stood for Euergetes. The queen sought help from her Syrian son-in-law Demetrius and fled to him with a great amount of treasure after her husband succeeded in fighting his way back to Alexandria. But Demetrius was killed after being defeated by a Pretender, Alexander, whom Euergetes supported.

---

[166] Strack, *Dynastie*, pp. 38 ff.

[167] Strack, *op. cit.*, pp. 38-50.

[168] Wilcken, *Urkunden*, I, p. 3, *Archiv.* IV, p. 224.

[169] Diod. XXXIV, 14.

Cleopatra, obtaining no help in Antioch from her daughter Cleopatra Thea, returned to Egypt and again became associated in the government with her brother and her daughter. The Edict of 118 B. C. which provides for the reform of various abuses and regulates certain matters in the kingdom bears the name of all three.

It seems highly probable that Cleopatra herself was quite as responsible for these reforms as her brother, who has received such high praise on the score of their excellence. Of course it is not known that either of them composed the decrees, which may have been the work of some administrative officers [170] of the realm. But it is at least as likely that Cleopatra, who showed her good sense and brains from the beginning of her career, had a hand in these arrangements as that Euergetes, after a long life of self-indulgence, suddenly was capable of settling affairs so competently. The Decrees are regarded by many as a complete vindication of his character (e. g.)—" It is impossible to turn from this really excellent list of reforms introduced by Euergetes II himself to the stories about him which pass for history without feeling that there is a very marked discrepancy. As Mahaffy has well pointed out,[171] the contemporary evidence of this reign does not in the least justify the abuse that has been heaped upon Euergetes II by his detractors from Polybius down to Revillout and which reaches its highest pitch in the melodramatic narrative of Justin. The new evidence as to his reign afforded by the present volume is still more in his favor. The problem is largely one of chronology, for if it can be shown that the actions attributed to him by historians did not take place at the time which they mention, there is good reason for doubting whether they took place at all ", etc.[172] Tarn [173] also considers that the series of decrees completely

---

[170] So Niese, III, pp. 272-273, n. 6.

[171] *Empire of Ptolemies*, pp. 385 ff.

[172] Grenfell and Hunt, *Tebtunis Papyri, Royal Ordinances*, I, p. 20.

[173] Tarn, *Hellenistic Civilisation*, pp. 32 f., 161 f. But cf. Rostovtzeff, *Social and Economic History of the Roman Empire*, p. 571:

disproves the Greek tradition which makes him a blood-stained tyrant, who committed many crimes.

The decrees begin with an amnesty for crimes committed before 118 B. C., except those of murder and temple-robbing, and contain various provisions for the remission of arrears of taxes, for the reform of customs, for regulating the ownership of land and houses, for protection of workers in the service of the king against exactions from officials, protection for royal cultivators and others working for the crown, etc. There is the enactment that native cases in the demotic shall go before *laocritae* to be decided by Egyptian law, while cases in which the documents are in Greek shall be decided by *chrematistae,* while in purely Egyptian cases the *laocritae* shall judge.[174]

The occasion of the decrees is admittedly the necessity of bringing back order to a land in confusion because of the civil dissension of the time of ἀμειξία and in the war between Cleopatra and Euergetes. Cleopatra certainly was not the woman to be overlooked in such a settlement, and if the arrangements were composed by the rulers themselves and not by their advisers, I strongly incline to the view that Cleopatra II, the first of the line to be co-regent with her husband, a woman of extraordinary ability, character, and nerve, had more to do with framing the decrees than Euergetes II. It seems to be as logical to argue that the man described by his contemporary Polybius and other historians could not have framed such edicts, as to argue that he did frame them (which is not proved) and that therefore the historians who say ill of him must have invented their stories of his wickedness.

" I feel convinced that P. Jouget's attacks on the ' rehabilitators ' of Euergetes II are fully justified. Euergetes made a virtue of necessity: his practice was probably very different from his words, which as a matter of fact were not even invented by him, but assumed at a very early time the conventional expressions used in amnesty decrees, just like the decrees of the priests and similar Egyptian documents of the earlier period."

[174] For a summary of the whole document see Bevan, *Egypt*, pp. 315 ff.

It has also been pertinently asked [175] why we hear of no attempt on his part to regulate affairs in his kingdom until two years before his death, after a long reign. He died in June, 116 B. C., and the name of his sister Cleopatra appears for the last time in a demotic papyrus of October 29, 116 together with that of Cleopatra III and Ptolemy VIII.[176] She outlived her husband and had a share for a few months in still another combination of rulers.

She was queen for fifty-seven years and was probably over seventy when she died. A tough unyielding nature which did not know how to acknowledge defeat, she retained her power and her prestige through every vicissitude of fortune. Her life with Philometor doubtless was one of harmony; at her turmoil of soul during the terrible years of marriage and warfare with the younger of her brothers we can only guess. She was buoyed up by that passion for power and for action that stamped the Macedonian, when not degenerated, in each country in which they established their rule. She established the principle of " Equal rights for Queens " in Egypt, and the length of her reign and the variety of its episodes place her beside Arsinoe II and Cleopatra VII in the significance and interest of her career.

CLEOPATRA III

The Cleopatra to whom the throne of Egypt was left by the will of her husband and uncle, Euergetes II, was the most domineering of the Macedonian-Hellenistic queens. She had in the highest degree the passion for sovereignty and grandeur and disposed of the lives of her sons and her daughters as she saw fit in the interests of her own rule. She is not said to have been a licentious or a particularly murderous woman, though she would no more than the rest of her line hesitate to commit dynastic murder, or murder for vengeance,

---

[175] Niese, III, p. 273. Cf. however, Bouché-Leclercq (*Lagides*, II, p. 83), who thinks that wisdom came to Euergetes II in his old age.

[176] *Pap. Tebtunis*, I, p. 32, 4.

12

such as putting to death the general who returned from Cyprus without the person of her son whom she had sent him to apprehend.

It is amusing to note that Mahaffy, the champion of her husband, to whom so much evil is attributed, regards Cleopatra as a "desperate queen whose long career is hardly to be paralleled in any other civilized society".[177] He continues—"Perhaps among the despots of the Italian Renaissance we might find a princess as daring and as unscrupulous but not so successful for forty-five years". Mahaffy is evidently starting her desperate career at the point of her alleged rape by her uncle and her subsequent marriage to him while he was her mother's husband. In this matter a girl of twelve or fifteen—she was born between 160 B. C. and 155 B. C.[178]—in the hands of a man of her uncle's age and character was surely more sinned against than sinning. On the whole a more reasonable case might be made for her decency and morals than for those of Euergetes II, though at present it is fashionable to praise him for good administration (at the end of his life) and to attribute his bad reputation to Greek propaganda.

Defending Euergetes II from the charge of violating Cleopatra before his marriage to her, Mahaffy [179] says that fortunately Polybius has told us the fact that the young princess was already betrothed by her father to his brother and that therefore he fulfilled his engagement to the legitimate heiress to the throne in marrying her. It is not certain that he was betrothed to her—it may have been her older sister Cleopatra Thea, afterward queen of Syria, who was betrothed to Euergetes II in 154 B. C., when Cleopatra III was but an infant. And if the argument of Mahaffy holds, and this alleged betrothal absolves Euergetes II from guilt, much more it absolves the girl, and Mahaffy is premature in dating her desperate career from this early point. True, she

---

[177] Mahaffy, *Empire*, p. 418.
[178] Strack, *Dynastie*, p. 198, n. 24.
[179] Mahaffy, *History of Egypt*, p. 187.

became what Justin drastically calls " matris pellex ", but she was also a legitimate queen of Egypt.

Of the life together of the mother and daughter and the king who married them and had children by them we have only official information. An inscription from Cos [180] tells of this composite family. It states that king Ptolemy and queen Cleopatra, the sister, and queen Cleopatra, the wife, Beneficent Gods, honor Hieron, son of Simos, of their foremost friends, and tutor of their children, with a gold crown and a gold statue because of his merit and devotion to them and their children. And in the reliefs added by Euergetes II to the temple at Kom Ombo he appears with his sister-wife Cleopatra and his wife Cleopatra receiving gifts from Horus and making offerings to various Egyptian gods.[181]

But officialdom, though it presents a fair picture of the family life of the three [182] and their children, cannot obscure the terrible hatreds and enmities that haunted such a household. War finally broke out between the Sister-Wife and Euergetes II, and he was forced to flee to Cyprus. Cleopatra III and her children went with him and there can be no doubt that she was in entire accord with him during the struggle with her mother. She bore him in all five children, Ptolemy Soter II (later called by the nickname-loving Alexandrians Lathyrus, Chick-pea), Ptolemy Alexander, Tryphaena, Cleopatra IV and Cleopatra Selene. Her husband is said to have killed his son and heir Memphites, child of Cleopatra II, while they were in Cyprus, and it may be that Cleopatra III acquiesced in the deed of her husband in the desire to have her own sons inherit. We know nothing of her during this period, and in 124 B. C. she and her mother reigned together with Euergetes II again; the rescripts of

---

[180] *O.G.I.* 141. Cf. *O.G.I.* 137, 138, 139, 140, 142.

[181] J. de Morgan, *Kom Ombo*, pp. 195 ff.

[182] Mahaffy, *Empire*, p. 385. " I gladly record the fact (i. e. of the honors to the tutor of the children) as giving us one more item of evidence by which to judge him less harshly."

reform of 118 B. C. were published in the name of the three sovereigns.

The evidence of papyri shows that Cleopatra II outlived her husband and reigned for a short time with her daughter Cleopatra III and her grandson Ptolemy Soter. Meyer [183] suggests that her death might have coincided with the forced divorce of his sister-wife Cleopatra IV by Ptolemy Soter II at the dictation of his mother. The suggestion is sometimes made that Cleopatra III had her mother murdered, but there is no proof of this.

The history of the reign of Cleopatra III after the death of her husband in 116 B. C. is that of relentless persecution of her older son, who was forced upon her as co-regent by the people of Alexandria. Euergetes II had left her the kingdom of Egypt with the right to choose whichever of her two sons she wished to share her power. He left the Cyrenaica to his illegitimate son, Ptolemy Apion. Cleopatra was forced to acquiesce in the arrangement by which Ptolemy Soter II shared her power, but her name preceded his in official documents.[184]

Her younger son, Ptolemy Alexander, whom she had wished to have associated with her in the government instead of Soter, she sent to Cyprus as viceroy; she then began to play the dictator in the affairs of her older son. She forced him to give up his wife, Cleopatra IV, whom he loved and was reluctant to divorce, and made him marry his younger sister Selene. Cleopatra IV, the elder sister, had doubtless inherited too strong a will and high a spirit from her mother to get on peaceably with her, and Cleopatra III saw in this daughter and queen a power that threatened her own. The daughter was rich and adventurous enough to go to Cyprus, the natural refuge of a Ptolemy, where her brother Alexander was governing, and raised an army.[185] Bouché-Leclercq [186]

---

[183] Meyer, *Klio*, II, p. 477.

[184] *O.G.I.* 167, 738, 739.

[185] Justin, XXXIX, 3.

[186] Bouché-Leclercq, *Lagides*, II, p. 93, n. 1.

even suggests, though only as a hypothesis, that there might have been a marriage between her and her younger brother in Cyprus, which did not last long and produced as its result Ptolemy Alexander II, whose mother is not known. Cleopatra IV went with her troops to Syria, where she offered herself and her soldiers to Antiochus Cyzicenus, her cousin, who was at war with his half-brother Antiochus Grypus. Both of these men were sons of Cleopatra Thea, sister of Cleopatra III of Egypt, and Tryphaena, the eldest daughter of the Egyptian queen, was the wife of Grypus. Cyzicenus married the Egyptian ex-queen, and she was in Antioch, which was in his power, when that city was besieged by Grypus. Antioch was captured and Cleopatra IV was at the mercy of her sister Tryphaena and her husband. The king wished to spare her; Justin puts in his mouth a speech in which he begs his wife to consider the claims of their common blood, and of the sanctity of the temple in which the unhappy queen had taken refuge. Tryphaena thought that she detected the plea of love and not of mercy in her husband's words, and was so enraged that she had her sister killed at the altar where she was clasping the image of Artemis.[187] When Cyzicenus was again victorious, he captured and killed Tryphaena, offering her to appease the spirit of his murdered wife (*eius supplicio uxoris manibus parentavit*).

Thus Cleopatra III had spread war and ruin among her children. Cyzicenus was henceforth her bitter enemy and Grypus her ally. The trouble between Cleopatra III and her son Soter II came to a head when Cyzicenus asked for and obtained from the Egyptian king six thousand men to be used in defence of the Greeks in Samaria who, brought to desperate straits by the siege of their city by the Jewish high-priest Hyrcanus, had appealed to Cyzicenus for help. Ptolemy Lathyrus, Josephus says, sent the troops without his mother's consent and she therefore turned him out of the government. The queen, like her mother Cleopatra II, was strongly pro-

---

[187] Justin, XXXIX, 3.

Jewish and appointed Jews to high position in her army. She seized this opportunity to get rid of her son and at the same time to strengthen herself with the Jewish population in Alexandria, which was second only to the Greek element in the city. Porphyry [188] doubtless gives the queen's version of the expulsion of her son. He says that Ptolemy Soter in the tenth year of his reign killed friends of his parents and because of his wicked acts was sent into exile by the Alexandrians. Pausanias [189] says that Cleopatra caused eunuchs who had been wounded purposely to be brought before the people and declared that they had received their wounds in her defence; in this way she so roused the mob against her son that he fled to save his life and Cleopatra summoned her younger son Alexander from Cyprus to reign with her in Alexandria. This was in the year 108. The queen sent an army to seize her older son when he was established in Cyprus, but the greater part of the soldiers revolted and went over to Ptolemy; only the Jews remained faithful, Josephus says, because of the honor which their countrymen had with the queen. Cleopatra had the commander of the expedition which had been sent to catch her son put to death for his failure to bring him back to Egypt.[190] Ptolemy retreated to Seleuceia-in-Pieria to avoid warring with his mother, not because his forces were unequal to hers (*quamquam Ptolemaeus verecundia materni belli non viribus minor ab insula recessisset.* Justin, *l. c.*). He soon returned and was established as king of Cyprus. The struggles between the Hellenistic cities and the Jews brought both Ptolemy and his mother into Palestine. The two kings in Syria were so busy fighting one another that no help could be expected from them and the people of Ptolemais sent to Ptolemy and asked him to come to deliver them out of the hands of Alexander Jannaeus. Ptolemy landed with a large

---

[188] Porphyry, *F.H.G.* III, p. 721.
[189] Pausan. I, 9, 4; cf. Justin, XXXIX, 4.
[190] Justin, *loc. cit.*

force in Sycamine only to find that those who had summoned him had been induced by one of their leaders to change sides and no longer desired his aid. Josephus tells of Ptolemy's campaign against Ptolemais and against Alexander Jannaeus in Judaea; he was victorious and the Jewish historian accuses him of abominable cruelties. He says that when Cleopatra saw that her son had grown so great and had laid waste Judaea without hindrance and had got Gaza and was almost at her gates, she was afraid that he would return as king of Egypt; she therefore put her army under her two Jewish generals, and ordered her son Alexander to come with the fleet to Phoenicia; she herself went at the head of the land forces to Palestine.[191]

Before leaving Alexandria she sent to Grypus, her former son-in-law who was king at Damascus, her daughter Selene, the ex-wife of Ptolemy, with troops and money for her dowry.[192] After making this political marriage for her youngest and only remaining daughter she took her little grandchildren to the island of Cos and left them in the temple of Aesculapius,[193] depositing there also her will and testament and a great amount of splendid treasures which Mithradates afterward seized in 88 B. C., among them a chlamys said to have been worn by Alexander the Great. She captured Ptolemais, forced her son to withdraw from his advance on Alexandria, and appears to have entertained the idea of recovering Coele-Syria, the old dower land of her grandmother, "the Syrian", for Egypt. But she was dissuaded by the Jews, to whom she attached so much importance; they warned her of the enmity she would arouse against herself among all the Jews everywhere if she seized Jannaeus and made herself mistress of the country. One of her Jewish generals had been killed while in pursuit of Ptolemy, and her son-in-law Grypus did not send her any aid. So she made a treaty of mutual aid and alliance with Alexander Jannaeus in Scythopolis and

---

[191] Josephus, *A.J.* XIII, 13, 1.
[192] Justin, *loc. cit.*
[193] Josephus, *loc. cit.*; Appian, *Mithr.* 23.

returned to Egypt, without having accomplished anything against Cyzicenus, her hated ex-son-in-law, or against Ptolemy Soter, her hated son. Perhaps it was at this time, though Justin places the event before her going to Palestine, that her son Ptolemy Alexander decided that he and Egypt had had enough of Cleopatra's arbitrary and cruel rule and retired from Alexandria, probably to gather an army against her. He returned at her request and Cleopatra's name soon after vanishes from the records. She died some time in the summer of 101 B. C., between September 16 and October 31.[194] Justin says that she was killed by Alexander and that the Alexandrians in rage rose against him and drove him out, recalling Soter. Pausanias also says that justice overtook her when she died by the hand of her son whom she had set in power. Soter however was not recalled until 90 and Cleopatra died eleven years before that. From the year 101 the coins bear only the date of Alexander, and the name of a new queen, Berenice, the sister, goddess Philadelphus,[195] appears. This is the daughter of Ptolemy Soter by his wife Cleopatra IV or his wife Selene.

Cleopatra III's love of pomp and magnificence is reflected in her devotion to religion and her eagerness for religious honors. She was worshipped as Isis, Great Mother of the Gods, and had a special priest called the Holy Foal. She had also the titles of Goddess Mother-loving, Saviour, Justice, and Victorious. She had at least three eponymous priestesses of her various aspects of divinity. Bouché-Leclercq brilliantly says [196] of her cults: " The stephanephoros of Cleopatra Nikephoros precedes the athlophoros of Berenice, her skeptophoros or phosphoros precedes the canephoros of Arsinoe, and her priestess precedes the priestess of Arsinoe Philopator. ' The Saving One ', ' Justice ', ' The Twin of Osiris Euergetes ',

---

[194] Meyer, *Klio*, II, p. 478; *Greek Papyri*, 2nd series, Oxford, 1897, 32; *Tebtunis Pap.* I, 106.

[195] Wilcken, *Urkunden*, I, pp. 458 f.

[196] Bouché-Leclercq, *Lagides*, III, p. 57.

takes rank before the queens of yesterday and leaves them only the place of the shadow beside the light ".

It is sometimes said that she shared the Ptolemaic interest in learning because she sent out the adventurer and explorer Eudoxus of Cyzicus, who had come to Egypt in the reign of her husband and had made various voyages of discovery for that king. Eudoxus brought back from a voyage to India a cargo of perfumes and of precious stones, all of which were taken from him by the Egyptian king. After the death of Euergetes II Cleopatra III sent an expedition on a larger scale to India under Eudoxus. He is said not to have returned until her reign was over.[197] His second cargo also was confiscated; so it is likely that the perfumes and other valuable things that he brought back prompted the queen to finance and patronize his expedition, rather than the geographical information and the lists of words from strange languages which he acquired.

Cleopatra III long outlived her sister Cleopatra Thea, the Syrian queen who was killed by her son Grypus in 121. She survived longest of the children of Cleopatra II and Philometor and was survived by both her sons and by her daughter Selene, who was married first to her brother Ptolemy Soter II, then to Antiochus Grypus of Syria, then to his half-brother and rival, Antiochus Cyzicenus, who had married her sister Cleopatra IV of Egypt and had killed her sister Tryphaena, wife of Grypus; after his death Selene's wealth made her so desirable that she succeeded in getting another husband, Antiochus Eusebes, by whom she had two sons. Antiochus Eusebes was the son of her preceding husband.

Cleopatra III was a woman of the same stamp as her mother Cleopatra II and her grandmother Cleopatra " The Syrian ", and had more scope for her activities than they, as she had a longer time to reign in widowhood and was able to keep her sons from exercising power. She has the reputation of being a worse woman than the earlier Cleopatras,

---

[197] Posidonius ap. Strab. II, 98 ff.

chiefly because she was a meddlesome despot. Both she and
her mother were reared in a court that was a hotbed of corrupt
and Oriental softness of living, and both preserved to an
extraordinary degree the only virtues that could flourish in
the Alexandrian palace, high courage, endurance, and ability
to rule. They were far better in these respects than the men
of the time. Like the other women of the dynasty, Cleopatra
appears to have had no lovers; her foible was autocracy, not
amorous adventure. "Her whim was her only rule up to the
day when her despotism was cut short by assassination." [198]

For a longer time and to a greater degree than with any
other woman of her dynasty her actual power was recognized.
Her energies were wasted in quarrels with her sons and in
spite of her iron will and great ability one does not get the
impression of such a genuine understanding of politics as that
which her grandmother and her mother both appear to have
possessed. The one touch of humanity in any record of her
is purely accidental; Appian says that her little grandson
was left in Cos in the temple of Aesculapius ὑπὸ τῆς μάμμης,
and that loving word for grandmother lends her a moment
of tenderness and reminds us that she very likely loved
her own little children and grandchildren. But most of all
she loved power. She was very probably nearing sixty when
she died; it is not unlikely that Justin is right in saying
that her son killed her and it is probable that no one mourned
her death. She was an energetic despot and a singularly
unsympathetic character. Though it was her passion to rule,
there is nothing to show that she was in any real sense a
great ruler.

SELENE, CLEOPATRA V

Cleopatra V was that Selene, sister and wife of Ptolemy
Lathyrus and perhaps mother of Berenice III, the story of
whose adventures in Syria when sent there by her mother to
marry Antiochus Grypus in 102 B. C. at the time when
Cleopatra III was invading Coele-Syria, has already been told.

---

[198] Bouché-Leclercq, *Lagides*, III, p. 58.

FIGURE 10.

SARDONYX CAMEO WITH HEAD OF A PTOLEMAIC QUEEN.   HELLENISTIC GREEK WORK.

Boston Museum of Fine Arts.

She was the wife of one king of Egypt and of three Seleucid kings, Antiochus Grypus, Antiochus Cyzicenus and Antiochus Eusebes, son of Cyzicenus and nephew of Grypus. Appian [199] states as his own opinion that the Syrians gave her last husband the title of Pious because he had honored his father and his uncle in marrying the lady of their choice, his step-mother.

We learn from Cicero [200] that her two sons by her last husband (*regis Antiochi filios pueros*) came to Rome in 75 B. C., sent by their mother to claim the throne of Egypt which was occupied by a bastard son of Lathyrus, Selene's brother and former husband, for her and themselves. Cicero says, " They did not come about the Syrian throne, for that they held without dispute, as they had inherited it from their father and their forbears, but they claimed that the throne of Egypt belonged to them and to their mother Selene." They apparently were very rich and their mother at that time was living in dignity and wealth in Ptolemais. Here she was captured by Tigranes of Armenia in 69 B. C. and taken by him to Seleuceia on the Euphrates where she was killed.[201] Her sons had failed in Rome to obtain a hearing for their claims, and the elder son, Antiochus, was shamefully robbed by Verres on a visit to Sicily on his way home to Syria. This son was Asiaticus, who became king in Antioch with the consent of Lucullus, but did not keep his ancestral kingdom long. Pompey refused to give back to him the kingdom which he had lost—Justin says " what Lucullus had given, Pompey took away ".[202] Syria became a Roman province, and Selene's son Antiochus XIII, who was all but the last of the Seleucid kings, was killed by an Arab chief. The outline which we have of the adventurous life of Selene is instructive in revealing how much the wealth and prestige of a daughter of the house of Ptolemy, combined with the high spirit inherited

---

[199] Appian, *Syr.* 69.

[200] Cicero, *Verres*, IV, 27.

[201] Strabo, XVI, 749; Josephus, *A.J.* XIII, 16, 5; *B.J.* I, 5, 3.

[202] Justin, XL. 2. Justin calls the young man son of Antiochus Cyzicenus.

from Cleopatra III, could achieve. If she was fourteen or fifteen at the time of her marriage to her brother in 116, she would be about sixty when she died in 69 B. C. A doubt has been expressed of the likelihood of Selene's being young enough in 90 B. C. when she would be about forty, to bear the two sons of whom we hear from Cicero, and it has been suggested that a younger Selene was their mother. Bevan says, " One must remember that women age more quickly in the south. It is not impossible that Selene might have borne children when over forty, but highly improbable." [203] I do not know what the statistics are for southern nations, but the bearing of children by women over forty is such a common phenomenon in England and America that it appears not improbable in a woman of such vigor and vitality as Selene's life shows her to have been. Appian makes the definite statement that she married the three Seleucids, Grypus, Cyzicenus and Eusebes, and we know from Justin that when she was sent by her mother to marry Grypus in Syria she was the ex-wife of her brother, the then king of Egypt. The fact that she sent her sons to Rome to claim the throne of Egypt from the bastard son of Ptolemy Soter II indicates that she reckoned on a very close connection with the ruling house of Egypt, and that close connection was hers if she was indeed the daughter of Euergetes III and Cleopatra III.[204]

BERENICE III,

ALSO CALLED CLEOPATRA [205]

Berenice III was the daughter of Ptolemy Soter II and of one of the two sisters whom he married; it is not known of which. The date of Berenice's birth is therefore uncertain.

---

[203] Bevan, *Egypt*, p. 334, n. 4, replying to Bouché-Leclercq, *Lagides*, II, p. 106, n. 3. *Cf. House of Seleucus*, II, p. 304.

[204] Dr. Constantine Kalamara of Athens has kindly sent me statistics of a considerable number of births in his obstetric clinic, in which the women bearing the children have been forty years old or over.

[205] Wilcken, *Urkunden*, I, n. 125, pp. 591 ff.; *O.G.I.* 740.

If the daughter of Cleopatra IV, she may have been born
before her father was associated in the government of Egypt
in 116 B. C.; if Selene was her mother, she could not have
been born before 114 B. C. When her father was exiled she
was left with her grandmother and her mother, if Selene was
her mother, in Alexandria. Her name first appears with that
of her uncle Ptolemy Alexander in a papyrus dated Oct. 31,
101, and she was doubtless married to him in 102-101 B. C.
She is called the goddess Philadelphus.[206] Her uncle had a
son of the same name as himself whose mother is not known.
Bouché-Leclercq [207] suggests the possibility that he might
have sprung from a temporary union of Cleopatra IV and her
brother Alexander at the time when she left Alexandria, divorced by her mother from Lathyrus, and came to Cyprus to
hire a mercenary army. This child had been brought up in
the island of Cos, left there by his grandmother when she was
invading Palestine in the war against Cyzicenus and her son
Ptolemy. Mithradates had taken charge of him in 88 and
reared him as an heir to a throne.[208]

Berenice had at least one daughter [209] by her uncle, but of
the fate of this girl nothing is known. A "proskynema" of the
royal family records a visit of king Ptolemy Alexander and
the queen and the children to the temple of Isis at Philae.
Her husband is said by Posidonius [210] to have been hated by
his people, but fawned upon by his *entourage,* and to have
indulged his appetites to the degree that he became extremely
fat and unable to proceed except with the support of a slave
on either side, yet he had some skill in leaping from couch
to couch in drunken dances in drinking bouts. He was
driven from his throne in 89 and though he displayed energy
in raising a mercenary army (which he paid by coining
Alexander's gold coffin, if he is the Ptolemy referred to in
the story of that episode in Strabo XVII, p. 794) he got back

---

[206] *Tebtunis Pap.* I, 106.
[207] *Lagides*, II, p. 93, n. 1.
[208] Appian, *Mithr.* XXIII.

[209] Porphyry, *F.H.G.* III, p. 722.
[210] Athen. XII, 550.

to Alexandria only temporarily and was again obliged to flee the country and went to Syria with his wife and daughter. He was killed next year in an encounter with the Alexandrians off Cyprus.

Berenice returned to Egypt to reign with her father, Ptolemy Soter, called Lathyrus, who came back from exile in the odor of sanctity since he had shown piety toward his mother when attacked by her in war,[211] and was now called ποθεινός, "the king of their desire". In the first three years of his reign he put down a native rebellion, and Pausanias says that he practically destroyed Thebes.[212] After that he reigned in peace keeping himself from entangling alliances with Sulla and Lucullus in 87-86 B. C. when Sulla was besieging Athens. He did offer Lucullus [213] a splendid emerald with his own head carved on it, and this the Roman general at first refused, but seeing the king's head upon it took it, for fear that a refusal might be counted an insult and endanger his passage to Cyprus, as Ptolemy was sending a convoy of ships with him. The Athenians were grateful to Ptolemy for help after Sulla's spoiling of their city and raised statues in bronze " of him and of Berenice, his only legitimate child ".[214]

Ptolemy died in 80 B. C. and Berenice was his heir. The two had been called in official documents " The Gods Philadelphoi Philometores Soteres ", the father taking the title Philadelphus from his daughter, Berenice Philadelphus. The country was without a male ruler and the women of the royal household according to Appian [215] desired a male kinsman. The child left in Cos by Cleopatra III in 102 B. C., and taken by Mithradates in 88 B. C. and educated by him for eight years, had escaped from the Pontic court to Sulla, who now sent him to be king of Egypt. Porphyry says that he came

---

[211] Justin, XXXIX, 5; Euseb. II, 364.

[212] Pausan. I, 9, 3.

[213] Plut. *Lucullus*, II-III. Plutarch makes the curious error of calling the old Ptolemy a lad at the time of this episode.

[214] Pausan. *loc. cit.*,

[215] Appian, *B.C.* I, 102.

in response to a call from the Alexandrians, which does not seem probable, nor is it likely that Berenice wished him to share her power. He married her and within three weeks had her assassinated, a deed that roused her subjects to frenzy, for they had loved her; the young murderer was seized by an angry mob that took him to the Gymnasium where he was killed.[216] Cicero says in a fragment, *de rege Alexandrino*,— " I see that it is a recognized fact that the king after killing with his own hands his sister, who was dear to her people and established in their affections, was himself killed by the fury of the mob ".

Berenice [217] was much older than the young man who married and murdered her; neither of them left children, and the next heir was an illegitimate son of Ptolemy Lathyrus who had been living at the court of Mithradates.

CLEOPATRA VI, TRYPHAENA, WIFE OF PTOLEMY XI, AULETES

Ptolemy Alexander II had shown the fruit of the royal training at the Pontic court under that expert in murder, Mithradates Eupator, by his assassination of his aunt Berenice, who had for dynastic reasons become his wife. The Ptolemy who succeeded him, called Auletes, had had the same environment and training as a protegé of the royal poisoner, and his younger brother Ptolemy had been reared at that court and possibly Cleopatra Tryphaena also, if she was one of the same group of illegitimate children of Lathyrus. It was a bad start for any young prince to be protected by the Pontic king, and of Ptolemy XI Cicero says that he was possessed of " neither royal birth nor royal spirit ".[218] Who

---

[216] Porphyry, *F.H.G.* III, pp. 722 f.

[217] Berenice III is called Cleopatra by Porphyry. In the Greek documents she is called Berenice up to 97 B. C. Later she is called Cleopatra and possibly in one papyrus Cleopatra Berenice. Spiegelberg, *Demot. Papyri aus den königlichen Mus. zu Berlin* (1902), 16; Strack, *Dynastie*, pp. 56, 107.

[218] Cicero, *De Lege Agraria*, II, 42, neque genere neque animo regio.

his mother was, is never stated. Mithradates thought well
enough of his chances in life, apparently, to betroth one of
his daughters to him during his stay in Pontus, for Appian
says [219]—" His two daughters, Mithradatis and Nyssa, had
been betrothed by Mithradates (ἠγγυημέναι) while still girls
to the kings of Egypt and of Cyprus, while being brought up
(συντρεφόμεναι) with them." This sentence has caused much
trouble because the tenses of the participles have not been
noted, and it has even been held [220] that Ptolemy XI was
betrothed to one of these girls between 69 and 63 (Strack,
p. 67). It is clear that the betrothal was a move on the part
of Mithradates at the time when he had the young Ptolemies
at his court and reflected that, bastards though they were,
they were the only Ptolemies of the male line left to inherit.

Since a document of the date Jan. 17, 79 B. C.[221] has been
discovered in which Ptolemy and Cleopatra Tryphaena appear
as " Gods Father-loving and Brother-and-Sister-Loving," it
is evident that a marriage was arranged for the young king
at once on his accession. If the new queen was his own sister
and had been brought up with him in Syria and Pontus, the
adjective Philadelphoi and the immediateness of the marriage
are accounted for. It seems very probable that Cleopatra
Tryphaena was a full sister [222] of her husband, and that the
marriage in the old Egyptian tradition and in that of the
Ptolemaic house was thought to give a sanctity to the new
rulers, whose illegitimacy was a bar to their being recognized
by Rome.

The Romans were claiming that Egypt was their property.
Cicero [223] says—" Every one knows the story that Egypt has

---

[219] Appian, *Mithr.* CXI.

[220] See Bouché-Leclercq, *Lagides*, II, 145, n. 1.

[221] Preisigke-Spiegelberg, *Prinz-Joachim Ostraka*, n. 1. Cf. pp. 20 f.

[222] Preisigke thinks that the occurrence of the word " sister " on
the slab proves that Auletes married his own sister, but the word
may be merely the conventional title. Cleopatra very likely was the
sister of Auletes, but the title " Sister " proves nothing.

[223] Cicero, *De Lege Agraria*, II, 41.

been left to the Roman people by the will of the king of
Alexandria ". He refuses to give his opinion in the matter,
but says that it is common talk that such a will exists.
Moreover the much-married queen Selene, Cleopatra V of
Egypt, who had married three Seleucids after her separation
from Ptolemy VIII, had two legitimate sons whom she sent
to Rome in 75 to claim the throne of Egypt. They would be
own cousins of the illegitimate Ptolemies who were now
reigning in Alexandria. Their claims were not recognized.
The question of recognizing Ptolemy Auletes was a burning
one at Rome. His brother Ptolemy was king of Cyprus and
in the end committed suicide rather than hand Cyprus and
his wealth over to the Romans. Ptolemy of Egypt was a
worthless man according to all accounts of him, but he was
in a terrible position. As Bouché-Leclercq says:[224] " He
bought day by day the right to rule, and the Roman senators
exacted a high price." Cassius Dio says:[225] " He had spent
large amounts of money on some of the Romans, partly from
his own pocket and partly borrowed, in order to be recognized
and to be called friend and ally, and he was now collecting
this sum by force from the Egyptians."

About Tryphaena, the queen, we know nothing certain except
her name. The question of the greatest interest in connection
with her is whether she was the mother of the famous Cleopatra VII. It is strange indeed that no one of the historians
in whose pages the name of the last Cleopatra of Egypt so
often gleams has any mention of her mother, who is as obscure as her daughter is illustrious. In the turmoil of
anxiety, debts, and bribery in which the life of Auletes was
passed his wife escapes notice almost completely. Her name
is not found in the papyri after August 7, 69 B. C., and
Strabo says that of the three daughters of Auletes only the
eldest was legitimate. As Strabo considers Berenice the eldest, this statement may be a mistaken echo of the fact that

---

[224] Bouché-Leclercq, *Lagides*, II, pp. 175-6.
[225] XXXIX, 12.

13

Berenice III was the only legitimate child of Lathyrus, for
the name of Cleopatra appears with that of her husband on
the pylon of the temple at Edfu:—" Ptolemy, young Osiris,
with his sister queen Cleopatra named Tryphaena "—with a
date corresponding to Dec. 5, 57 B. C. Further Porphyry [226]
says that two daughters of Auletes, Cleopatra Tryphaena and
Berenice, ruled together for one year while the king was in
Rome, and that after the death of Cleopatra Berenice ruled
alone for two years. A reign of two sisters is unheard of in the
Ptolemaic dynasty. Either Cleopatra, a daughter of Auletes,
ruled alone for one year,[227] a fact that is nowhere attested, or
else we have a natural arrangement of the mother Cleopatra
reigning alone, as guardian of the younger children, in her
husband's absence, or perhaps the mother, who may have been
somewhat incompetent, reigned with her spirited daughter for
one year after her husband disappeared. He was even thought
dead by his subjects. As Bouché-Leclercq says, all difficulties
are resolved if we accept the evidence for the prolongation
of the life of Cleopatra Tryphaena until 57 B. C. It is not
possible in any case to reconcile the two authorities Porphyry
and Strabo, since the latter is evidently thinking of Berenice,
though he does not mention her name, as the queen appointed
by the Alexandrians, whom he calls the only legitimate
daughter of Auletes. He speaks of three daughters, and the
other two would of course be Cleopatra VII and Arsinoe, both
well known to history. If there was a daughter Cleopatra
Tryphaena, as Porphyry states, who succeeded Auletes in 59
B. C. during his exile in Rome, she would be the eldest and
on Strabo's statement the only legitimate daughter, and this
gives four daughters to Auletes, not three. If we agree that
both Strabo and Porphyry cannot be right in their data and
admit some inaccuracy in both, the matter can be made
clear by accepting Cleopatra Tryphaena as the only legitimate wife of Auletes, who for some unknown reason is not

---

[226] Porphyry, *F.H.G.* III, p. 723.

[227] This was the opinion of Strack (*Dynastie*, pp. 67 f.), though
he later modified it (Cf. Bouché-Leclercq, *Lagides*, IV, p. 327).

mentioned in the papyri after 69 B. C., but is mentioned as wife of Ptolemy XI on the pylon of the temple at Edfu in an inscription of the year 57 B. C. The strange facts that no mother of the great Cleopatra, Arsinoe, and the two brother Ptolemies is ever mentioned, and that no charge of illegitimacy was ever brought by Rome against Cleopatra and her two brothers are explained, if all these children of Auletes were also children of his wife Cleopatra Tryphaena. She was apparently a lady of no spirit, though she bore three daughters who were notable for their daring and boldness. She seemingly made no impression on the course of events of her time, when Rome was threatening Egypt and her husband was harassed by debts and political difficulties in Rome and in Egypt, finding his distractions from his troubles in fluteplaying and less innocent amusements. We should be glad to know more of the mother of three such remarkable daughters as Berenice IV, Cleopatra VII, and Arsinoe, the youngest, who for a short time commanded an Egyptian army in revolt against Caesar and Cleopatra and afterward suffered the proud humiliation of walking in Caesar's triumph in Rome.

If Cleopatra Tryphaena was the mother of all the children of Auletes who appear in history, she bore him five children, Berenice, Cleopatra, Arsinoe, Ptolemy XII, and Ptolemy XIII, and reigned for one year in Alexandria before her death, during her husband's exile in Rome.

If Auletes was, as Cicero says in his fragment, *De Rege Alexandrino,* a boy in Syria when called to Egypt to be king at Alexandria, he was perhaps fifteen years old at the time, and was the son of some concubine of Lathyrus whom the latter had had while he was king of Cyprus before he returned to Egypt. If Cleopatra Tryphaena was his full sister, she was perhaps younger than he. Ptolemy Lathyrus returned to Egypt in 88 B. C. and took no new wife, perhaps being contented with the mother of his illegitimate children. If Cleopatra Tryphaena was hardly more than a child at the time of the marriage to Auletes in 79, she may not have had

children for some years. Arsinoe III in similar case did not
bear her son Ptolemy V until after eight years of marriage
to her brother Ptolemy IV. We do not know the date of the
birth of queen Berenice, Cleopatra Tryphaena's oldest child,
but she was old enough to be regent with her mother in
58-57 B. C.

Indeed this wraith-like queen gives almost an impression
of unreality in the dearth of information about her. It is
significant of the unavoidable fate of Egypt that henceforth
the complications with Rome afford the most important
knowledge that we have of the affairs of the old Ptolemaic
realm. We know that Cleopatra Tryphaena was the wife of a
wastrel king who bought from the Romans the right to reign;
she was probably the mother of the most famous woman of
all time. But what quality of greatness or of beauty Mark
Antony's "Serpent of old Nile" inherited from her we do
not know.

BERENICE IV

Berenice IV, who reigned at Alexandria from 58 B. C. to
55 B. C., was the eldest, and Strabo says the only legitimate
daughter of Ptolemy Auletes. The reasons for considering
this statement of Strabo's incorrect have already been discussed. The exact date of Berenice's birth is not known;
it may be, as I have suggested before, that her mother was
too young to bear children at the time of her marriage with
her fifteen-year-old husband, and Berenice's birth may have
been delayed for some years after 79 B. C., in which year
Ptolemy Auletes and Cleopatra Tryphaena were married.
The father of Berenice had a very precarious seat on the
throne of Egypt because of his own illegitimacy and the
designs of Rome upon Egypt. He spent much of his life
and substance in bribing eminent Romans to obtain for him
recognition as king of Egypt and friend and ally of Rome;
he attained this recognition at last in 59 B. C. by the payment
of a very large sum of money to Julius Caesar, consul that
year in Rome. This arrangement did not end his troubles,

for he had to collect the money by forcible means in Egypt.[228] Dio says that the Egyptians were enraged at his procedure and much roused against him because he would not listen to their demand that he require the Romans to give Cyprus back to Egypt, or else renounce their friendship. This was a counsel of perfection that the king could by no means follow. He slipped away to Rome, accused his subjects of expelling him, and sought from the Romans a forcible restoration to his land. The Alexandrians did not know nor care where he had gone and even entertained the pleasant thought that he might be dead. Dio [229] says that they placed Berenice his daughter on the throne, but it appears from Porphyry [230] that Cleopatra Tryphaena, the mother of Berenice, ruled for a year; possibly Auletes had left his affairs in his wife's hands. The two sons were little children, and it would be according to precedent for the mother to be left guardian of the male heir. Berenice, according to Porphyry, reigned for two years alone after her sister's (*sic*) death.

When the Alexandrians heard that their king was alive and in Rome, they promptly sent one hundred men to that city to defend them against the charges made by Auletes and to state their own grievances. Auletes had influence enough to get rid of the envoys by assassination, or intimidation or bribery. The scandal reached the ears of the Senate, and Marcus Favonius urged action of some kind, since so many foreign envoys had been killed and so many Romans bribed. Auletes, however, was temporarily in funds again and the investigation came to nothing. A thunderbolt which struck the statue of Jupiter on the Alban Mount was regarded as an indication that bribe-taking by so many eminent Romans was not approved by Heaven, and a Sibylline oracle was read to the following effect: " If the king of Egypt come requesting aid, do not refuse him friendship and do not help him with

---

[228] Cassius Dio, XXXIX, 12, 1-2.
[229] Cassius Dio, XXXIX, 13, 1.
[230] *F.H.G.* III, p. 723. (Porphyry calls Cleopatra Tryphaena a sister of Berenice).

numbers, or you will have struggles and perils." Cato made
this oracle public, and there was much discussion of what
should be done for Ptolemy,—whether Spinther should restore him without an army, or Pompey should escort him
home with two lictors. Ptolemy was all for the latter course,
but the senators thought that Pompey might get too much
out of this arrangement and so opposed it. Ptolemy, in
despair, went to Ephesus and took sanctuary with the goddess
Artemis in her temple at the end of the year 57. Here he
hoped that he might bribe Gabinius, the proconsul of Syria,
to restore him.[231]

In Alexandria the court was looking for a suitable man to
marry Berenice, and first asked one of the sons of Selene who
had come to Rome in 75 to claim the throne of Egypt. This
young man was a cousin of Auletes and a grandson of
Euergetes II. An embassy went to offer him Berenice's
hand, but he died before the negotiations were completed.
The Alexandrians next thought of another young Seleucid,
Philip II, great-grandson of Euergetes II and son of Philip,
last Seleucid king of Syria, who had been expelled by
Pompey. Gabinius, who was Pompey's man, objected to the
match as against the interests of Rome, and Philip did not
dare to accept the hand of the Egyptian queen against the
command of the Roman pro-consul.[232] The next year
Gabinius prepared to restore Auletes, and the Alexandrians
in haste secured a Seleucid of doubtful antecedents and worse
than doubtful manners. He was so ill-bred that the Alexandrians, always quick in nicknaming their rulers, at once
called him " Fish-packer " (κυβιοσάκτης), and Berenice, adept
by inheritance in what is called politely " dynastic murder ",
had him strangled [233] after a few days of his society. In all
haste then, for circumstances pressed and her father's return
was imminent, she allied herself to an energetic man,
Archelaus, an old friend of Mark Antony, who gave himself

[231] Cassius Dio, XXXIX, 15-16.
[232] Porphyry, *F.H.G.* III, 716.
[233] Strabo, XVII, 796; Cassius Dio, XXXIX, 57.

out as son of Mithradates the Great and had been given by
Pompey the position of high priest in the temple at Comana.
Gabinius had got money from Archelaus for letting him go
to Egypt and money from Ptolemy as a bribe to restore that
monarch to his throne. This latter task, Plutarch says,
Gabinius did not much like, but was "absolutely enslaved"
by the ten thousand talents which Auletes offered him. Mark
Antony was with him in command of the cavalry of the invading army.[234] He captured Pelusium and its garrison and
when Auletes came, mad with the desire for vengeance and
determined to kill all the captives, Antony prevented his
murderous designs, thereby acquiring merit with the Alexandrians which was to serve him in good stead later. He sought
out and buried the body of Archelaus, who was killed in the
fighting, and this, too, was remembered with gratitude by the
conquered people. He saw in Alexandria a young girl of
fourteen who was in every sense of the word to be his "fate".
This was the princess Cleopatra. Appian[235] says that Antony
was teased by the sight of her beauty at that time. Plutarch
speaks of Archelaus as fallen in battle, whereas Cassius Dio
says that Gabinius put to death Archelaus and many others
and then restored Egypt, which was entirely in his power, to
Ptolemy. The king killed his daughter Berenice at once, and
being in need of great sums of money to pay his Roman debts,
he also killed many of the wealthiest Alexandrians. He was
restored in the year 55 and died four years later, the most
worthless of all the Ptolemies.

Berenice passes from the stage of the Ptolemaic royalties
a victim of her father's baseness and of Roman avarice. The
two qualities which her short life and reign display are those
manifested over and over again by the royal women of Macedonian blood, high courage and the unscrupulous cruelty
which she showed in her instant strangling of her lout of a
husband, the "Fish-packer". A phrase used by Cassius
Dio [236] about her—"fearing the Romans"—illuminates the

---

[234] Plut. *Ant.* III.
[235] Appian, *B.C.* V, 8.
[236] XXXIX, 57.

later conduct of her young sister Cleopatra in all her relations
with the Roman generals with whom she allied herself.
Cleopatra in her childhood saw her father ceaselessly beseeching Rome for recognition as king of Egypt; she saw Rome
restoring her father and killing the king-consort, the husband
of her sister, the Queen; she saw her sister who had dared
defy Rome killed without mercy. What wonder that the
vision of Rome was always with her, that she sought the
Roman invader in her war with her brother and found her
strength and her pride in alliances with Romans, giving up
everything for the sake of being recognized by Rome as queen
of Egypt, and in the end cherished as her dearest wish that
of being queen also in the great city where her father had
begged and bribed for her ancestral throne?

CLEOPATRA VII (Fig. 11)

Cleopatra VII was queen of Egypt from the death of her
father Auletes in 51 B. C. until 30 B. C., when she came into
the power of Octavian and ended her life rather than walk
in his triumphal procession. In her the Ptolemaic dynasty
established by Alexander's friend and general, Ptolemy the
Macedonian, son of Lagos and Arsinoe, had its final flowering.
The women of the line had almost without exception retained
the dominant qualities of the Macedonians, while the later
kings were sunk in sloth and sensuality. Her mother I
believe to have been Cleopatra Tryphaena, the only wife of
Ptolemy Auletes, but since the evidence is meagre it is disputed whether Cleopatra VII was the legitimate child of two
illegitimate royalties, or the illegitimate child of one of them.
Who her mother was may be a matter of dispute, but what
is undoubted is that Cleopatra herself was of the same breed
as the Eurydices, Arsinoes, Berenices, and Cleopatras who
preceded her in Macedonia, Egypt, and Syria, and showed
themselves " no unequal rivals of the men ". She is more
famous than all the rest, not that she was more beautiful or
more strong of character, but she had enchanting ways which

Fig. 11.

Bust of Cleopatra VII of Egypt.

British Museum.

were irresistible—the world is still caught in her "strong toyle of grace"—and destiny made her not only queen of Egypt but mistress of the greatest Romans of her time.

The percentage of Macedonian, Persian, and possible Greek blood in her has been carefully reckoned and the suggestion has not been lacking that she had a Jewish strain; this last supposition is based on such slight evidence as her curving nose and her facility in languages. She was, whatever the mixture of her blood, the last royal Macedonian, and in her their glory ends in a sunset of splendor. Auletes had bequeathed the kingdom to his elder daughter and elder son, Cleopatra and her brother Ptolemy XII, who were respectively about seventeen and ten years old at the time of their father's death. A copy of his will had been deposited by him at Alexandria and one had been sent to Rome. Caesar [237] is a witness for this fact. The charge of the Palace and the government was in the hands of the kind of men who flourished in the Alexandrian court-life since the time of Ptolemy IV, the most important of whom at this time was the eunuch Pothinus. Associated with him was a Greek from Chios who was tutor of the young king; his name was Theodotus, and he is branded forever in history as the one who, to gain favor, as he thought, brought the head and signet-ring of the foully murdered Pompey to Caesar. There was also the commander of the troops, Achillas, whom Plutarch [238] calls an Egyptian.

Cleopatra appears in action from the beginning of her reign. Valerius Maximus [239] relates that when the Gabinian soldiers who had settled in Egypt and had become part of the permanent population of Alexandria killed two young Romans, sons of the pro-consul of Syria, Marcus Calpurnius Bibulus, who had been sent to call them back to Syria, the young queen sent the murderers to the pro-consul for punishment. This first act of her reign of which we know indicates her intention to keep on good terms with Rome. Bibulus

---

[237] Caesar, *B.C.* III, 108.
[238] Plut. *Pompey*, LXXVII.
[239] Valerius Maximus, IV, 1, 16.

was a friend of Pompey, and Cleopatra's father had been restored to Egypt partly by the good offices of Pompey. So when his eldest son, Gnaeus Pompey, came to Alexandria two years later in 49 B. C. seeking ships, men, and money from the queen and her brother, he was given sixty ships and five hundred Gabinian soldiers besides supplies of corn. Plutarch suggests [240] that Cleopatra had her first Roman love-affair with the young Pompey. But the young man sailed away with his fleet to Corcyra (he was killed fighting in Spain in 45 B. C.) and the next year Caesar came to Egypt and into Cleopatra's life. Her strong will had already asserted itself in a manner that caused the court triumvirate of Pothinus, Theodotus, and Achillas to fear her, and they resolved to get rid of her. She was accused of wishing to put her brother aside and in the fourth year of her queenship she was driven from Egypt by the eunuch and his fellows. But she was, and intended to remain, *basilissa* of Egypt. She was rich, and without difficulty raised a mercenary army, probably in Arabia, and returned to regain her crown. Caesar writes that when he came to Egypt in pursuit of Pompey, he found at Pelusium the boy-king with a great force, at war with his sister Cleopatra, whose camp was but a short distance from that of Ptolemy.

The great Pompey had tried to land at this time, seeking succor from the young king whose father he had befriended. Plutarch in his great tragic way tells of the coming of the fugitive to Alexandria and of his assassination in the boat which brought him to the shore, by the hand of a soldier who had earlier fought under his banner. This was done by order of the creatures who ruled the young king, and according to Plutarch Caesar burst into tears when he was given Pompey's seal with the lion carved on it. Now that his great enemy was murdered he turned his attention to the affairs of Egypt. The story of his dealing with the Alexandrians and the young monarchs is told in the books on the Civil War and the Alexandrine War which go under Caesar's name. The

---

[240] Plut. *Ant.* XXV.

Alexandrians were enraged when they saw Caesar marching through their streets with the *fasces* of Roman authority borne before him by the lictors, and he was threatened by the crowds who thought that the majesty of their rulers was insulted.[241] When his men were killed by the eunuch Pothinus, Caesar at once proceeded to get young Ptolemy in his power. He leaves it for Plutarch and Dio to tell of the romantic flight of the young queen from her camp at Pelusium to Alexandria, where she arrived in a little boat and was carried wrapped in a roll of bedding into the presence of the Roman general, thus escaping assassination by the eunuch who hated her. Plutarch says that Caesar was at once captivated by the dash and beauty of the girl as she suddenly emerged from the bundle of bed-covers, but Caesar himself writes nothing of this. Dio[242] says that when Ptolemy saw his sister with Caesar the next day, he rushed out of the palace before the crowd and threw down his diadem, crying that he had been betrayed. The Roman guards seized him, and the mob threatened to kill Caesar, who came forward and spoke to them, promising to carry out their wishes. In an assembly of the Alexandrians he, representing the Roman people, read the will of the late king of Egypt and ordered that Cleopatra and Ptolemy should marry and rule Egypt under the protection of Rome. He also proposed, according to Dio, to let Arsinoe and the younger Ptolemy rule in Cyprus, which was now a Roman possession. The young king and Cleopatra celebrated their marriage with a great festival,[243] and Caesar remained in the Palace with the four young Ptolemies, of whom the eldest was his mistress. Arsinoe, jealous of her sister's power, or incited by Pothinus, escaped with her eunuch Ganymedes and went to the army at Pelusium, where she was proclaimed queen of Egypt.[244] Although but seventeen years old she demanded to share the

---

[241] Caesar, *B.C.* III, 106.

[242] Cassius Dio, XLII, 35 ff.

[243] Plut. *Caes.* XLIX.

[244] Cassius Dio, XLII, 39; Caesar *B. C.* III, 112.

command of the army and the direction of the war with
Achillas. Caesar gives an interesting account of the mongrel
character of the troops under Achillas. Arsinoe soon quar-
reled with the Egyptian and had him killed; she then took
the entire command without let or hindrance, putting her
eunuch in charge of the fighting-men. His method was to
increase the largesses to them with which Arsinoe and
Achillas had been vying for their favor, but he was hated by
the soldiers for his cruelties, and they soon grew sick of the
whims of their girl-commander (multitudinem confectam
taedio puellae) and sent to Caesar asking for their king,
whom Caesar kept under his eye in the Palace. He allowed
the boy to go after giving him good advice. According to
the author of the Alexandrine War Ptolemy, after weeping
crocodile tears and begging to be allowed to stay with Caesar,
bounded away like a hind let loose and belied the tears which
he had shed in Caesar's presence by the fierceness of the war
which he waged against the Romans. In the final battle
which gave Caesar the victory and the possession of Egypt
the young king was drowned in the Nile in the attempt to
escape.[245] Caesar then gave the kingdom to the younger
brother and to Cleopatra, " who had remained loyal to him
and under his protection," [246] and decided to take Arsinoe
to Rome with him to prevent any uprising to put her on the
throne.

The writer of the Alexandrine War cynically enough defends Caesar from the charge that his motive in releasing
the young Ptolemy was an impulse of generosity (bonitas)
and says that the act was one of the shrewdest possible
political moves. (Quasi vero id Caesar bonitate tantum
adductus ac non prudentissimo consilio fecisset. ibid. 24).
Caesar's best asset was Cleopatra, and it suited his book to
have the young king out of the way and also to put the
princess Arsinoe in a place where she could not create dis-
affection among the Alexandrians. It was easy to arrange

---

[245] Caesar, *Bell. Alex.* 31.   [246] Caesar, *B.A.* 33.

that his mistress Cleopatra and the remaining brother, who was about twelve, should reign together as Father-loving Gods.[247] Cleopatra was already (January, 47 B. C.) with child by Caesar, and it is probable that she did not intend that the new boy-king Ptolemy XIII should be her permanent co-regent. With Arsinoe in Rome and Ptolemy XII drowned in the Nile the young queen of Egypt had little to fear, so long as she had at her side the greatest Roman of the moment. They took a pleasure-trip together up the Nile in a splendid boat, and they would have gone into Ethiopia if the soldiers had not rebelled against this plan. In June their son was born, said to be very like his father in features and to walk like him when he grew older.[248] It is quite clear from Plutarch's statement that Caesar had gone to Syria before Cleopatra's child was born. He says: "He left as sovereign of Egypt Cleopatra, who shortly afterward bore him a son, and marched to Syria." [249] Weigall [250] is entirely incorrect about this when he says, "Plutarch's statement may be interpreted as meaning that Caesar departed to Syria after the birth of his son." The tense of the verbs makes this inference impossible. The child was named for his father and was known by the diminutive Caesarion. Three legions under the command of Rufinus had been left by Caesar to guard Cleopatra's power. The old Palace triumvirate, Pothinus, Theodotus, Achillas, had all been killed and Cleopatra reigned secure, supported by the Roman legions.

In Caesar's great triumph in 46 B. C. he celebrated the subjugation of four peoples, the Gauls, Pontus, Libya, and Egypt, and in the processions walked a little boy, Juba of Mauretania, who was some day to marry the last Cleopatra, daughter of Mark Antony and the Queen of Egypt. "Most

---

[247] Cassius Dio, XLII, 44.

[248] Plut. *Caesar*, XLIX; Suet. *Caesar*, 52.

[249] Καταλιπὼν δὲ τὴν Κλεοπάτραν βασιλεύουσαν Αἰγύπτου καὶ μικρὸν ὕστερον ἐξ αὐτοῦ τεκοῦσαν υἱὸν ὃν Ἀλεξανδρεῖς Καισαρίωνα προσηγόρευον ὥρμησεν ἐπὶ Συρίας. Plut. *Caesar*, XLIX.

[250] Weigall, *Cleopatra*, p. 128, n. 1.

blest of captives," Plutarch calls him, because of the fact
that in his captivity he was to learn Greek and Latin and
become a very learned prince; in the Egyptian procession
the Princess Arsinoe in chains roused pity for the shame put
upon her, and anger against the conqueror, for the Romans
had never before seen a queen led in chains in a triumphal
pomp.[251]   Mahaffy, who is inclined to see no evil in con-
querors like Caesar, ascribes Arsinoe's walking in chains in
the procession to the dark influence of Cleopatra, who, he says,
must have pressed Caesar to this treatment of her sister " or
such a scene would never have taken place ".   This hypothesis does not ascribe too much malice to Cleopatra, but it surely
ascribes a scrupulousness to Caesar which was not native to
him.   Caesar had Vercingetorix put to death at the end of
his triumph over the Gauls,[252] a barbarous killing of a gallant
enemy, not to be condoned by the fact that such murders
were in vogue until Mark Antony set the fashion of letting
captive kings live after the triumphal pomp in which they
had walked.   Arsinoe in chains and Cleopatra his mistress
both showed the power of Caesar and the weakness of conquered Egypt.   Of Cleopatra he placed a statue of gold in
the temple of Venus Genetrix, mother of the Julian race, and
the queen's image stood beside that of the goddess.[253]

In 46 B. C. Cleopatra joined Caesar in Rome, bringing
with her the little Caesarion and her young brother, king
Ptolemy.   It is probable that the birth of Cleopatra's son
sealed the doom of the young king; he died, Josephus [254]
says by poison, either in Rome or in Alexandria just after
Cleopatra returned to her kingdom after Caesar's death.
She stayed in Caesar's Gardens across the Tiber, where she
held a sort of court.   It was said that Caesar intended to get
a law passed to allow him to have more than one legal wife,
and without doubt the queen herself hoped to be his wife and

---

[251] Cassius Dio, XLIII, 19.

[252] Cassius Dio, XLIII, 19.

[253] Appian, B.C. II, 102; Cassius Dio, LI, 22.

[254] Josephus, A.J. XV, 4, 1.   Cf. Pap. Oxyr. XIV, 1629.

to share the Roman and Egyptian rule with him. She was well aware that no one could rule in Egypt without the backing of the most powerful Roman.

Our information about her stay in Rome is scanty and chiefly derived from the meagre references to her in letters of Cicero of the year 44. The first of these occurs in a letter to Atticus dated in the middle of April, 44, about a month after the assassination of Caesar. He writes (*A.* XIV, 8)— Reginae fuga mihi non molesta—"the Queen's flight is no sorrow to me". From this it is obvious that Cleopatra within a month after the death of Caesar had sailed to Alexandria. The next mention of her is in a letter of May 11 (*A.* XIV, 20). The interpretation of this passage is disputed and like all the mentions of Cleopatra, " regina," as Cicero always calls her, is brief and allusory. The Latin reads :—Tertullae nollem abortum; tam enim Cassii sunt jam quam Bruti serendi. De regina velim atque etiam de Caesare illo. There are here sharp antitheses between *Tertullae* and *regina; nollem* and *velim; Cassii* etc. and *Caesare illo*. I accordingly understand that Cicero means " I am grieved to hear of Tertia's loss of an expected child, for the world has need of the propagation of the stocks of Brutus and Cassius. I should be glad of such a loss in the case of the queen and that (expected) scion of the breed of Caesar." Mahaffy [255] and Bouché-Leclercq [256] condemn this interpretation and wish to understand *scribas* in the second sentence. But it is clear from the tenor of the letter that Cicero throughout it is commenting on what Atticus has written to him, not asking for information. Moreover, another child was the natural result of the continued union of Caesar and such a fecund woman as Cleopatra, who desired to have heirs for Caesar and the Roman-Egyptian empire which she anticipated; such child-bearing contrasted her favorably with Caesar's childless wife. In a letter to Atticus of May 17 (*A.* XV, 1a) of the same year, about a week later than the one just considered, Cicero writes—"De regina rumor

---

[255] Mahaffy, *Empire of the Ptolemies*, p. 463 n. 1.
[256] Bouché-Leclercq, *Lagides*, II, p. 223 n. 2.

exstinguetur "—" the rumor about the queen will die down ".
This may refer to the gossip about an expected child. The
next week, May 24 (*A*. XV, 4) he writes, " De Menedemo
vellem verum fuisset. De regina velim verum sit." (Another
antithesis of the verbs like those in the sentence cited above)—
" I wish it had been true in the case of Menedemus and I
hope it may prove true of the Queen." On June 13 (*A*. XV,
15) he writes; " I hate the Queen. The sponsor of what she
promised me, Hammonius, knows that I am justified—learned
books they were and things suitable to my dignity, such as I
could speak of in a public assembly. Sara I recognized as a
scoundrel and one who gave himself airs with me. I saw him
once only at my house. When I asked him quite politely
what I could do for him, he said it was Atticus whom he
wished to see. The Queen's arrogance when she was living
in the Gardens across the Tiber I cannot recall without the
keenest anger. No more to do with that gang! They think
that I have no spirit and that I can stomach anything."
The next day, June 14, he writes to Atticus (*A*. XV, 17)—
" De regina gaudeo te non laborare, testem etiam tibi pro-
bari ", " I am glad that you are not troubled about the Queen
and that the witness is satisfactory to you."

From these brief and cryptic allusions to the Queen little
is clear except Cicero's dislike of her arrogance. Since the
question of the paternity of her son Caesarion was one destined to be hotly discussed in Rome, it seems not unlikely
that Cleopatra would wish to have another child by Caesar
at the time when she was living in his house,[257] when there
would be no doubt that Caesar was the father. This I take
to be the rumor of which Cicero speaks—either a false one,
or else the shock of Caesar's death, bringing destruction of
all her fantastic hopes, and the hardships of the flight by sea
to Egypt produced the effect for which Cicero expressed his
hope in the letter to Atticus of May 11, 44 B. C.

Her brother Ptolemy is mentioned in a document [258] of

---

[257] Cassius Dio, XLIII, 27, 30.
[258] *Pap. Oxyr.* XIV, 1629.

the date of July 26, 44 B. C. His name and Cleopatra's appear together. Porphyry [259] says that he died by the treachery of Cleopatra in the fourth year of his and eighth year of her reign. Josephus [260] says that the queen poisoned her brother who was but fifteen years old. According to the Oxyrhyncus document the death of the young king must have taken place after the return to Egypt.

Suetonius [261] says that Cleopatra was sent back to Egypt by Caesar, but there can be no doubt from the evidence of Cicero's letters that her flight followed the assassination of the Dictator. Rome was very likely a dangerous place for her and her little son.

With Ptolemy XIII poisoned and the princess Arsinoe in the temple at Ephesus where her father also had been a " suppliant ", the only representatives of the house of Ptolemy in Egypt were Cleopatra and Caesarion, who now are named together in the inscriptions:—[262] " Queen Cleopatra Father-loving Goddess and King Ptolemy, who is also Caesar Father-loving Mother-loving God."

In the civil strife that followed the death of Caesar both of the contending parties demanded the aid of Cleopatra's fleet. It is sometimes said [263] that she did nothing for either the victorious or the defeated side, but waited to see who would be in the ascendant. This view is directly contrary to the historical evidence of Dio and Appian. Dio says that she secured the recognition of her son Caesarion as king of Egypt because of the force that she sent to Dolabella.[264] Appian [265] tells of the demand of Cassius for Egyptian ships and of his getting some from the viceroy of Cyprus without Cleopatra's consent. He says that the Queen excused herself on the

---

[259] Porphyry in *F.H.G.* III, p. 724.

[260] Josephus, *A.J.* XV, 4, 1.

[261] Suet. *Caesar*, 52.

[262] *O.G.I.* 194; cf. *Annales du Service des Antiquités de l'Égypte*, 1908, p. 241.

[263] Bevan, *Egypt*, pp. 372-374.

[264] Cassius Dio, XLVII, 31, 5.

[265] Appian, *B.C.* IV, 61, 63, 82.

14

ground of the famine and pestilence that afflicted Egypt that
year, but that her real reason was that she was co-operating
with Dolabella because of her relation to the dead Caesar.
This was the reason for her sending him her four legions.
She also had another fleet ready to send which was delayed
by bad winds and weather.   After Dolabella's defeat by
Cassius and his suicide Cleopatra attempted to join Octavian
and Antony with a strong fleet which was dispersed by a
storm, and Murcus, who was off Taenarum, lying in wait for
Cleopatra, learned of the breaking up of her ships and saw
the wreckage carried by the waves as far as Laconia.[266]
Cleopatra was so ill that she was unable to take the ships out
again, and before long the news of the victory of the Caesar-
ians rendered her help unnecessary.   Appian [267] says that
when she and Mark Antony met in Cilicia and he reproached
her for not taking an active part in the struggle, she did not
defend herself but simply enumerated what she had done
for the Caesarian cause—she sent legions to Dolabella, defied
Cassius, who threatened her twice, and finally sailed herself
to join the ships of Octavian, but was driven back by the
storm.   Bevan does not take this seriously, and calls it a
feminine explanation—" the weather had been atrocious and
she had been so dreadfully ill ".   But there is no suggestion
in Appian's account of the interview between Antony and
Cleopatra that Cleopatra stated anything but facts, and those
facts are told by Appian himself in his previous book.

After the battle of Philippi Octavian went back to Italy
so ill that it was thought that he would not reach Rome alive.
Antony, who because of Octavian's ill health at the time of
the battle had got most of the glory of the victory, went to
Greece and then to Asia, where he was greeted with the
utmost adulation; kings waited at his doors and queens vied
with one another to gain his favor by their gifts and their
beauty.   In Ephesus he was hailed by the inhabitants dressed
as maenads, satyrs, and fauns, as Dionysus the Gentle, the

---

[266] Appian, *B.C.*, IV, 82.   [267] Appian, *B.C.*, V, 8.

Giver of Joy. According to Plutarch he showed himself charming and cruel by turns. There was, he says, a slowness of perception and a lack of subtlety in his nature that kept him from understanding himself and others. He was a handsome, blustering soldier, given to love of women and to practical joking. He had the strong Roman aquiline features and a frame like that of a sculptured Heracles. Cicero says that he had the jaw and chest of a prize-fighter. Both in his virtues and in his vices he was akin to the Macedonian type, and it is the most dazzling of these, Demetrius the Besieger, that Plutarch chooses to compare with him.

This conquering hero came through the subservient Greek and Asian towns to Tarsus, and there he summoned the Egyptian queen to come to answer for her inactivity in the war. She came and caught Mark Antony " in her strong toyle of grace ". Whether he had seen her in Rome is uncertain; it seems almost incredible that he should not have seen her during her year and a half of residence in the city in Caesar's Gardens, but there is no record of this. He had seen her in Alexandria when he was there as Gabinius' master-of-horse at the time of the Roman restoration of her father, and had then caught fire from her beauty. All who write of her tell of a charm, a " magic ", that was in her voice and in all her ways. She had brains as the queens before her had, and more than any of them she had accomplishments and culture. She had a remarkable command of languages and a liking for books. Dellius, the " Leaper " from side to side in the Civil Wars, was sent to summon her, and perceiving her cleverness, beauty, and charm in speech and voice, felt sure that she would have success with Antony, lover of women. He bade her put on her best, like Hera in the Iliad, going to make Zeus on Ida her lover, and to have no fear of Antony, sweetest and kindest of captains. She was sure of her victory over Antony, says Plutarch, for her beauty was at full bloom and she was not the inexperienced girl who had won Gnaeus Pompey and Caesar, but a woman who knew the world and men.

" Si le nez de Cléopâtre," says Pascal, " eût été plus court, toute la face de la terre aurait changé ". If her profile as it appears on busts and coins is correctly rendered, she had something to spare of length on her curving nose, and Plutarch says it was not her beauty that was beyond compare, but the delight of her presence and the music of her marvellously modulated voice.

She took with her for Antony gifts of treasures suitable to come from the rich land of Egypt, but she relied most on her own enchantments and power over men. Many letters came from him and his friends to hasten her, but she laughed at them all and came sailing up the Cydnus, a baroque Aphrodite, with the glitter of gold and silver. " When she first met Mark Antony she pursed up his heart upon the river of Cydnus." Cassius Dio says merely, " Cleopatra came to meet him in Cilicia," but Plutarch has told of all the splendor of her barge in a famous description. Shakespeare has taken Plutarch's tale and transmuted it into still more famous poetry.

> " I will tell you.
> The barge she sat in like a burnished throne
> Burnt on the water: the poop was beaten gold;
> Purple the sails, and so perfumed that
> The winds were lovesick with them; the oars were silver,
> Which to the tune of flutes kept stroke and made
> The water which they beat to follow faster,
> As amorous of their strokes. For her own person
> It beggared all description: she did lie
> In her pavilion—cloth-of-gold of tissue—
> O'er-picturing that Venus where we see
> The fancy outwork nature."

The pseudo-classical was in all this expressed by the wealthy and beautiful Macedonian-Egyptian queen in its most splendid and romantic form.

"Aphrodite comes to feast with the new Dionysus for the blessing of Asia " was the cry of the surging multitudes that welcomed the gleaming barge as it was steered to the shore by her maids-in-waiting, arrayed as sea-nymphs and Graces, steering at the rudder and working at the ropes. Antony

> " Enthroned i' the market-place did sit alone,
> Whistling to the air, which, but for vacancy
> Had gone to gaze on Cleopatra, too, and made a gap in nature."

The end of the meeting was that Antony, whose taste in women had been always for the coarser sort, was overwhelmed by this woman in the magnificent style; he felt himself a rough soldier and a boor as he sat at her side at the supper she gave him in a banqueting-room lighted with such dazzling brilliance as he had never seen. The queen answered his clumsy and bold jests smartly and wittily, and fell in with his soldier's humor without reluctance or reserve. According to all the historians she captured him at once.[268]

Antony was married to the strong-minded and fighting Fulvia, whose domination over him had, Plutarch [269] says, rendered him so tame in the hands of women that his married life had been a good schooling for Cleopatra's control of him. This control for the time was complete. Antony was a man of a kind common in every age: strong in action and weak in will, gallant and brave where physical courage was required, but incapable of self-control and victim of his appetites. A handsome, brawling soldier of this type is often generous, but usually lacks brains.

At Cleopatra's bidding [270] Antony had Arsinoe in Ephesus assassinated, as well as Serapion of Cyprus, who had given ships to Cassius, and a young Pretender in Aradus, who said he was the Ptolemy who had been drowned in the Nile.

Antony came to Alexandria late in 41 B. C., and the " Inimitable Life " [271] that began for him and the Egyptian queen and their chosen friends sprang from Cleopatra's wit and

---

[268] Plut. *Ant.* XXVIII.

[269] *Ibid.*, X.

[270] Josephus, *A.J.* XV, 4, 1; Appian, *B.C.* V, 9.

[271] Plut. *Ant.* XXVIII; *O.G.I.* 195 (*Bull. dell' Instit.* 1866, p. 199), Ἀντώνιον μέγαν ἀμίμητον, Ἀφροδίσιος παράσιτος τὸν ἑαυτοῦ θεόν.

power of splendidly dramatizing their daily existence. It
was a life of magnificent folly, and Antony, Plutarch says,
was like a school-boy on holiday, utterly disregardful of what
Labienus was doing among the Parthians and of the war
which his wife Fulvia was carrying on in Italy against
Octavian. Plutarch tells many tales of the ways in which
Cleopatra feasted, played with, and mocked at her Roman
miles gloriosus, with a thousand fashions of flattering him
and pleasing him. In a manner of living as though taken
from the Arabian Nights Entertainment, they gambled,
drank, hunted and fished together, and wandered about Alexandria by night in disguise, frightening people by peering in
at their windows and suddenly starting up in their doorways,
jeering at the folk whom they met. The Alexandrians liked
this sort of rough humor and said that Antony left his tragic
mask in Rome and wore his comic one for them. The two
lovers flung away the wealth of Egypt with both hands, and
Plutarch says Antony flung away the most costly of all riches,
that is, time. Fulvia and Lucius Antonius, Antony's wife
and his brother, were engaged in the Perusian war against
Octavian; Pacorus had entered Palestine; Labienus had invaded Asia; Herod, driven out of Palestine by the Parthians,
was on his way to seek the protection of Antony. At last in
the spring of 40 B. C. these events were hammering too loudly
at his doors to let Antony forget them; his brother was captured at Perusia, and Fulvia, his militant wife whom nothing
daunted, was on her way to him. So waking [272] from his
Egyptian slumber (ἐξυπνισθείς) and coming to his sober senses
(ἀποκραιπαλήσας), he left his " Serpent of old Nyle " and
returned to Italy, met on the way at Athens by Fulvia and
by his mother Julia. After he left Alexandria Cleopatra had
twin children, Alexander Helios and Cleopatra Selene.

The friends whom Antony met on his way home, who had
fled from Fulvia's war, told him that she had provoked the
whole trouble with the determination to get Antony away

---

[272] Plut. *Ant.* XXX.

from Cleopatra by arousing war in Italy. He did not greet her with kindness, and she died in Greece, worn out by her exertions and emotions. Plutarch thinks that she died before reaching her husband, and Appian [273] suggests that a stormy interview with him drove her to suicide.

The death of this restless and contentious woman did much to reconcile Antony and Octavian,[274] and the renewed friendship was strengthened after the signing of the Treaty of Brundisium, by which the East was given to Antony, and by the marriage of Antony to Octavian's half-sister Octavia. This lady received permission from the Senate to marry Antony while still in the period of mourning for her late husband, the consul Claudius Marcellus. Political marriage though it was, Octavia with the grave beauty of a Roman matron and the Julian intellectual capacity, her brother's darling, won the heart of her new husband for a time; he did not return to Cleopatra and their twin boy and girl for some years. Octavia had a daughter by Antony in their first year together. This "marvel of a woman" [275] ($\chi\rho\tilde{\eta}\mu\alpha$ $\theta\alpha\nu\mu\alpha\sigma\tau\grave{o}\nu$ $\gamma\nu\nu\alpha\iota\kappa\acute{o}\varsigma$) kept the peace between her husband and her brother when their alliance threatened to break in 37 B. C.; Antony in return for ships ceded to Octavian got a promise of legions for his eastern campaign on which he immediately started. His wife had spent the winter of 39 B. C. with Antony very happily in Athens, and in 37 B. C. when she interceded between her brother and her husband, she had borne to Antony a daughter and was pregnant again. After their return to Italy she accompanied him on his way to the East as far as Corcyra with the entire brood of children, those of Fulvia and her own little daughters.[276] What Cleopatra felt during the three years and more in which Antony had left her for the lady "of holy, cold, and still conversation" is not recorded, but whatever grief or anger had been in her heart,

---

[273] Appian, *B.C.* V, 62.
[274] Appian, *B.C.* V, 59.
[275] Plut. *Ant.* XXXI.
[276] Cassius Dio, XLVIII, 54; Plut. *Ant.* XXXV.

she was willing to come to the ruler of the East and again
become his mistress or his wife.   She met him at Antioch
and he won her favor by giving her [277] Phoenicia, Coele-Syria,
Cyprus, and part of Cilicia and the balsam fields of Jericho,
" balm of Gilead ", and the perfume-yielding territory of the
Nabathaean king in Arabia.   Svoronos (*Münzen der Ptolemäer*, IV, 386) has shown that the new reckoning of her
regnal years which appears on coins of Berytus, starting with
the year 36 B. C., is based on this new aggrandizement of her
territory and her political power.   Antony also acknowledged
his paternity of the twins whom she had borne in the year 39
B. C. after he had gone to Italy.   He was in a beneficent mood
at Antioch and bestowed tetrarchies and kingdoms where he
would upon his favorites, depriving of the same those whom
he disliked.

> " in his livery
> Walked crowns and coronets; realms and islands were
> As plates dropped from his pocket."

When Antony started on his Parthian campaign to bring
back the banners of Crassus and the Roman captives, Cleopatra went with him to the Euphrates river; she came back
by way of Damascus and Judaea and had an interview with
Herod, who was now her vassal.   Josephus has a story that
she attempted to seduce Herod, but that he, loving his wife
Mariamne, was so revolted by Cleopatra's advances that he
planned to kill her.   Realizing that this course might have
unpleasant consequences for himself he gave her fine presents
and escorted her to the border.   Herod himself is evidently
the authority for this tale of Cleopatra's attempt to seduce
him, and the story is obviously a lie.   Cleopatra was at the
time pregnant and the little Ptolemy was born at the end of
the year.[278]   Herod, whose fixed idea was to get rid of Cleopatra, would not stop at inventing a scandalous tale to calum-
niate her and cast an excellent light on his own character.   The
magnificent army which Antony led against the Parthians

---

[277] Plut. *Ant.* XXXVI.
[278] Gardthausen, *Augustus*, II, p. 170 f.

came back, not as conquering heroes, but in rags and starving. Antony never appears in the pages of history more to our liking than as Plutarch describes him going about among his wounded soldiers, suffering with them and saying and doing what he could to help them, while they clung to his hands and told him to look after himself and they would be all right if only all should be well with their *imperator*. Plutarch says that his power over his troops and their eagerness in his service were unrivalled. They loved their rough-and-ready, spendthrift commander, who kept company with them so easily and could match their coarse jests. Now he came back to Cleopatra for comfort "like a little girl running to her mother and wishing to be taken in her arms ".[279] He summoned her to meet him at a place on the seacoast between Sidon and Berytus and could hardly endure the interval of waiting for her to come. He gave himself up to drinking, but constantly jumped up and left the drinkers to look out to see if Cleopatra's ship was sailing up the harbor. She came with garments for the ragged soldiers and Egyptian gold to pay them. When the news of Antony's disaster reached Rome Octavia wished at once to sail to the help of her husband. Such magnanimity seems astonishing, but has never been uncommon in a wife of her type toward a man of the type of Antony. Octavian permitted Octavia to sail with supplies, which he could well afford to do, for he had taken Sicily from Sextus Pompey and Africa from Lepidus. Moreover Antony was a triumvir, and the triumvirate had been reduced to two by the suppression of Lepidus.

Plutarch says that Octavian had not thought of his sister's love for Antony in giving her permission to join her husband, but foresaw that she would be rebuffed and that this insult, added to the fact that Antony had given Roman provinces to Cleopatra, would afford him excellent reason to war against him.

Octavia reached Athens with her ships and supplies before

---

[279] *Il.* XVI, 7-8.

receiving Antony's letter telling her to remain there as he was off again for Asia. She was grief-stricken, understanding very well what his real motive was and who was with him, but in her magnanimous way wrote to ask him where she should send the garments for the soldiers and the mules and money and presents for his captains, as well as two thousand splendidly equipped soldiers for his praetorian cohort. Niger, a friend of Antony, brought the message, which overwhelmed Cleopatra with the knowledge that Octavia was ready to cross swords with her for the possession of her husband, and with the fear that the beauty and grandeur of Octavia's character and the influence of Octavian might prevail to win back Antony for his wife and Rome. In that event she would lose not only her lover, who was the father of three of her children, but also her hope of becoming a great empress, and might perhaps lose the queenship of Egypt as well.[280]

She may have loved Antony—she evidently found him a congenial companion—and by this time he regarded her as his Egyptian wife and may have gone through some form of marriage ceremony with her. But her strongest feeling was the desire to be queen and empress, the same feeling essentially that stirred in so many of the Macedonian queens.[281] Mahaffy asks if human nature had deserted the Hellenistic queens and the Hyrcanian tiger of the poet taken its place. He forgets that the tiger lived in the nature of the Ptolemies as well as of the Cleopatras and that far more deeds of cruelty and murder are attributed to the kings than to the queens of the house. Cleopatra, like the rest of her line, would stop at nothing to secure her own power, and it is absurd to call her a woman " who fought all her life for the fulfillment of a patriotic and splendid ambition ".[282]

Plutarch says that when she feared that Antony would be

---

[280] Plut. *Ant.* LIII.

[281] From the year 36 B. C. the head of Cleopatra was substituted for that of Octavia on the coins of Antony. Cf. Babelon, I, p. **196**. Cf. Servius, *Aen.* VII, 684.

[282] Weigall, *Cleopatra*, p. 410.

won back by Octavia, she conquered him by her weakness and her tears. It was her last resource, as it has been that of many other women before and since Cleopatra, and there is no reason for calling her a " comédienne " as does Bouché-Leclercq,[283] who thinks that she did not dupe even Antony. Whether she loved him or not, her humilation and the fear of seeing her kingdom made a Roman province were keen enough to warrant all her weeping. She persuaded him to return with her to Alexandria, deferring the eastern march until the following spring. Bouché-Leclercq thinks he was afraid of undertaking the new campaign so soon after defeat. Octavia returned to Rome, where she resisted her brother's order to leave the house of Antony. She stayed in it with all his children and befriended so far as she could any of her husband's friends who came to her for help.

The next year Antony returned from his Asian campaign, bringing with him as captives king Artavasdes of Armenia and his family and an immense amount of loot. He betrothed his little son Alexander to Iotape, daughter of the Median king Artavasdes (enemy of the Armenian of the same name). He left most of his troops in Armenia in expectation of a grand campaign against the elusive Parthians in the following year.

Cleopatra assumed the titles of New Goddess and New Isis [284] and wore the sacred costume of Isis when she appeared in public. The highest moment of her life came now, for Antony against all Roman precedent and custom triumphed in Alexandria. This greatly shocked Rome, where it was said that Antony flung away for the sake of the Egyptian woman the beautiful and sacred things of his country. This triumph in which the New Isis, Cleopatra, sat enthroned [285] on a gold throne in the Serapeum and in hieratic pose received the

---

[283] Bouché-Leclercq, *Lagides*, II, p. 269.

[284] Plut. *Ant.* LIV.

[285] Bouché-Leclercq calls Cleopatra " the divinity who in this sacrilegious parody was to replace Jupiter of the Capitol ". *Lagides*, II, p. 277.

homage of the *triumphator* and the captive princes, was to
her only a foretaste of the triumph of which she was dream-
ing, in which the city should be Rome and Octavian should
bow before her asking for grace and pity.　To be empress
of Rome appears now to be her fixed idea, and her oath was
"As surely as I shall yet dispense justice on the Roman
Capitol ".[286]　But this day of triumph in Alexandria was not
destined to have a repetition in Rome.

The Armenian princes, chained in gold fetters, would not
bow the knee in worship of Cleopatra, and merely greeted her,
calling her by her name; they paid dearly later for their
refusal, but were not now punished by death, as Vercingetorix
had been after Caesar's triumph.

Shortly after this triumph another great ceremony was celebrated which announced to the world that Antony and Cleopatra were emperor and empress of the East and that their
children were the heirs of their glory.　The royal pair sat
on gold thrones, and on seats below them were Caesarion, and
Alexander Helios and Cleopatra Selene and the little Ptolemy
Philadelphus.　When the Gymnasium was filled, Antony before
all proclaimed Cleopatra queen of Egypt, of Cyprus, of Libya,
and Coele-Syria, with Caesarion as co-regent; next he named
his sons by Cleopatra kings of kings and assigned to Alexander Armenia, Media, and Parthia (when the last-named
should be subdued), and little Ptolemy was proclaimed king
of Phoenicia, Syria, and Cilicia.　Alexander wore the tiara
and upright *kitaris* of a Persian monarch, as befitted his
name, and Ptolemy wore the soldier-boots, the military cloak,
and the flapping hat of the Macedonians with the diadem
about it.　A far cry from the first Ptolemy, son of Lagus, to
this little half-Roman Ptolemy!　The boy was the last Ptolemy in Egypt, and Ptolemy, son of his sister Cleopatra, was
the last of that name of the royal blood in Africa.　Cleopatra
Selene sat below the other children, but she was the only one

---

[286] Cassius Dio, L, 4-5; Zonaras, X, 29.

of them all destined to survive to sit upon a throne, though her brothers were hailed by Antony as kings of kings.

This is Plutarch's account. Cassius Dio differs a little,[287] adding that Antony commanded that Cleopatra be called queen of kings (βασιλίδα βασιλέων), and Caesarion king of kings, and declared that she had been the true wife of Julius Caesar and that Caesarion was his true son. Dio also adds that the little Cleopatra was to be queen of the Cyrenaica.

A splendid spectacle this of the Roman soldier and the Macedonian-Egyptian queen, the two most magnificent people in the world, at the time the most loved and the most hated, sitting on their gold thrones, with their little sons and daughter on the silver platform at their feet and princes of the east walking in chains before them. Never have Shirley's verses had a better illustration than in the splendor and in the fate of Antony and Cleopatra.

> The glory of our blood and state
>   Are shadows, not substantial things;
> Man has no armour against fate—
>   Death lays his icy hands on kings.
> Sceptre and crown shall tumble down
>   And in the dust be equal made
> With the poor crooked scythe and spade.

After this triumph coins were struck with the head of Antony and a little Armenian tiara and the device *Antoni Armenia Devicta* on one side, and the bust of Cleopatra wearing a diadem with the inscription *Cleopatrae reginae regum filiorum regum* on the other.[288] Kahrstedt (*op. cit.* p. 278), discussing the coins inscribed Thea Neotera, says that they all belong to the last years of her life and bear out what Plutarch relates about her assuming the garb and title of New Isis. Kahrstedt ascribes the coins to the period after the Alexandrian Triumph of Antony when Cleopatra had been proclaimed Queen of Kings. Cf. also Svoronos, *Münzen der Ptolemäer*, IV, 377 and 386.

---

[287] Cassius Dio, XLIX, 41.
[288] Babelon, I, pp. 195 f. Cf. also 94.

Of the splendidly licentious life in the Alexandrian court accounts appear in the historians, some so extravagant that they appear to exceed the possibilities of even Cleopatra's fantasy. Antony was Osiris, or he was Dionysus with ivy-crown and thyrsus, followed by Egyptian and Roman revellers. " He has thrown away all the noble titles of his own land and has become one of the cymbal-bearers of Canopus ", Octavian said of him.[289] He was much given to drunkenness at this time, or had the reputation at Rome, and his Isis was said to protect herself from the effect of too much wine by the magic power of an amethyst ring which she wore for an anti-dote.[290] The Romans found it particularly disgusting that the Roman ex-consul Munatius Plancus (Horace's *Consule Planco*) should appear in one of the revels naked and painted sea-green to represent old Glaucus, with a crown of reeds and a trail of fishes.[291] The blame for all the excesses of Antony was fastened by his countrymen on Cleopatra, who, they said, had taken away his senses by some enchantment (Cassius Dio, L, 5). Cleopatra swallowed her pearl ear-pendant in a cup of wine; Antony walked abroad with a gold sceptre in his hand [292] and a Persian scimiter at his side, wearing a red cloak fastened with brooches of precious stones. They flung away fortunes on a single feast, and stories of their oriental prodigality were heard everywhere in Rome. Antony gave his daughter Antonia to the wealthy Oriental Pythodorus.[293]

In the spring of 33 Antony marched as far as the Araxes river, apparently intending to renew his attack on the Parth-ians. He went no farther however, and contented himself with making a treaty with the Median king for alliance against both the Parthians and Octavian. He took back the girl Iotape, affianced to his son Alexander.

---

[289] Cassius Dio, L, 27.

[290] *Anth. Pal.* IX, 752.

[291] Vell. Pat. II, 82-83.

[292] Florus, IV, 11; Cassius Dio, L, 5, 3.

[293] This marriage was inferred by Mommsen, *Eph. Ep.* I, pp. 270 ff. from *O.G.I.* 377, but is denied by Dessau, *Eph. Ep.* IX, pp. 691 ff.

Antony now made one of his magnificent gestures to Rome. He wrote to the Senate saying that he would resign from his office if Octavian would do the same and would submit all his authority to the power of the Senate and the Roman people.[294] This was of course a great piece of bluffing, for Antony was a natural gambler with life; he hoped that the Roman people, dazzled by what he had achieved, would make Octavian give up hostilities or would turn against him if he refused to do this.

Cleopatra, who now in the belief of the Romans and in fact had complete control of Antony, desired to put the matter to the touch and bring the quarrel between Octavian and Antony to the decision of open warfare. Her Caesarion was the storm-centre, for the friends of Octavian declared that he was not the son of Caesar, and one of the reasons for the bitterness of Octavian was that Antony maintained that Cleopatra had been the wife of Caesar and that Caesarion was his lawful son. Cleopatra as mother of Caesar's son and wife of Antony had a chance of realizing her ambition to be empress of Rome and the East. After Antony's return from Asia she went with him to Ephesus and they passed the winter there. There the fleet assembled for the war against Octavian. The new consuls, Domitius Ahenobarbus and Sosius, who had defended Antony and attacked Octavian on the first day of their term of office, fled to Antony on the second day of that term and arrived at Ephesus with other senators who were on Antony's side. They urged Antony to send Cleopatra back to Egypt to await the outcome of the war in Alexandria. He saw the wisdom of their representations, for her presence was a detriment in many ways. She was heartily disliked by many Antonians who had no desire to see her and her son " dispensing justice on the Capitol ". We read much in the Roman writers about the disgrace of a woman living in the Roman camp.

---

[294] Cassius Dio, XLIX, 41.

Romanus eheu -posteri negabitis-
emancipatus feminae,
fert vallum et arma miles et spadonibus
servire rugosis potest,
interque signa turpe militaria
sol adspicit conopium.[295]

But Cleopatra would not go home. She had furnished two hundred of the eight hundred ships of the fleet and two thousand talents, and she bribed Canidius to represent her claims to Antony. She said that besides the great contributions which she was making, Egypt would be angry if their queen was slighted and the Egyptian soldiers in the fleet would be slack if she were not there for them to fight for; in fine she was the best ruler and adviser among all those assembled, since she had been queen of her own kingdom so long and had shared Antony's fortunes, learning from him how to deal with affairs of state.[296]

Antony yielded the point, and he and Cleopatra sailed to Samos with their forces complete and there made holiday. "And while all the world was groaning and travailing together around them, one island resounded day after day with the sound of flutes and harping, and the theatres were packed to see new plays performed. Every town joined in the festival, sending oxen for the sacrifice, and kings vied with one another in receptions and gifts. And the folk said 'What will they do for their triumphal feast after the victory when they lavish all this on the feast before the battle?'" The kings of the east were there:—

Bocchus, the king of Libya; Archelaus,
Of Cappadocia; Philadelphos, king
Of Paphlagonia; the Thracian king, Adallas,
King Malchus of Arabia; King of Pont;
Herod of Jewry; Mithridates, king
Of Comagene; Polemon and Amyntas,
The kings of Mede and Lycaonia,
With a more larger list of sceptres.

---

[295] Horace, *Epod.* IX, 11 ff.
[296] Plut. *Ant.* LVI.

Shakespeare has here permitted himself some license of change from Plutarch,[297] by whom kings present are reported to have been Bocchus of Libya, Torkondemus of upper Cilicia, Archelaus of Cappadocia, Philadelphus of Paphlagonia, Mithradates of Commagene and Sadalas or Adallas of Thrace, while Polemon of Pontus, Malchas of Arabia, Herod the Jew, Amyntas of Lycaonia and Galatia, and the king of the Medes sent troops. They were, says Dio,[298] " practically all the kings and rulers whose territories bordered on the parts of the Roman empire subject to Antony, some in person and some represented by lieutenants." But no matter what Shakespeare's divergences from the written story are, not even Plutarch, to whom he owes all but his own genius in writing the play, has told the splendor and the shame of the great pair as he has told it.

When the revels on Samos were over, Antony left his players and musicians at Priene, and he and Cleopatra sailed on to Athens, where his wife Octavia had stayed with him in the first years of their married life and where she had come later in her distress for him bringing him ships and supplies for his defeated army. The Athenians had a high regard for Octavia, and Cleopatra was jealous of her prestige among them. She demanded and received public honors from them. They sent a delegation with Antony, in the role of Athenian citizen, at its head to convey their decree to her, and her statue in the costume of Isis was placed on the Acropolis beside that of Antony.

It was Octavia as much as Octavian that she wished to conquer, and she now insisted that Antony should send a bill of divorcement to his Roman wife and the order to leave his house. Octavia obeyed, taking with her all his children except the eldest boy Antyllus, who had joined his father in Athens. Her greatest sorrow was the thought that she had been the cause of the civil war. Plutarch says that many of the

---

[297] *Ibid.* 61.

[298] Cassius Dio, L, 6.

15

Romans, especially those who had seen Cleopatra, pitied Antony for what he had been made to do to Octavia.[299]

Cleopatra grew more arrogant and insulted important Roman friends of Antony, Titius and Plancus (him who had been the sea-green Glaucus in Alexandria), who fled to Octavian [300] and told him many secrets, especially about Antony's will, which was in the keeping of the Vestal Virgins. Octavian took it from the Vestals and revealed its terms to the people. In it Antony left directions that he should be buried in Alexandria at the side of Cleopatra, wherever he should die, and testified that Caesarion was the son of Julius Caesar. He left splendid gifts to his Egyptian children.[301]

A spate of news set in at Rome about the insolent behavior of Cleopatra and the servile position of Antony, who was accused by Calvisius of having given the queen two hundred thousand volumes from the library at Pergamum, and of having insulted men of dignity and rank by reading love-letters from her, written on tablets of crystal and onyx, when he was giving audience to tetrarchs and kings. He was said to have left the court where Furnius, a noble Roman, was pleading when he saw Cleopatra's litter passing through the market-place and to have accompanied her with his hand on the litter, and he had allowed the Ephesians to greet Cleopatra as sovereign in his presence. Antony's friends were so stirred by this scandal that they sent Geminius to Athens to tell him that he should send the queen home. He found it difficult to get audience with Antony, for Cleopatra believed that Octavia had sent him, and therefore she heaped insults on him, making him the butt of her jests at meals and seating him among the meanest guests. He was ordered at a feast to tell his errand and said that his business was one of soberness, but that drunk or sober he knew one thing—all would yet go well

---

[299] Plut. *Ant.* LVII.

[300] Cassius Dio, L, 3; Plut. *Ant.* LVII.

[301] Plut. *Ant.* LVII. Rostovtzeff holds that this will was probably forged by Octavian, Plancus, and Titius (*Social and Economic History of Rome*), p. 494. Cf. p. 29.

if Cleopatra would be off for Egypt. Antony raged at him and Cleopatra threatened; he went back to Rome and joined Octavian's party.[302]

Cleopatra was honored and fêted in Athens, but from now on the stars in their courses fought against her. The " Inimitable Life " was over, and her dream of living it as Empress of Rome and the East was destined soon to end. War was declared against her by Octavian, acting as *fetialis* before the temple of Bellona in Rome and launching the spear as symbol of war against a foreign enemy. He did not declare war against Antony,[303] knowing that he would not desert her and the Romans would be able to accuse him of fighting for " the Egyptian " against his own land.

When Antony and Cleopatra moved with their immense fleet and army toward Patras with many Asiatic princes and their forces, it was a movement of the east and what remained of Hellenism in the world against the west and Italy.[304] More than two-thirds of Antony's legionary soldiers were eastern troops, though commanded by Italian officers, and in the fleet the percentage was far greater.[305] As Kromayer says, Antony was perforce an oriental king, even though he promised to restore the republic in Rome and to give back the state and the entire control of it two months after his victory to the Senate and the Roman people.[306] If forced to choose between Italy and the Orient, the composition of the armies under his command made the choice of the East and Egypt inevitable for him. Some of his Roman advisers thought otherwise and both at Patras and later in the camp at Actium urged him to give up the idea of a naval battle, to which the queen was obstinately attached, and to send her back to Egypt with her ships and march into Thrace or Macedonia to meet Octavian by land wherever the latter

---

[302] Plut. *Ant.* 59.
[303] Cassius Dio, L, 6; Plut. *Ant.* 60.
[304] Kromayer, *Hermes*, XXXIII (1898), pp. 67 ff.
[305] *Ibid.* p. 68.
[306] Cassius Dio, L, 7.

wished to give fight. Even Canidius urged this course in view of the constant desertions to Octavian's side of kings and Roman citizens. Luck went against Antony in skirmishes on land, and Deiotarus of Paphlagonia and Rhoemetalces of Thrace deserted [307] to Octavian not long after Domitius Ahenobarbus had given up hope of Antony and sailed over in a small boat to the camp of the enemy. When supplies began to fail the army, Antony put the question to his advisers whether they should stay and risk a battle or should transfer the scene of war elsewhere. Cleopatra, who would be entirely ruined in the event of a defeat by land, urged taking all the legions except enough to garrison some strong places in Greece back to Egypt in the fleet. The troops were hungry and disheartened and suffered from the unhealthy site of their camp. Cleopatra had lost her nerve because of some bad omens; swallows had built in the rafters of her tent and on her admiral-ship, and the statues which the Athenians had set up on the Acropolis in honor of her and Antony had been struck by lightning and dashed down into the theatre.[308] She did not dare sail away openly because that course would ruin her and Antony with their allies as well as with the Romans,[309] but she filled Antony with her fears of losing Egypt and the East and persuaded him to give up the idea of an invasion of Italy and to sail back to Egypt. However luxurious her *conopium,* the long months of camp life on the Ambracian coast had been full of hardships, and with the fear of malaria added she was filled with eagerness to return to her own kingdom, from which a victory of the enemy would shut her out forever. Dellius and Amyntas had been wavering in their allegiance to Antony, who had sent them into Thrace and Macedon to get cavalry troops; he was so distrustful of them [310] that he went himself to meet them on the pretext of an intention to succor them if they should be attacked. These two men now went over to

---

[307] Plut. *Apophtheg. Augusti,* 2.
[308] Plut. *Ant.* 60.
[309] Cassius Dio, L, 15.
[310] Cassius Dio, L, 13.

Octavian. Horace with the zeal of a new proselyte sings in the ninth epode of the Gauls who turned their two thousand steeds around and raised the shout of " Caesar ", referring to Amyntas [311] and his Galatians:

> ad hoc frementes verterunt bis mille equos
> Galli canentes Caesarem.

Antony now had the ships which the reduced numbers of his troops did not permit him to man, burned, and he ordered all soldiers to embark on the remaining ships. Twenty-two thousand men went on board, and the captains were told to take on board all the large sails,[312] an order which they could not understand, as the sails could not be of use in a battle so near the coast. Antony designed them for the long voyage to Egypt. He also had all Cleopatra's wealth of treasure which she had brought with her placed on her ships.[313] Dio says that in the battle Antony entered on the fight unwillingly. Cleopatra's sixty ships were placed behind the battle line.[314] There can be no doubt from Dio's statements that the flight to Egypt was prearranged between Antony and Cleopatra and that the rest of the fleet was to follow by order of Canidius as soon as they should be able to break through. Cleopatra, Cassius Dio says, tossing up and down in the waters behind the main line and also tossed in mind as well as in body, feeling sick and terrified, and " being a woman and an Egyptian woman at that ", of a sudden, when a favorable breeze sprang up, gave the signal for flight to the ships under her command and broke through to the confusion of both friend and foe, doing what Kromayer says [315] the moment demanded, for the shock of the forward movement of sixty ships brought a violent forward movement into the fight,

---

[311] Bouché-Leclercq, *op. cit.* II, pp. 300 f., n. 3.

[312] Plut. *Ant.* LXIV.

[313] Plut. *Ant.* 64; Cassius Dio, L, 15.

[314] Kromayer, *Hermes*, XXXIV, 1899, pp. 35 f., classes these ships among the non-combatants.

[315] Kromayer, *Hermes*, XXXIV, p. 46.

which had become stationary. Antony delayed no longer; he had known that he was to follow when Cleopatra should attempt to escape, and abandoning his disabled admiral-ship he went into a quinquireme and sailed after the queen. When she saw him coming, she raised a flag of recognition and took him aboard her boat. This was all by arrangement, and Plutarch's romantic account of Cleopatra's treacherous flight and the frantic pursuit of her ship by Antony, because the very soul of him was escaping from him, is not in accord with either probability or the facts.[316] Plutarch says that after Antony came on board Cleopatra's ship, he kept by himself for three days without speaking to her until after they came to Cape Taenarum, where her women-in-waiting brought them together. This does not signify, as it is generally understood to do, that he was enraged with her for a treacherous flight, but reflects the despair in which he was plunged by the fact that his high hopes had shattered. All that was left for him and for Cleopatra was to hold Egypt against Octavian. He was still the most famous soldier in the world, and with the forces at his command and the wealth of Egypt he might have made good once more against the disorder and confusion that prevailed in Italy, if he could have summoned the energy of his younger days.

Cleopatra was eager to get back to Egypt, fearing a revolution if the news of the disaster at Actium should become known before their arrival; she sailed into the harbor of Alexandria with the prows of their ships wreathed, and songs of triumph were sung to the sound of the flute by the musicians on board as though she was returning from a victory. Dio says [317] that she at once had those who were pleased with the result at Actium put to death, and she began to collect whatever wealth she could lay her hands on by confiscating the property of the murdered men and of others, and by seizing temple-treasures; she also looked about for allies and reinforcements, and in order to ingratiate herself with the

---

[316] Plut. *Ant.* 66.   [317] Cassius Dio, LI, 5.

Median king Artavasdes, she sent him the head of his old
enemy, the Armenian of the same name, who had walked in
gold chains in the triumph of Antony in Alexandria. She
collected treasure with feverish haste, prosecuting what Plutarch calls [318] a vast and mad enterprise; that is, to build
ships in Alexandria and in the Red Sea [319] and launch them,
laden with her treasure, in the Arabian Gulf in order to flee
with troops and treasure to some safe land, such as India or
southern Persia. But the ships were burned a little later by
the Arabs of Petra at the command of Quintus Didius,
governor of Syria, who went over to the side of Octavian.

Antony had hoped that his land force at Actium would
hold together, but Canidius came telling him that his troops
had surrendered to Octavian. After a time Antony aban-
doned the house that he had built in his first despair to live
in as a hermit and joined Cleopatra in the Palace, where a
melancholy repetition of the old gaieties and revels began, the
Inimitable Livers ironically changing their names to Com-
panions to the Death. As Octavian drew nearer and the
legions in Cyrene deserted to his cause, the queen was trying
the effects of poisons on various prisoners and was deter-
mining that the bite of the asp was superior to all drugs in
the easy death which it produced. Antony's son Antyllus and
Cleopatra's son Caesarion were enrolled as citizens, which was
an occasion for prolonged feastings for the Alexandrians.

When Octavian reached Asia in the late spring of the year
30 Antony's prestige was gone. He and Cleopatra both sent
embassies to Octavian with gifts: Antony asked that he might
live as a private citizen in Egypt or in Athens; Cleopatra
without the knowledge of Antony sent a gold sceptre and
crown and the royal chair,[320] asking that her children might

---

[318] Plut. *Ant.* 69.   [319] Cassius Dio, LI, 5-6.

[320] δίφρος—Bouché-Leclercq (*Lagides*, II, 320) and others understand the word to mean chariot, which is most unlikely. The
sceptre, crown, and throne formed the regalia of Egypt. The δίφρος
is perhaps the δίφρος ἐπίχρυσος on which Antony sat (Cassius Dio,
XLIX, 40) at the Triumph in Alexandria.

rule in Egypt. Octavian received her presents and secretly
sent word to her that if she would kill Antony or expel him
from Alexandria he would pardon her and give her the kingdom of Egypt. She still had a weapon in her wealth and
Octavian's eagerness to get it. She had her treasures brought
to a splendid monument which had been constructed for her
beside the temple of Isis, and in this she heaped her gold,
silver, emeralds, pearls, ivory, ebony, and precious fragrant
spices, and a quantity of tinder and tow. Octavian was afraid
that the queen would set fire to all this vast wealth, which he
needed so desperately to pay his debts in Italy. According to
Dio he even sent word to her that he was in love with her,
thinking that this would be the most effective bait with a
woman of her temperament to induce her to kill Antony and
keep herself and her treasures intact for his triumph. The
long conversations of the messenger Thyrsus with Cleopatra
made Antony suspicious, and he had him flogged and sent
him back to Octavian with the message that the latter could
take it out on the back of a deserter from Antony, his freed-
man Hipparchus.

Antony won one last victory before his life, so full of glory
and of shame, ended in suicide and in Cleopatra's arms. The
van-guard of the Roman troops was met by him at the Hippo-
drome at the Canopic Gate, and he defeated them and chased
Octavian's cavalry back to their camp. Exulting that he had
once more struck a blow, he rushed to the Palace fresh from
the battle with his armor on, kissed Cleopatra as of old, and
with his old grand gesture placed before her the soldier who
had fought most gallantly. The soldier received from Cleopatra a gold breastplate and a gold helmet. He took them
and that night went to Octavian's camp.[321] Antony now
challenged Octavian to a duel. The answer came from him
that many ways to die were open to Antony.[322] He resolved
to attack Octavian by land and sea and that night gave a
banquet to his friends, telling them to drink deep, for the

---

[321] Plut. *Ant.* 74.   [322] *Ibid.* 75.

next day they might be serving other masters and he be lying on the ground, " dust and a shadow ". That night after the drinking was over, he walked alone through the silent city, which was strangely quiet in fear of the hovering danger. Of a sudden he heard the sound of music in the air and the voice of a great multitude leaping and singing. The rushing sounds went toward Canopus, where Octavian lay encamped, and men said that Dionysus, the god whom Antony loved, was leaving him.[323] The next day Antony led his infantry from the city and placed them on high ground. He watched his fleet sail out to meet Octavian's ships. When the fleets met, Antony's men raised their oars in token of friendship, and both fleets joined and sailed back together. As Antony watched this, at the very moment he was deserted by his cavalry, who went over to the enemy, and his foot soldiers were routed. He went back, crying that Cleopatra, for whose sake he had begun the war, had betrayed him. She was afraid of his furious rage and fled to her tomb, which she barred and bolted, and sent messengers to tell Antony that she was dead. Believing that this was true and knowing that without her he could do nothing to save their children and his son Antyllus, he asked his servant Eros to kill him. Eros drew his sword, but turned it on himself. Antony then thrust the sword into his own body, but the wound was not yet deadly. Cleopatra sent her secretary to summon him to her, and when he found that she was living he asked to be taken to her. Cleopatra dared not open the tomb below, and she with Iras and Charmion drew him up by ropes into the upper room. What follows Plutarch has told in his moving narrative, derived from the account left by Olympus, the physician of Cleopatra. Who can read untouched by the sense of tears in human things the dying words of Antony and the grief of Cleopatra, no more an empress,

> but e'en a woman and commanded
> By such poor passion as the maid that milks
> And does the meanest chores.

---

[323] *Ibid.* 75.

It is one of the great moments in the drama of life and of
history, and Antony dying in Cleopatra's arms has a greater
glory than any conqueror. No moment in the life of Julius
Caesar or of Augustus was destined to move the world of men
and give the κάθαρσις of life's drama as was the passing of
the spirit of Mark Antony.

> She shall be buried by her Antony.
> No grave upon the earth shall clip in it
> A pair so famous.

What of Cleopatra after this? She had her children and
her kingdom still to think of and hoped that with her treasures which Octavian coveted she might make some bargain
with him. He is said to have gone into his tent and wept
a tear when he heard of Antony's death, but his emotion did
not prevent him from having young Antyllus killed. Cleopatra conferred with him through the bolted gate of her tomb,
asking for the kingdom for her children. By a ruse Procu-
leius succeeded in climbing into the window of the tomb with
two men, and the queen, seeing that she was a captive, tried
to kill herself. She was too precious an adornment of the
triumph of Octavian to be allowed to do this and so was
treated with great courtesy. She had sent Caesarion into
India, but he was also betrayed and brought to Octavian, who
hesitated what to do with him, but decided that since he was
a Caesar he was better dead than living. The boy was not
put to death until after the death of his mother. Octavian
could not very well have taken the great Caesar's son to Rome
to adorn his triumphal procession.

Plutarch says on the authority of her physician Olympus
that Cleopatra's dearest wish was to die and that she planned
to starve herself to death, but Octavian threatened her with
harm to her children if she would not submit to live. He
came to see her in her prison and of his visit two differing
accounts are left, that of Plutarch derived from Olympus and
that of Dio, who gives the official account and presents us
with a picture of an unscrupulous and naïve seductress who

tries to win Octavian by kissing pictures and letters of Julius Caesar and then makes overtures to him with sweet words and glances. When he refused to look at her and answered her coldly and said no word about the kingdom and no word of love, Dio says, she gave way and begged him to let her die and be buried in the same tomb with Antony. This he says was also requested in a writing which she left when she died. Octavian spoke kindly to her, giving her some hope, for he wished to bring her to Rome to cast lustre upon his triumphal procession. He allowed her to go with Iras and Charmion to Antony's tomb, where she prayed to her husband's spirit to keep her from the ignominy of being shown in a Roman triumph and to let him share her tomb. The end of her prayer is either a marvel of Plutarch's tragic style, or else as affecting words as ever any woman spoke: " Of all my thousand sorrows no one is as bitter and as great as this brief space that I have lived away from you."

All the world knows the story of the asps brought in a basket of fresh figs and the death by the asp-stings of the queen and her two hand-maidens. She had sent Octavian a letter signed and sealed and after dining she sent every one from her except Iras and Charmion. When Octavian read the letter and found that she entreated him to bury her in the grave with Antony, he sent messengers at once to find what had happened. When they entered her room they saw Cleopatra lying dead in royal splendor on a gold couch and Iras dying at her feet. Charmion, just falling, was still busy with the arrangement of her mistress's diadem. When a messenger said to her angrily, " Charmion, is this well ? " she answered " Well indeed, and fitting for the descendant of so many noble kings ", and fell beside the couch. This was the epitaph of Cleopatra.

It has been suggested that Octavian had her put to death and that the story of the asp-bite was the invention of the Romans to hide the murder, but it seems improbable that Octavian should have wished to kill her before she walked in his triumph. According to Dio he did all that he could

to have her restored to life after he came and saw her dead,
and when unable to bring her back, " he marvelled at her
and pitied her, but chiefly felt pain for himself as deprived
of the chief glory of his victory ".

Dio sums up her character in this way: " She was insatiate
in the pursuit of love and insatiate in her greediness for
wealth; she was greatly ambitious and eager for fame and
was haughty and insolent; she got the kingdom of Egypt
because of a man's passion for her and she hoped by the
same means to become queen of Rome, but of that she failed
and so lost Egypt. She held under her sway two of the
greatest Romans of her time and because of the third she
took her own life." [324]   Tarn says of her — " Cleopatra's
courage is as indisputable as is the complete absence of
moral scruple in the use of her person and her lovers for her
one end. But what she really was, and what that end was,
it seems difficult to know: whether she was a mere courtesan,
crazy to be empress of the Roman world, or whether she was
a great patriot, who with a woman's weapons all but reversed
Fortune's wheel at the eleventh hour and almost succeeded in
avenging Rome's treatment of the Hellenistic states by making
her Hellenistic kingdom Rome's co-partner in Empire."

The accusation of lust is not justified by the facts of her
life. She was faithful in her relation to the two Romans,
Julius Caesar and Antony; she hoped to be the wife of the
first and was actually the wife of the second. The fact that
they each had un-royal wives in Rome would not constitute
a difficulty from the point of view of a Ptolemaic queen.
She is often called a " royal courtesan " by historians, because
she bore children to the two Romans to whom she was according to her own conception married, but she would not have
been regarded by the same historians as unchaste if she had,
according to Ptolemaic custom, borne children to her own

---

[324] Cassius Dio, LI, 15. Cf. Bouché-Leclercq, *Lagides*, II, p. 336, n.
1, on the abuse heaped on Cleopatra by Roman writers: " C'est
l'éternel refrain." Tarn, *Hellenistic Civilisation*, pp. 42 f.

brothers. She was like all the Ptolemies proud, cruel, domineering, and unscrupulous, but lacked the vices of the male Ptolemies of drunkenness and lust. Like all the women of the line she had no especial interest in love-intrigue, but was bent on securing political and imperial power.

Mahaffy finds that she was already false to Antony at Actium and there computed with the utmost care the chances of the rivals, hoping that her charms might still work to secure another great Roman for her own. His views about the psychology of female love, in which he thinks nothing is more frequent than " a strong passion co-existing with selfish ambition, so that a woman embraces with keener transports the lover whom she has betrayed than one whom she has not thought of betraying ", must surely have been gathered from an extensive reading of melodrama rather than from an experience of the facts of life. It is as foolish to condemn her and all of the women of her line, as Mahaffy in an unguarded moment does [325] (" What Arsinoe, what Cleopatra from first to last ", etc.) for crimes condoned in the case of the men, as to present her as a " sympathetic " heroine, " a dainty little queen with her fat baby at her breast ", " a lonely and sorely-tried woman who fought all her life for the fulfillment of a patriotic and splendid ambition ".[326]

She and Mark Antony had a strange, wild life together, a life that was not good for the blustering, brave, and vacillating Roman soldier, who should have been killing Parthians and Medes and strengthening the boundaries of the Roman empire. Had he done his duty as a soldier, we should have missed a splendid page of history filled with documents of the human heart and soul and we should have lost one of the greatest of tragedies, written by a man who understood the fiery spirit of Cleopatra. She cheated Octavian of his triumph over her, and her splendid immortality of fame he could not take from her, though he got her emeralds and pearls and frankincense to pay his soldiers and his debts in Italy. More than any other Macedonian except Alexander

---

[325] Mahaffy, *Empire*, p. 445 ff.   [326] Weigall, *op. cit., passim.*

the Great, to whom she is akin in her brilliance, her intellectual power, and her ambition, she has exercised the spell of her magic over those of her time and every generation since. She was not a pattern of virtue, nor a monster of wickedness, nor a good bourgeois wife, nor a great and splendid patriot, but a Ptolemy with the virtues and vices of her race. Flowering in splendor on the old decaying stock of the royal Macedonian house of Egypt, she was throughout her tumultuous and dramatic life

non humilis mulier.

Strabo, writing under Augustus when order had been brought by the Romans into the disordered kingdom, says that under Cleopatra the land was mismanaged because of the debauchery of its rulers and that the natural wealth of the state was lost because of misrule.[327] Cleopatra attended to the needs of the army and the fleet, but her own personal affairs and her precarious position as ruler so occupied her mind, that she apparently paid no attention to the administration of Egypt. She was absent in Rome from 46 to the spring of 44 B. C. The canals of the Nile were neglected, and mud so accumulated in them that this caused the failure of the Nile to rise and the consequent famine, in the year 44-43.[328] The Turin *stele* from Thebes,[329] which is dated in the names of Cleopatra, Father-loving Goddess, and of Ptolemy also Caesar, Father-loving, Mother-loving God, was set up by priests of Amon Ra at Thebes and elders of the place and the rest of the people, in honor of Callimachus, who is said in it to have cared for Thebes in times of deep distress and to have relieved the city in a season of want and famine, nobly shouldering their burden alone, shining out like a splendid star and a Good Dæmon to those who had lost hope. He is also said to have seen to it, like his father's father, that the feasts and assemblies in honor of the Egyptian

---

[327] Strabo, XVII, 797.
[328] Pliny, *N.H.* V, 58; Appian, *B.C.* IV, 61; Josephus, *Apion*, II, 60.
[329] *O.G.I.* 194.

gods should be held in holy and fitting manner. He is given the title of Saviour of the City, and statues of gold and hard stone are to be set up in conspicuous places in the temple of the god and in the city. There is no reference at all in the body of the inscription, after the dating, to the queen. In another inscription Cleopatra and Ptolemy Caesarion issue a decree (year 41 B. C.) that Alexandrians who work in the country as farmers shall not be liable for taxes beyond the regular dues for corn-land and vineyards. This decree was a response to a delegation of Alexandrians who came before her to ask her interest in their case. Aside from this decree there is no particular evidence that she looked to the affairs of her kingdom from the point of view of her subjects. Orosius [330] tells of a factory of hers for making textiles and rugs, of which the Roman senator Quintus Ovinius was superintendent, a post which cost him his life when Octavian got control of Egypt. It is not strange that after the bad régime of Ptolemy Auletes his daughter, brought up in the tradition of negligence and wastefulness, did not know enough or care enough about the administration of the country to improve in any way on the bad management of her immediate ancestors. Strabo says [331] that things went on from bad to worse under the last Ptolemaic rulers and that the Romans corrected the abuses of the Ptolemies and utilized the natural resources of the country, which was so rich that even to the worst spendthrift and waster among the kings, that is, Auletes, father of Cleopatra, it brought in a revenue of twelve thousand talents yearly. [332]

Building of Egyptian temples went on under all the Ptolemies, good and bad. Cleopatra's name and that of Caesarion appear on the temple at Denderah where a colossal Egyptianizing figure represents Cleopatra as the goddess Hathor. Caesarion is in Pharaonic dress, offering incense to Isis.

---

[330] Orosius, VI, 19, 20.

[331] Strabo, XVII, 798.

[332] Rostovtzeff, *Social and Economic History*, pp. 258, 264; *A Large Estate in Egypt in the Third Century B. C.*, pp. 3-4, 126-129.

CHAPTER IV

CLEOPATRA SELENE OF MAURETANIA, DAUGHTER
OF THE GREAT CLEOPATRA

It was after Dolabella had informed Cleopatra of Octavian's intention to send her and her surviving children to Rome that she decided upon suicide. The three children of her and Mark Antony, Alexander Helios, Cleopatra Selene, and the little Ptolemy, walked in the triumph of Octavian in 29 B. C., and a statue of their mother with an asp on her arm was borne in the procession. The children were then given over to the care of Octavia, who brought them up together with her own two Antonias, Major and Minor. Iullus Antonius,[1] son of Fulvia and Mark Antony, was also a member of the household. Antyllus had been killed by order of Octavian in Egypt.

When Cleopatra Selene was of marriageable age, Octavian married her to the Numidian prince Juba, who had as a child walked in the procession of Caesar's triumph in 46. He had been brought up in Italy, where he had taken to study and had developed a passion for historical research. Augustus was fond of him and took him on a number of his campaigns. After the Spanish campaign of 25 Juba was given a kingdom in Africa consisting of part of Gaetulia[2] and also Mauretania.[3] In the year 20 the head and name of Cleopatra first appear with Juba's on the coins issued by him. The following epigram written by Crinagoras of Mitylene, who was in close relation with Octavia's household, and also wrote epigrams for Antonia, daughter of Octavia and half-sister of Cleopatra, may refer to the wedding.

---

[1] Iullus Antonius married Octavia's daughter Marcella and was put to death in the year 2 B. C. for adultery with Julia, daughter of Augustus (Tacitus, *Annals*, IV, 44).

[2] Drumann-Groebe, *Geschichte Roms*, I, p. 383, n. 16.

[3] Cassius Dio, LIII, 26, 2.

" Great lands of the earth, whose borders touch, which the
Nile with waters swelling separates from the black Aethio-
pians, you have got sovereigns in common by marriage and
you make one race of Egypt and Libya. From generation
to generation may the sceptre pass from father to son, firmly
established forever over both lands." [4]

Cleopatra issued coins in her own name,[5] and her head and
legend were associated with those of her husband on his
coinage. Juba's coins for the most part have their inscriptions in Latin, while the inscriptions of Cleopatra's coins are
always in Greek. Of the coins on which both appear, Juba's
head is on the obverse with the inscription in Latin and
Cleopatra's on the reverse with Βασίλισσα Κλεοπάτρα in Greek.

She doubtless considered her own lineage superior to that
of her husband, and the types on her coins are chiefly concerned with the worship of Isis. The crocodile also appears
among them. Her husband traced his descent to Heracles
and his types often refer to that god.

She had a son whom she named Ptolemy, showing the same
pride in her race in keeping the famous name that she shows
in the inscriptions and types on her coins. She was the last
Cleopatra and he was the last royal Ptolemy. She is often
said to have had a daughter Drusilla but that rests on no
certain ancient authority. Tacitus [6] says that Antonius Felix,
procurator of Judaea from 52 to 60 A. D., married a grand-
daughter of Cleopatra and Antony, whose name he gives as
Drusilla. This Felix according to Josephus [7] and to *Acts*,[8]
was married to a Jewish Drusilla, the sister of the younger
Agrippa and of Berenice. Suetonius says that Felix was the

---

[4] *Anthologia Graeca*, IX, 235. Gsell (*Histoire Ancienne de l'Afrique
du Nord*, VIII, p. 218) argues that this poem is falsely ascribed to
Crinagoras and really celebrates a much earlier royal marriage, that
of Ptolemy III and Berenice of Cyrene.

[5] Kahrstedt, *Frauen auf antiken Münzen*, *Klio*, X, p. 301.

[6] Tacitus, *Histories*, V, 9.

[7] Josephus, *A.J.* XX, 7, 2.

[8] *Acts of the Apostles*, XXIV, 24.

16

husband of three queens, by which he doubtless means three members of royal families. It is possible that two of them were named Drusilla, but it is more likely that Tacitus has made an error, misled by the name of the Jewish Drusilla. Cleopatra Selene would probably have named her daughter Cleopatra as she named her son Ptolemy. There seems to be no reason for her giving her a name that belonged to the family into which her half-sister Antonia Minor married. It is true that Pallas and his brother Felix were freedmen of Claudius, Antonia's son, and Drumann [9] says, " Drusilla vermählte Claudius mit seinem Freigelassenen und Günstlinge Antonius Felix Statthalter in Judaea ". There is here however a chronological difficulty. Gardthausen has proved against Mommsen and others, who advocate a later date (36 B. C.) for the birth of Cleopatra Selene, that she must have been born in 40 B. C.[10] She was married no later than 20 B. C. If Drusilla was born in the early years of Cleopatra's married life, she could hardly have been married to a man who was still in active life as procurator of Judaea between 52-60 A. D. We have no information about the birth years of Pallas and his brother Felix, but it is not likely that either was born before 10 A. D. at the earliest. If Felix married his first wife when he was twenty, that is, about 30 A. D. or later, that wife could hardly have been a daughter of Cleopatra Selene. And indeed there is absolutely no evidence that the grand-daughter of Antony and Cleopatra mentioned in Tacitus was a daughter of Juba and Cleopatra Selene. Alexander Helios and Ptolemy both went with Cleopatra to Mauretania on her marriage.[11] We hear nothing further of their fortunes, but the grand-daughter in question if her existence is admitted, might be a child of one of them. But I believe that Tacitus has been misled by the name of

---

[9] Drumann-Groebe, I, 383.

[10] Gardthausen, *Augustus*, II, pp. 170 f., " Das Alter der Kinder Cleopatra's ".

[11] Cassius Dio, LI, 15.

the Jewish wife and if Felix married three queens, as
Suetonius says, he married three oriental [12] queens.

The date of the death of Cleopatra Selene is not known. It
has been inferred that she lived to 11 A. D. from the fact that
coins of hers exist which are assigned to that year and later.
If she lived to that year (in which she would be fifty-one years
of age), her husband must have married again in her life-
time. It seems unlikely that such action of a vassal-king
would meet the approval of Augustus. Juba is called by
Plutarch the most cultivated of kings, the one most given to
historical research, and one of the most learned of writers.
It may have been on a journey to Asia in search of historical
material that he met a lady who had a great power over men,
Glaphyra, the daughter of king Archelaus of Cappadocia.
This captivating and trouble-making princess was first married to Alexander, son of Herod, who, Josephus says, loved
her more than his own life.[13] She made herself very unpopular at the Jewish court by boasting of her Persian blood and
high descent and by scoffing at the Jewish wives and daughters of Herod because they were not as nobly born. They
hated her and in revenge accused her falsely of an affair with
her father-in-law Herod. After Herod killed her husband on
the charge of a conspiracy against him, she was sent back
with her dowry to her father's court, and there Josephus says
Juba met and married her. He evidently soon left her, and
Archelaus, the brother of her first husband, fell in love with
her and put away his wife Mariamne in order to marry her.
It caused scandal among the Jews that he married his
brother's widow when there were living children of his brother
and Glaphyra. The statement of Josephus that she married
Archelaus after the death of Juba is a palpable error, as that
marriage took place in 3 A. D. and Glaphyra died in 6 or 7
A. D., whereas Juba lived to the year 23 A. D. We hear of
the marriage with Juba from Josephus only.

---

[12] So Dessau, *Römanische Kaiserzeit*, II, 1, pp. 162 f. and II, 2,
800, n. 1.

[13] Josephus, *A.J.* XVI, 10, 7; cf. *B.J.* I, 23, 1; 24, 2-3.

If we believe on the testimony of the coins that Cleopatra lived until after the year 11 A. D., it is probable that she was left as regent of the kingdom during her husband's absence and that they reigned together again after the interlude of his marriage with the Cappadocian princess. It has been held that the epigram of Crinagoras [14] refers to her death on the occasion of an eclipse of the moon of March 22, 5 B. C. " The moon rising in the evening dimmed her light, shrouding her grief in darkness because she saw her namesake, lovely Selene, sinking down to dusky Hades. She had shared the beauty of her light with her and mingled her death with her own darkness."

Her son Ptolemy succeeded his father and reigned until 40 A. D., when he was killed by Caligula, who wished to get possession of his wealth. The kingdom was divided into two Roman provinces. No marriage or children of his are recorded, and no more is known of the descendants of Mark Antony and Cleopatra except the mysterious mention by Tacitus of a grand-daughter who married the procurator Felix, and it is likely that she is a double of the real wife of Felix, the Jewish Drusilla.[15]

With the murder of Ptolemy of Mauretania the House of Ptolemy, son of Lagus, so far as history knows it, became extinct. The last Cleopatra appears, from her coins and her naming of her son, to have been a woman of pride and distinction. Why her husband left her for Glaphyra, if indeed he did leave her, is an unexplained mystery. Mommsen has supplied with the names of Glaphyra and Juba the inscription *I. G.* III, I, 549. If this is correct we have the Athenians honoring Glaphyra by a decree while she was the wife of Juba. But the restoration is uncertain.

---

[14] *Anth. Graec.* 7, 633. Gsell (*op. cit.* pp. 220 ff.) believes that Cleopatra Selene died soon after the birth of her son Ptolemy and before her husband's marriage to Glaphyra. He thinks that coins continued to be struck in her name after her death.

For these coins see Regling, *Zeitschrift für Numismatik*, XXVIII, 1910, p. 11.

[15] Dessau, *Röm. Kaiserzeit*, II, 2, 1, 800, *Anmerkung* 1: " Eine Verwechselung liegt also vor."

EPILOGUE

We have followed in the three countries, Macedonia, Syria, and Egypt, the succession of the queens from the early time when the daughters of the royal house were of significance politically only when they were given in marriage as "a strong compulsion", as Herodotus [1] says, to insure the validity of a treaty, to the time of the last Cleopatra of Egypt, who ruled as an absolute monarch, without regard to the brother-kings who for a brief part of her reign were nominally her co-regents. In the three centuries and more between Eurydice I and Olympias of Macedonia and Cleopatra VII of Egypt the prestige and power of the Hellenistic queens grew to a height beyond the most fantastic dreams of those early queens. It is in Egypt that this change, which Strack [2] suggests might be called the "Emancipation of the Queens", takes place. The steps of progress have been noticed in the life of each queen who contributed to it, but it will be well to sum them up now in retrospect. In Macedonia, it will be remembered, the queens diminished in political importance after the struggle of Olympias and Eurydice II for political power at a time when the reigning kings were of no significance, the one being weak-minded and the other an infant. For as soon as the strong Cassander took charge of affairs, there was no more talk of women in power in Macedonia, and except for the activities in Asia of Stratonice II, ex-queen of Demetrius II, no Macedonian queen appears with the old, bold spirit of the fourth century royal woman. The wives of Philip V counted for nothing in the state and their names are uncertain or unknown. The last queen Laodice, after her splendid naval escort by the Rhodian ships when she was a bride, is heard of only in connection with the capture of her husband by the Romans.

In Syria there were two queens who made an impression

---

[1] Hdt. I, 74.

[2] Strack, *Dynastie*, p. 2.

on world-politics. Laodice I was the more effective of these two and evidently had general charge of the war known by her name.[3] Her son Seleucus Callinicus, however, fought the battles and gained the glory, and Laodice did not establish her rule permanently. Likewise Cleopatra Thea had but a brief period of real power before she was succeeded and poisoned by her son Antiochus Grypus. The last queens of Syria, the three Egyptian sisters, Tryphaena, Cleopatra IV of Egypt, and Cleopatra V Selene, were active women and concerned in affairs, but none of them succeeded in getting an independent place as ruler. Tryphaena and Cleopatra IV were both killed in the struggle for power between the brothers Grypus and Cyzicenus, Antiochus VIII and Antiochus IX respectively.

In Egypt the story is different. At the beginning of the Lagid rule in that country the king had all the authority in his hands as absolute and sole ruler;[4] after ten generations it is a woman who has that power. Under the first five Ptolemies the queens have no acknowledged share in the government and for the most part count for no more than the queens in Macedonia or Syria. But actually the woman who was probably the greatest of all the Hellenistic queens, Arsinoe II, governed Egypt through her brother. Neither the strong Berenice II nor her persecuted daughter Arsinoe III attained to equality in the kingship, and Cleopatra I, who was regent during the infancy of her children, did not claim or receive the position of reigning monarch. Her daughter Cleopatra II is the first of the Egyptian Ptolemaic queens to have a place beside her husband as a monarch possessed of equal rights with the king. On the passage of the Louvre Papyrus 2386, " Since the king and queen hold that all should receive justice under their sway ", Wilcken[5] notes that the mention of the queen is of importance for Cleopatra's

---

[3] Wilcken, *Papyruskunde*, I², p. 1; p. 5, l. 7, τοῖς περὶ τὴν Λαοδίκην.

[4] Wilcken, *Papyruskunde*, I², p. 2; Strack, *Dynastie*, p. 2.

[5] *Urkunden*, I, 2, p. 523.

position in the government. In the Zois Papyrus [6] the word
βασιλεῦσι, kings, refers to Ptolemy and Cleopatra.[7] A similar
use of the Latin word *reges* for the two monarchs appears
in Livy [8] and indicates that Cleopatra II is queen beside her
husband with authority equal to his. Later, when at war
with her younger brother, she assumed the titles Thea Philometor Soteira in the thirty-ninth year of Euergetes II (132-
131) and began to count therefrom her own regnal years.[9]
Although she was forced to come to terms with her brother
and her daughter Cleopatra III and again to rule with them,
she never gave up her position as reigning monarch of Egypt
with the same rights as the king, a position which she was
the first of the Ptolemaic queens to achieve. Her daughter
Cleopatra III succeeded in maintaining the same power when
associated with her sons in the kingship, and her name has
official precedence in the documents over that of the son with
whom she reigns. Neither of her two daughters who married her son Ptolemy Soter had any share in the government.   Ptolemy Soter's legitimate daughter Berenice
reigns with her uncle Ptolemy Alexander as Cleopatra
Berenice,[10] and with her father on his return to Egypt in
89 B. C. She has a special title Philadelphus, which her
father assumes. During the exile of Auletes his daughter
Berenice reigns for two years, and after Ptolemy's death his
daughter Cleopatra reigns, having successively each of her
two brothers as nominal sharers of the royal power. In
Macedonia there was no powerful queen after the fourth
century; in Syria Cleopatra Thea was not able to emulate
the success of her mother and sister in Egypt; and in Egypt
itself it was not until Cleopatra II that the co-regency of
the queen with the king was established. " After the achievement of political equality on the part of the queen from the

---

[6] *Ibid.* no. 114, p. 527.

[7] *Ibid.* p. 533.

[8] XLIV, 19. Cf. XLV, 13.

[9] *Urkunden*, I, 1, p. 3; Strack, *Dynastie*, pp. 42-44.

[10] *Urkunden*, no. 125, pp. 591 f.

time of Cleopatra II the throne remains for the queen who outlives her husband with the requirement that she must summon a male member of the family to share the government with her ".[11] It may be noted that a queen who has once had such royal power, *e. g.* Cleopatra II, cannot be set aside by her husband even if, as in the case of Euergetes II, the husband takes another wife. Cleopatra III forced her son Ptolemy Soter to divorce his wife Cleopatra IV, but that lady had never reigned.

It has seemed necessary to dwell at some length on the gradual achievement of equality in power by the Ptolemaic queens, as well as on the fact that the great majority of queens in Macedonia and in Seleucid Syria, though possessing wealth and prestige, had no share in the kingship. The power of the Hellenistic queens is often represented as much greater than it actually ever was except among the later Ptolemies, and exaggerated statements are made which are based on the occasional appearance of a woman in war or in politics, rather than on a consideration of the real status of the queens. For example Bevan [12] says with reference to the regency of Cleopatra I, " In these Macedonian houses, as we have seen, a woman is the equal of a man ". This was never true in Macedonia and seldom (and never for a long period) in Seleucid Syria. The gradual attainment of such equality in Egypt has been discussed above.

Further it may be remarked that the queens enjoy a greater reputation than they merit for military exploits. In barbarous Illyria and in old Macedonia it appears to have been a custom for princesses to appear on the battlefield. At least we read in Polyaenus of Cynane going with her father Philip on an Illyrian campaign and slaying an Illyrian queen in battle. This I believe, is the only case where a royal Macedonian woman is said to have killed an enemy on the field of battle. It is probable that after the dramatic entry of Olympias and Eurydice on the field at Euia they neither of

---

[11] Strack, *Dynastie*, p. 75.   [12] Bevan, *Egypt*, p. 282.

them led a charge, but rather were placed in safety behind
the fighting men. The kings always charged at the head of
their troops.[13] Cratesipolis, Diodorus says, herself drew up
her mercenaries against the line of the rebellious Sicyonians
and conquered them.[14] Cynane led an army into Asia to
take her daughter to marry Arrhidaeus, and we read of
Cleopatra II, Cleopatra III, Cleopatra IV, and Stratonice II
at the head of armies; but it is probable that the real command lay with their generals who directed the movements of
the troops. Laodice I had a war named after her, but there
is no record of her fighting in it. Her son Seleucus had
charge of that. The pre-eminence of the queens lay in
diplomacy and government rather than in warfare. Arsinoe
II took an extraordinary interest in the navy; Cleopatra VII
maintained a great fleet and though given to seasickness did
not hesitate to put to sea with her fighting ships. At Actium
she and the ships laden with her treasures were placed behind
the great turreted battleships. She was not expected to take
any part in the fighting. The Hellenistic queens were of an
extraordinary hardihood and courage, but it is not likely that
the men wished to have them mingling in the battle. There
were no female soldiers. The author of the Alexandrine War
speaks of the fact that the soldiers under Arsinoe, sister of
Cleopatra VII, were sick of their girl-commander.[15]

As for the character of the queens, I have repeatedly said
that they must be judged by the standards of the men of
their times, for the striking phenomenon with these women
is the fact that so many of them approached more nearly
than women in any other period to the character and achievements of the men of their race. It has been said of them that
" It is only in the intensity and recklessness with which they
pursue their ends that we see any trace of womanhood left
in them." [16] It would be truer to say that some of them

---

[13] Tarn, *Hellenistic Military and Naval Developments*, pp. 30 f.
[14] Diod. XIX, 67; Macurdy, *A.J.P.* L, 1929, pp. 273 ff.
[15] *B.A.* XXIII, confectam taedio puellae.
[16] Bevan, *House of Seleucus*, II, pp. 279 f.

approach masculine intensity and recklessness in pursuing
their ends, for it is, in general, in the ranks of men rather
than among women that reckless adventurers on the grand
scale are to be found. No woman of them all rivalled the
splendid recklessness of a Philip or an Alexander, the spirit
that Demosthenes says drove Philip on from Illyria to
Chalcidice, from Thessaly to Thrace, running over the countries like a forest-fire or a hail-storm, sacrificing any part of
his body, his eye, his hand, his leg, for the sake of ambition
and glory.[17] There is no match for that among the most
intense of the Hellenistic queens.

One who attempts to apply the standards and conventions
of a different social system to the rulers of the Hellenistic
period whether men or women is plunged into contradictions
and dilemmas at once. Cleopatra VII is often condemned by
moralizing writers for her relations to Caesar and Antony
more harshly than she would have been if she had borne children to her brothers. The Hellenistic rulers had not learned
" the supreme beauty of the gentler virtues ",[18] most of which
would have seemed imbecility to them, but it must be repeated that the queens as a whole were less cruel and less
given to dynastic murder than the kings, that they were more
temperate in their lives and were not given to drunkenness
and sensuality, as were the later kings in Egypt at least.
Some few queens, such as Olympias and Cleopatra Thea,
appear to have been extraordinarily cruel, not exceeding
however in this respect what is told of such kings as Philip
V and Ptolemy VII, Euergetes. No king, not even her own
son Antigonus Gonatas, equalled the beauty of mind and
character and the nobility of Queen Phila I of Macedonia.

Through the Hellenistic centuries these women kept until
the end the intrepid virtues of the old Macedonians. There
have been no more fearless women than Cleopatra Selene,
the last Seleucid queen, and Cleopatra VII, the last of the
Ptolemies, each of them μείζων ἢ κατὰ γυναῖκα. It is not among

---

[17] Dem. XVIII, 67.
[18] Lecky, *History of European Morals*, I, p. 228.

the delicate ladies of Athens, nor even among the hardy
Spartan women, that we find the like of the greatest Hellenistic queens. For that we must go to the women of the Attic
stage, to Medea, to Antigone, to Electra, to Jocasta, and
to Clytaemnestra.

NOTE ON THE BATTLE OF ACTIUM

Tarn's article on the battle of Actium (*J.R.S.* XXI, 1931,
pp. 175 ff.) reached me after this book was in page proof. I
have been convinced by it that Antony " had not one plan,
but two alternative plans: to win a victory if possible, but if
not possible, to make for Egypt." I am not convinced, however, by his statement that it is absurd to suppose that
Cleopatra was stationed in rear in order to be protected from
fighting. It is true that Cleopatra was brave enough to fight,
and in her youth had commanded an army, but in the circumstances, it was more important that she should save the
treasure, which had been placed on her ships, and that she
should come back safe to her children and her kingdom than
that she should risk her life in a hopeless combat. The escape
had been planned with Antony, and the chivalry with which
Tarn credits him would see to it that Cleopatra should not
be placed in desperate danger. Tarn says that the suggestion
that any Macedonian princess was not going to fight can only
raise a smile; but with all the bravery which was characteristic
of them not many Macedonian princesses are on record as having actually taken part in battles. If Antony had been successful in his movement against Agrippa, of course Cleopatra
would have come up with her ships and doubtless have done
her part, but neither she nor Antony wished to risk her life
unnecessarily. Their children were in Egypt.

Various Coins.

FIGURE 12. 1. Gold Stater, Philip II of Macedonia. Reverse. Biga. E. T. Newell. 2(a). Gold octadrachm. Reverse. Jugate heads of Ptolemy I and Berenice I. (b). Gold octadrachm. Obverse from different coin. Coin of Ptolemy II and Arsinoe II, jugate busts. E. T. Newell. 3. Gold octadrachm of Arsinoe II, Philadelphus, wife of Ptolemy II. Obverse. E. T. Newell. 4. Silver tetradrachm. Obverse. Berenice II, wife of Ptolemy III. In collection of Dr. J. Hirsch (by kind permission). 5. Gold hexadrachm from Cyrene. Obverse. Berenice II. 6. Obverse of a gold octadrachm. Arsinoe III. Vienna. 7. Silver tetradrachm. Obverse. Cleopatra Thea and her son Antiochus VIII. E. T. Newell. 8. Cleopatra VII, bronze. Obverse. E. T. Newell. 9. Silver tetradrachm. Cleopatra VII, Struck at Askalon. Obverse. British Museum. 10. Silver denarius. Cleopatra Selene, wife of Juba II of Mauretania. Reverse. E. T. Newell. 11. Silver drachm. Antonia Tryphaena, of Pontus, mother of Polemon II, daughter of Pythodoris and Polemon I, wife of Cotys of Thrace. E. T. Newell.

BIBLIOGRAPHY

(Full titles of books and articles chiefly referred to in text and notes.)

Abel, O., *Makedonien vor König Philipp*, Leipzig, 1847.

Annales du Service des Antiquités de l'Égypte, 1908, 1920 (see under Edgar C. C.)

Beloch, K., *Griechische Geschichte*, 2nd ed. III¹, III², IV¹, IV², Berlin and Leipzig, 1922-1923, 1925-1927.

Berve, H., *Das Alexanderreich auf prosopographischer Grundlage*, Munich, 1926.

Bevan, E., *The House of Seleucus*, London, 1902.

———, *A History of Egypt under the Ptolemaic Dynasty*, London, 1927.

Bouché-Leclercq, A., *Histoire des Lagides*, Paris, 1903-1907.

———, *Histoire des Séleucides*, Paris, 1913-1914.

Buecheler, F., *De Bucolicorum Graecorum aliquot carminibus*. *Rhein Mus.* XXX, 1875, pp. 33 ff.

Bury, J. B. and others, *The Hellenistic Age*, Cambridge, 1923.

Charles, R. H., *The Apocrypha and Pseudepigrapha of the Old Testament*, Oxford, 1913.

———, *The Book of Daniel*, Edinburgh, 1913.

Dessau, H., *Geschichte der Römischen Kaiserzeit*, vol. II, Berlin, 1930.

———, *De Regina Pythodoride et de Pythodoride iuniore*, *Ephemeris Epigraphica*, IX, 1910, pp. 691 ff.

Dittenberger, W., *Sylloge Inscriptionum Graecarum*, 3rd. ed., Leipzig, 1915-24.

———, *Orientis Graeci Inscriptiones Selectae*, Leipzig, 1903-1905.

Drumann-Groebe, *Geschichte Roms*, vol. I, Berlin, 1899.

Edgar, C. C., *Zeno papyri*, *Annales du Service des Antiquités de l'Égypte*, XIX, 1920.

Ferguson, W. S., *Hellenistic Athens*, London, 1911.

Gardthausen, V., *Augustus und seine Zeit*, Leipzig, 1891-1904.

Grenfell, B. P. (with Mahaffy), *Revenue Laws of Ptolemy Philadelphus*, Oxford, 1896.

———, *Greek Papyri, chiefly Ptolemaic*, Oxford, 1896.

Grenfell and Hunt, *Greek Papyri*, second series, Oxford, 1897.

———, *The Tebtunis Papyri*, vol. I, London, 1902.

———, *Oxyrhynchus Papyri*, Part XIV, London, 1920.

Gsell, S., *Histoire Ancienne de l'Afrique du Nord*, vol. VIII, Paris, 1928.

Hoffmann, O., *Die Makedonen, ihre Sprache und ihr Volkstum*, Göttingen, 1906.

Hogarth, D. G., *Philip and Alexander of Macedon*, New York, 1897.

Holleaux, M., *Études d'histoire hellénistique, Klio*, VIII, 1908, 267 ff.

Jacoby, F., *Die Fragmente der griechischen Historiker*, vol. II D, Berlin, 1930.

Kahrstedt, U., *Frauen auf antiken Münzen, Klio*, X, 1910, 261 ff.

Koerte, A., *Hellenistische Dichtung*, Leipzig, 1925.

Klotzsch, C., *Epirotische Geschichte*, Berlin, 1911.

Kornemann, E., *Zur Geschichte der antiken Herrscherkulte, Klio*, I, 1902, 51 ff.

————, *Die Ehe der θεοὶ Φιλομήτορες, Klio*, IX, 1909, p. 138.

————, *Zur Geschwisterehe im Altertum, Klio*, XIX, 1925, 355 ff.

Kromayer, J., *Antike Schlachtfelder in Griechenland*, vol. II, Berlin, 1907.

————, *Kleine Forschungen zur Geschichte des zweiten Triumvirats, Hermes*, XXXIII, 1898, 1 ff.; XXXIV, 1899, 1 ff.

Macurdy, G. H., *Queen Eurydice and the Evidence for Woman-power in Early Macedonia, American Journal of Philology*, XLVIII, 1927, 201 ff.

————, *Basilinna and Basilissa, A.J.P.*, XLIX, 1928, pp. 276 ff.

————, *The Political Activities and the Name of Cratesipolis, A.J.P.*, L, 1929, 273 ff.

Mahaffy, J. P., *Empire of the Ptolemies*, London, 1895.

————, *History of Egypt under the Ptolemaic Dynasty*, London, 1899.

————, (With Grenfell), *The Revenue Laws of Ptolemy Philadelphus*, Oxford, 1896.

Meyer, Ernst, *Untersuchungen zur Chronologie der ersten Ptolemäer auf Grund der Papyri, zweites Beiheft zum Archiv für Papyrusforschung*, Leipzig and Berlin, 1925.

Meyer, P. M., *Neue Inschriften und Papyrus zur Geschichte und Chronologie der Ptolemäer, Klio*, II, 1902, pp. 477 ff.

Mommsen, T., *De Titulo Reginae Pythodoridis Smyrnaeo, Ephemeris Epigraphica*, I, 1872, 270 ff.

Niese, B., *Geschichte der griechischen und makedonischen Staaten seit der Schlacht bei Chaeronea*, Gotha, 1899-1902.

Oldfather, W., *Lokris*, in Pauly-Wissowa, XIII[1].

Otto, W., *Priester und Tempel im hellenistischen Aegypten*, Leipzig and Berlin, 1905, 1908.

Pfeiffer, R., *Callimachi Fragmenta nuper reperta*, Bonn, 1923.

Pfuhl, E., *Ikonographische Beiträge zur Stilgeschichte der hellenistischen Kunst, Jahrbuch des d. arch. Instituts*, XLV, 1930, 1 ff.

Preisigke F., *Die Prinz Joachim Ostraka*, Strassburg, 1914.

Prott, H. v., *Das ἐγκώμιον εἰς Πτολεμαῖον und die Zeitgeschichte, Rhein. Mus.*, LIII, 1898, pp. 460 ff.

Rehm, A., *Das Delphinion in Milet*, Wiegand, *Milet*, I³, Berlin, 1914.

Roos, A. G., Λαοδίκειος πόλεμος, *Mnemosyne*, LI, 1923, pp. 262 ff.

Rostovtzeff, M., *Queen Dynamis of Bosporus*, *J. H. S.*, XXXIX, 1919, pp. 88 ff.

————, *Iranians and Greeks in South Russia*, Oxford, 1922.

————, *A Large Estate in Egypt in the Third Century B. C.*, Madison, 1922.

————, *Social and Economic History of the Roman Empire*, Oxford, 1926.

Schwahn, W., *Die Nachfolge Alexanders des Grossen*, *Klio*, XXIII, 1930, pp. 211 ff.; XXIV, 1931, pp. 306 ff.

Spiegelberg, W., *Demotische Papyri aus den königlichen Museen zu Berlin*, 1902.

Stähelin, F., s. v., *Kleopatra*, in Pauly-Wissowa, XI¹, 738-789.

Strack, M. L., *Dynastie der Ptolemäer*, Berlin, 1897.

Tarn, W. W., *Antigonos Gonatas*, Oxford, 1913.

————, *Hellenistic Civilisation*, 2nd ed., London, 1930.

————, *Hellenistic Military and Naval Developments*, Cambridge, 1930.

————, *Philip V and Phthia*, *C. Q.*, XVIII, 1924, pp. 17 ff.

————, *Queen Ptolemais and Apama*, *C. Q.*, XXIII, 1929, pp. 138 ff.; *C. A. H.*, VI, Chapters XII-XV; VII, Chapters XXII-XXIII.

Tillyard, H. J. W., and Wace, A. J. B., *The History of Demetrius the Fair*, *B. S. A.*, XI, 1904-5, pp. 113 ff.

Vallois, R., *Le Temple Délien d'Arsinoé Philadelphe. Comptes Rendus de l'Académie des Inscriptions et Belles-lettres*, 1929, pp. 32 ff.

Weigall, A. E. P. B., *The Life and Times of Cleopatra*, Edinburgh and London, 1914.

Wilamowitz-Moellendorff, U. v., *Lesefrüchte*, *Hermes*, LIV, 1919, pp. 46 ff.

Wilcken, U., *Urkunden der Ptolemäerzeit*, Berlin, 1922-1924.

————, *Grundzüge und Chrestomathie der Papyruskunde*, vol. I (*Grundzüge*), Leipzig and Berlin, 1912.

————, *Arsinoe II*, Pauly-Wissowa-Kroll, *Real-Encyclopädie*, II, 1282 ff.

INDEX

Achillas, 185, 188.
Actium, battle of, 211 *ff.*, 233-5.
Acts of the Apostles, 225.
Aeacides of Epirus, 38 *f.*, 45.
Aegae, 31, 44.
Aemilius Paullus, 74.
Aeschines, *The False Legation*, 19 *f.*; scholium on II, 32, 18.
Agathé Tyche, temple of, at Delos, 125.
Agathocleia, mistress of Ptolemy IV, 135, 138, 140.
Agathocles, son of Lysimachus, 56 *f.*, 104, 113 *f.*
Agathocles of Syracuse, 67.
Agathocles, favorite of Ptolemy IV, 135, 140.
Alcetas, king of the Molossi, 22, 38.
Alcetas, brother of Perdiccas, 49 *f.*, 55.
Alexander III of Macedon, the Great, 4, 8, 13, 24, 26, 28 *ff.*, 45, 54, 55, 108, 130, 173, 222, 234.
Alexander IV, 37, 40, 43, 55.
Alexander V of Macedon, 53, 54, 55 *ff.*, 104.
Alexander I of Epirus, 26, 30 *f.*, 35, 47.
Alexander Balas, 93 *ff.*, 155.
Alexander Helios, son of Antony and Cleopatra, 198, 203, 204 *f.*, 206, 210.
Alexander Jannaeus, 166, 167.
Alexander Zebinas, 97, 99.
Alexandria, 103, 108, 127, 129, 130, 133, *et passim*.
Alexis, comic poet, 120.
Amastris, wife of Craterus, Dionysius, and Lysimachus, 60, 107, 113, 117.
ἀμειξία, time of, 158, 160.
Amphipolis, 41, 43 *f.*
Amyntas III of Macedon, 14, 17-19, 22.
Amyntas, nephew of Philip II, 32, 48 *f.*
Anklets, for men, 81.
Antaeopolis, 154.

Antigone, mother of Berenice I, 103, 105.
Antigone, daughter of Berenice I, wife of Pyrrhus, 106.
Antigonus the " One-eyed," satrap of Phrygia, 47, 50, 61.
Antigonus Gonatas, 68, 69, 70, 119, 124.
Antigonus Doson, 72, 104.
Antioch, 6, 9, 57, 64, 71, 84 *f.*, 88 *f.*, 91, 95 *f.*, 97, 155, 159, 165, 171, 200.
Antiochis, daughter of Antiochus III, 141.
Antiochus I, Soter, 66, 68, 69, 78-81.
Antiochus II, called God, 79, 82, 87 *f.*, 123.
Antiochus III, " the Great ", 91 *ff.*, 136 *f.*, 141 *f.*
Antiochus, son of Antiochus III, 91 *f.*
Antiochus IV, Epiphanes, 74, 145, 148 *ff.*
Antiochus VI, Dionysius, 95 *f.*
Antiochus VII, Sidetes, 93, 96 *f.*
Antiochus VIII, Grypus, 93, 96, 97, 99, 165, 167, 169, 170, 171, 172, 230.
Antiochus IX, Cyzicenus, 97, 100, 165, 171, 172, 230.
Antiochus X, Eusebes, 171, 172.
Antiochus XIII, Asiaticus, 101, 171.
Antiochus Hierax, 4, 83, 86, 90 *f.*
Antipater, the Regent, 8, 9, 31, 32, 33 *ff.*, 38 *f.*, 45 *ff.*, 50 *f.*, 58 *ff.*, 66, 69, 102, 109.
Antipater, son of Cassander, 53, 54, 55 *f.*
Antonia Euergetis, daughter of Mark Antony (?), 11, 206.
Antonia Tryphaena, wife of Cotys, 11.
Antonius, Lucius, 198.
Antonius, Marcus (Mark Antony), 10 *ff.*, 112, 183, 194-219, 220, 224, 234.
Antyllus, son of Mark Antony, 215, 218, 224.

241

17